Reclaiming the Disabled Subject: Representing Disability in Short Fiction is a wonderful blend of scholarship and creativity that highlights the importance of disability in Indian literature and culture. Noting that disability is at once widely distributed through Indian society, the editors also note that it is hiding in plain sight. The successful aim of this groundbreaking edition is to bring disability into the perspective it deserves both from a literary and political viewpoint.

—Lennard J. Davis,
Professor of English at the University of Illinois at Chicago, School of Arts and Sciences,
Professor of Disability and Human Development at the School of Applied Health Sciences and
Professor of Medical Education at the University of Illinois College of Medicine

While postcolonial studies is a dynamic discourse and the number of academic works dealing with non-Western countries and their cultures has increased considerably in recent years, the 'contact zones' between critical disability studies and postcolonial studies are still underdeveloped. The same is true for literary and cultural disability studies. In particular, literary narratives about the experiences and lives of people with disabilities living in countries of the global South are rare. With a series of Indian short stories dealing with disability, this anthology aims to fill these gaps. It offers fascinating insights into a rich literary culture while highlighting the narrative power of disability. It thus contributes to breaking down traditional perceptions and challenging marginalising and exclusionary views of disability.

—Anne Waldschmidt,
Professor of Disability Studies, University of Cologne, Germany, and co-editor of *Culture – Theory – Disability: Encounters between Disability Studies and Cultural Studies*

RECLAIMING THE DISABLED SUBJECT

RECLAIMING THE DISABLED SUBJECT

Representing Disability in Short Fiction

Edited by

SOMESHWAR SATI
G.J.V. PRASAD AND
RITWICK BHATTACHARJEE

1

(Volume 1)

BLOOMSBURY

NEW DELHI • LONDON • OXFORD • NEW YORK • SYDNEY

BLOOMSBURY INDIA
Bloomsbury Publishing India Pvt. Ltd
Second Floor, LSC Building No. 4, DDA Complex, Pocket C – 6 & 7,
Vasant Kunj, New Delhi, 110070

BLOOMSBURY, BLOOMSBURY ACADEMIC INDIA and the Diana logo
are trademarks of Bloomsbury Publishing Plc

First published in India 2022
This edition published 2022

Bloomsbury Academic
An imprint of Bloomsbury Publishing Plc

ISBN: HB: 978-93-54353-30-7; eBook: 978-93-54353-36-9
ePdf: 978-93-54351-29-7

2 4 6 8 10 9 7 5 3 1

Typeset in Minion Pro by Manipal Technologies Limited
Printed and bound in India by Replika Press Pvt. Ltd.

To my parents Prof. Rameshwar Sati and
Dr Uma Sati, brother Amreshwari,
wife Arti and son Praneel

—Someshwar Sati

To Vidya Sagar and Rasa

—G.J.V. Prasad

To my parents Ravi and Swapna Bhattacharjee, brother Rajarshi,
and Cujo, Saikat and Soumya

—Ritwick Bhattacharjee

CONTENTS

ACKNOWLEDGEMENTS

This book is a product of years of work put in by people across the nation and world. Not only have several hands been busy at making this book see the light of day but three major institutions have provided their support and space towards its production. The editors of the book would thus like to extend their heartfelt gratitude to the Jawaharlal Nehru Institute of Advanced Studies (JNIAS), Jawaharlal Nehru University (JNU), for hosting the workshop in 2016 that ultimately enabled different people from across different disciplines to come together and translate disability-centric stories. The editors are also thankful to the International Association of Translation and Intercultural Studies (IATIS) for funding the same workshop. We are extremely grateful to Dr Hephzibah Israel from the University of Edinburgh for not only facilitating our interactions with IATIS but also guiding us whenever and wherever required. Finally, we would also like to extend our immense gratitude to Chandra Sekhar from Bloomsbury for having been extremely helpful, patient and understanding with this project. The current project would not have been possible without the constant support and interactions with all the aforementioned people.

—The Editors

This is a project that has been successful only because of the many people who have not just been involved with it in a participatory capacity but also those who have helped me read, write, record and think about the various aspects of this book. I am and shall be eternally grateful to all these students, friends and well-wishers for having made this project possible. Their names, in no particular order, are Aashish Jain, Ishita Bajaj, Ishita Mehta, Jahnavi Vaid, Manya Arora, Shambhavi Shukla, Sourabh Yadav, Anukriti Bajpai, Sakshi Sharma, Simran Bhagat, Ritika Mishra, Shambhavi Sinha, Utkrishta Sharma, Raj Sunaina Rao, Vani Wadhwa, Manisha Ray, Deepanjali Gurung, Deep Chatterjee, Kajal Punn, Anurima Chanda, Nina Sood, Shantam Goel, Vasundhara Chaudhry, Dr Bickram Phookun and Chandana Dutta. Finally, I extend my gratitude to my father Prof. Rameshwar Sati, my mother Dr Uma Sati, my brother Amreshwar, wife Arti and son Praneel for allowing me to have a life that would ensure a work like this.

—Someshwar Sati

First and foremost, I must acknowledge the role of Someshwar Sati, who conceived of this project and whose determination and drive ensured that the workshop we organised resulted in translations as well as theorisations. I must extend my utmost thanks to the ever-cheerful staff and friends that ran JNIAS, JNU, during the time the workshop was held—Mr Surendra Singh Rawat, Mr Nanda Ballabh and Mr Ravi Kumar; they ensured that the workshop was conducted smoothly and successfully. I must thank all the participants in the workshop—it was their enthusiasm and commitment that proved to us that we were on the right track. I must extend my thanks to the two guiding stars in my life who ensure that I keep my promises to others and do my work even if not on time, who motivate me in every aspect of my life—my daughter Shubha and my wife Kamala.

—G.J.V. Prasad

This book has been conceptualised and finalised in unprecedented times, not only for the world at large but also for me and my family. So, I am eternally grateful to all those people: doctors, nurses and health staff who have seen me and helped me out through the multiple medical emergencies that have beset me over the year. I am also thankful to the entire Bloomsbury team who have been working despite the pandemic to ensure that this book sees the light of day. Finally, I would also like to thank my friends, Saikat Ghosh and Soumya Bharadwaj, who have motivated me to finish writing and working on this project.

—Ritwick Bhattacharjee

INTRODUCTION

G.J.V. Prasad, Someshwar Sati and Ritwick Bhattacharjee

Recently, we came across a research scholar who is pursuing her PhD on the representations of marginalised subjectivities in Bengali literature. We seized this opportunity and asked her whether she could help us identify and locate a few disability-centric short stories in Bengali. She stopped, cast a puzzled look and, after taking a deep breath, confessed that she had never come across a text of the kind. Surprised, we immediately inquired if she had ever heard of Rabindranath Tagore's 'Subha'. At this, she burst out laughing, '"Subha", of course, "Subha", Tagore's "Subha", the touching story of a mute girl. There is of course "Drishtidaan" as well. Who can forget the memorable character of the blind Kumu?' she added. Soon enough, she began listing several other examples; at least 15 of them. Despite the long list she eventually gave us, what was troubling was her subsequent revelation that although she had read each one of these stories several times, she had never thought of them as narratives around and/or of disability. For this reason, the realisation of the pervasive presence of disability in Bengali literature came to her as a great shock. Today, as we write an introduction for an anthology of Indian short stories based on disability, our encounter with the research scholar continues to haunt us. A question loomed large: Why is it that a scholar, pursuing her research on the representations of marginalised subjectivities, is unable to identify and recognise a disability text even when she has encountered one?

Many of us have been reading, studying and even teaching the Indian short story for quite some time now, little suspecting that this corpus of literature abounds in representations of disability. Rabindranath Tagore, Sadat Hassan Manto, Dharamvir Bharti and other leading Indian literary artists have all produced narrative gems on the subject. Then, the marginalisation of disabled people in society has not resulted in their representational erasure from literature, at least not from the pages of the Indian short story. But, unfortunately, the social marginalisation of disabled people is matched by an equally conspicuous indifference within our classrooms of pedagogical practices that look upon disability as a legitimate tool of critical enquiry.

Each one of the authors mentioned above figures prominently in both undergraduate and postgraduate syllabi across the country. Yet, their representations of disability are hardly ever discussed by teachers and students. Rabindranath Tagore, for example, is read across the nation as an icon of Bengali literature. His interventions in discourses of Indian nationalism, socialism and womanhood are widely debated by students and teachers alike. However, our students are never told that Tagore has, through a sensitive portrayal of the mute girl Subha, radically altered the conceptual terrain within which disability has been traditionally understood. They are not told how, from a clinically diagnosed medical condition of a human body gone wrong, disability in Tagore's hands becomes a matter of social oppression. Nor are they told that by endowing Subha with intense sexual passion, Tagore revolutionises the way the sexuality of a disabled person has been viewed. Clearly, disability is yet to become a part of our academic consciousness.

It is puzzling to think that this is the state of affairs in a society (and culture) that prides itself on having a 3,000-year-old tradition of producing disability narratives. Since the early days of our great epics, disability has been a running theme across the entire corpus of Indian literature. From the blind king Dhritarashtra and his lame brother-in-law Shakuni in the Mahabharata, through the blind parents of Shravan Kumar and the hunchback maid Manthara in the Ramayana, down to the mute Subha, the blind Kumu and the cognitively impaired Thakara and the other disabled characters that appear in the stories collected in this volume, the Indian creative imagination has always been fascinated by the experience of disablement. Curiously, though, seldom has the Mahabharata or the Ramayana or, for that matter, any other major text or period in the Indian literary tradition been discussed from the disability perspective in seminars and conferences across the country. The institutionalised approach to the reading of literature in India is yet to be coloured by a disability perspective. Predictably, our academia is still to evolve a category or body of writing that can be referred to as Indian disability literature. This has adversely affected our ability to identify, recognise, locate, read, appreciate and instinctively recall Indian disability narratives.

The erasure of disability from both our classrooms and academic practices are symptomatic of a much wider social bias in which the various forms of inequalities associated with a corporeal difference are considered natural. For this reason, the status of common sense accorded by our society and culture to the hegemony of normalcy and notions like 'disability limits the body and minds of disabled people' or 'disabled life is a lesser form of existence' usually go unnoticed and unquestioned. This anthology of disability short stories presents a counterpoint to the academic and social attitude that treats the phenomenon of disability as given, and not worthy of public and scholarly discussion. It is in this spirit of critique and protest that the stories collected here have been compiled and edited. Given the intellectual climate of our academia, the appearance on the publishing horizon of an anthology of disability short stories would be wholly unexpected. This anthology lays emphasis on the persistent and pervasive presence of disability within Indian literature even as it acknowledges that, unfortunately, disability is yet to become a part of our academic consciousness. This acknowledgement allows this anthology to intervene; to create what has been missing and to present a world hitherto hidden behind a normalised and darkened veil of ignorance.

While the 'liberal' intellectuals in our academia are never tired of flagging post-colonial, Marxist, feminist, Dalit and other similar concerns pertaining to marginalised people and their identity, when it comes to the question of disability, the very same intellectual academic orientation appears to be coloured by a 'politics of disavowal' (Berube 1997). To Michael Berube, the 'politics of disavowal' is a 'piece with a larger and more insidious cultural form of resistance' (ibid.) which is intrinsically linked to 'the psychological distance most people put between themselves and disability' (ibid.). How should we account for this phenomenon? Could it be possibly traced to the processes of literary canonisation in India or, for that matter, even to the trajectory that the constitutional history of India has taken?

The Politics of Disavowal

In most Indian languages, the process of literary canonisation began soon after Independence in the 1950s. The principal concern at that time was obviously to cater to the political demands and ideological imperatives of an emerging discourse of nationalism. Throughout the country, intellectual efforts were primarily directed towards establishing the universal dimensions of literature that was authentically Indian. Intellectuals throughout the country were primarily interested in constructing an imagined community of the Indian nation and sculpting the category of the new Indian citizenry. Within such a scheme of things, disabled people were subjects of little interest. Nobody was keen on exploring the relationship of disabled people with the newly born nation. No one was interested in asking questions, such as what is the place of disabled people in independent India or how they relate to the category of the Indian citizen? In fact, the relationship between this new sense of nation-ness and the disabled population of the country was a fraught one. The articulation of any question that touched upon this relationship would have automatically undermined the ideological imperatives of an emerging discourse on nationalism.

The real damage was done a few years earlier during the framing of the Indian Constitution. This document, while delineating the principles of social justice and equality, laid special emphasis on promoting the educational and economic interests of the weaker sections of society—particularly the Scheduled Castes and Scheduled Tribes—and on protecting them from all forms of discrimination and exploitation. The disadvantaged and deprived status of disabled people, however, found little or no mention in the Constitution. No specific provisions of positive discrimination by the state were made for their upliftment. They were not even included in the National Census until 1981. It was only in the 49th year of our Independence that a bill advocating equal rights for persons with disabilities was passed by the Parliament. The Persons with Disabilities (Equal Opportunities, Protection of Rights and Full Participation) Act 1995, however, reflected the government's charitable and patronising attitude towards disability and presented a set of welfare measures concerned with service delivery and the basic survival needs of disabled people (Sati and Prasad 2019). Even the promotion of the educational and employment needs of this community through reservations was looked upon as a welfare measure. The inevitable consequence of such a legal framework was that in the sociocultural imagination, disability continued to be couched within a discourse that perceived the phenomenon in medical terms: as a kind of personal tragedy arising out of a biological deficit and functional limitation. For this reason, the general population of the country continued to perceive disabled people as incapable and dependent rather than normal, independent citizens of the nation. Critics of the Act believe that this legislation, in many ways, deepened the chasm in India's social fabric as disabled people were mocked and derided for unnecessarily draining the resources of the nation.

But the signing and ratification of the United Nations Convention on the Rights of Persons with Disabilities (UNCRPD) by the Indian Government in 2007 marked a major shift in the state's official position towards disability—from charity and welfare measures to right-based policy initiatives. The UNCRPD advocated full and effective participation along with systematic inclusion of the disabled body in society to ensure and promote the full realisation of all fundamental rights and human freedom without discrimination of any kind on grounds of disability. On 16 December 2016, the Indian Parliament finally passed The Rights of Persons with Disabilities Bill, 2016, that enshrined the above principle. Thanks to this historic legislation, which speaks the global language of human rights and entitlement, disability in India today is a thriving developmental category (Sati and Prasad 2019).

It is a matter of little coincidence that this volume of short stories makes an appearance at this particular juncture of history when the disabled population of India is beginning to be recognised as a presence within the corridors of political power. This makes us wonder whether there exists a political praxis between the struggles of disabled people and the academic pursuit of Disability Studies. Critical assumptions, ideological orientations, pedagogical practices and historical circumstances have, in the past, been hostile to the idea of using disability as an academically acceptable theoretical paradigm for analysing literature. But things are hopefully on the verge of change and the publication of this book is a clear case in point.

This anthology, however, does not claim to account for all the different forms of disability representations to be found within the pages of the Indian short story. To make such a claim would not only be ambitious but also disingenuous. The objective of this volume is far more modest—to provide the reader with a broad overview and representative illustrations of the dominant and recurring images of disability found within this corpus of literature. While the anthology samples a wide range of disability representations to be found within the Indian short story, the introduction to the volume sets out certain parameters within which these representations can be read, interpreted and understood. The attempt here would be to outline a thematic typology of disability representations. These categories, however, are in no way exhaustive, nor are they mutually exclusive. Various types of disability representations overlap with each other creating a complex picture of the phenomenon. At best, this classification would provide the reader with an enabling map that would guide him or her through the various stories and help him or her to correlate them and arrive at a general understanding of how disability is materially experienced in and through bodies, and how this experience is discursively reflected or even refracted in and through literature.

Defining Disability

In society at large, disability is viewed within the discourse of medicine essentially as a physical, sensory, cognitive or psychiatric deficit that incapacitates an individual from performing one or more of life's normative daily functions. Most people take this medical approach to disability for granted without realising that such a model inevitably creates a hierarchy of power between the disabled body and the non-disabled world. It is, therefore, mandatory to, first and foremost, deconstruct this discourse of medicine and free the phenomena from its confinement to the 'hallways of hospitals, therapeutic tables and rehabilitation centres' (Sati and Prasad 2019).

The medical model suggests that disability inheres in the biological deficit of the individual and its resultant functional limitations draw attention away from the social disadvantage, social exclusion and oppression experienced by disabled people. More importantly, a highly medicalised discourse individuates the phenomenon and traces it to the predicament of a particular individual and perpetuates the existing hierarchies of power. For this reason, the anthology moves beyond this highly medicalised and individualistic approach to disability and espouses a more progressive understanding of the phenomenon—one that places disability and disabled people within a broader social context. In other words, this volume is in tune with the dominant academic trends in contemporary Disability Studies that seek to effect a paradigm shift: from disability as a personal medical predicament to disability as social pathology.

Disability Studies according to Dan Goodley is 'a broad area of theory, research and practice that are antagonistic to the popular view that disability equates with personal tragedy'. 'While we may,' as Goodley writes, 'identify people as having physical, sensory, cognitive or mental health impairments, Disability Studies place the problems of disability in society' (2012). To him, 'if we locate disability in the person, then we maintain a disabling status quo. In contrast, by viewing disability as a cultural and political phenomenon, we ask serious questions about the social world' (ibid.).

In discussing disability, this anthology adopts a definition of disability that is consistent with the social model outlined before. It, therefore, goes without saying that at the heart of this volume, there lies a heuristic separation between impairment and disability. While the former defines the phenomena within a discourse of medicine as a deviation from a biomedical norm (including functional limitation) and relates to, as WHO notes, 'any loss or abnormality of psychological, physiological or anatomical structure or function', the latter refers to it in a social context and evokes, as the disadvantage or restriction of activity, caused by a contemporary social organisation, which takes little or no account of people who have physical impairments and thus excludes them from participation in the mainstream of social activities (Shakespeare 2006). This, however, does not mean that disability has everything to do with social barriers and nothing to do with an individual's impairment. The rationale for effecting a semantic distinction between the two terms is a practical one. This is not intended at privileging one category over the other but to differentiate the experience of corporeal difference from the prejudices, discriminations and other negative social responses that disabled people have to encounter daily. Such a distinction is imperative to understand and mitigate the oppression done in the name of disability. Tobin Siebers, thus, notes that disability is a 'social location complexly embodied' (2008).

The current book, in a sense then, advocates an ideologically specific definition of disability. But, given the rise of disability activism along with multiple human rights and identity movements associated with it, there is also a pressing need to view disability as a form of identity like those based on race, class, gender, caste and sexual orientation as well. Not doing so would inevitably lead to a deficient understanding of the phenomena. Far from articulating a medicalised and individual identity, this anthology expresses a feeling of solidarity and belonging to a community that prides itself on being corporeally different and able to navigate the world in non-normative ways, despite facing several physical and attitudinal barriers. There is, in this way, an understanding of disability here that values both disability scholarship and disability political activism. Therefore, while charting the growth and evolution of Disability Studies as a distinct academic discipline, the following section recognises and charts the transfer of ideas and ideologies from the realm of activism to that of research.

Origins of Disability Studies

The publication in 1995 of Lennard Davis's *Disability Studies Reader* announced the arrival, within western academia, of a new field of academic enquiry. Ever since, this field that goes by the name of Disability Studies has developed, expanded and acquired an interdisciplinary dimension. What follows is a brief outline of the growth and development of Disability Studies. This has been presented not as a comprehensive or conclusive history of the field—such histories do already exist—but rather as a means of conveying to the reader the general understanding of the field that the editors have relied upon in making this volume.

The genesis of Disability Studies as an academic discipline can be traced back to the voices of disability activists who, inspired by the political campaigns for civil rights launched by other marginalised groups, particularly the African–Americans, began, in the late 1960s and early 1970s, to push for the recognition, respect and dignity of disabled people. Until then, the dominant societal response to disability was to individuate the phenomena within the discourse of medicine—as a particular individual's medical problem—and perceive it negatively as a personal tragedy. An over-medicalised and individualist conception of disability, as the one referred to above, would be of no help to the generation and promotion of disability pride, which is a prime requisite to launch a politically organised challenge to social exclusion and various other forms of oppression that disabled people are subjected to. The ideological exigencies of forging and consolidating a coherent sense of collective identity that lies at the heart of political activism, thus, necessitated a paradigm shift in the way the experience of disablement was perceived and understood. Disability activists, primarily in the United Kingdom (UK) and the United States of America (USA) began, accordingly, to place disability within a much broader social context; transforming it from a 'personal predicament' to a 'social pathology'.

In the UK, the tone for such a paradigm shift was set by the Union of the Physically Impaired Against Segregation (UPIAS): a small network of disabled people set up in 1974 to protest against the exclusion of disabled representatives from mainstream social and economic activities; particularly their incarceration in residential homes. The UPIAS, in its policy statement, thus went well beyond the medicalised and individuated understanding of disability, and redefines the phenomena as a complex form of oppression:

> In our view, it is society which disables physically impaired people. Disability is something imposed on top of our impairments, by the way we are unnecessarily isolated and excluded from full participation in society. Disabled people are therefore an oppressed group in society ... [disability, now, is] the disadvantage or restriction of activity caused by a contemporary social organisation which takes little or no account of people who have physical impairments and thus excludes them from participation in the mainstream of social activities. (qtd Shakespeare 2006)

Across the Atlantic, in the USA, political activists and scholars associated with the independent living movement, while developing a social approach to disability, did not go as far as redefining the phenomena as a form of social oppression. Instead, they opted to follow the American tradition of political thought and perceive people with disabilities as a minority group. This minority model, as it were, gave disability, according to David Mitchell and Sharon Snyder, 'primary positioning … as located in the environment rather than the person. It also [solidified] a rights-based argument about the ability of people with disabilities to actively participate alongside able-bodied people as full citizens on the basis of equal access' (2012). Whether it was the UPIAS' intellectual orientation to frame the experience of disablement within a narrative of social oppression, or it was the American political propensity to categorise the disabled community as a minority group, disability activism both in the UK and the USA not only profoundly influenced governmental policies and legislation but also structured and defined the academic contours of subsequent developments in and as Disability Studies. Earlier, disability research was, thus, primarily defined by a sociological, political orientation and research on disability was largely carried out within the auspices of the social sciences.

The Rise of Literary and Cultural Disability Studies

The 1990s, however, witnessed a sea change in the disciplinary landscape of Disability Studies. With the rise of the prominence of Cultural Studies as a widely institutionalised field of academic enquiry, scholars within the humanities began to use literature as a key paradigm for their critical analysis of disability. Isolated examples of such intellectual endeavours can be traced back to Helen MacMurphy who, writing in 1926, draws upon cognitively impaired characters from various literary narratives, including Shakespeare's King Lear and Charles Dickens's Tiny Tim, to understand the experience of disablement and build a case for the better treatment of disabled people living in state institutions in the United States. But it was only with the publication of Leonard Davis's *Enforcing Normalcy* in 1995 and Rosemary Garland Thomson's *Extraordinary Bodies* in 1997 that a sustained and substantive engagement with disability became a living reality within the field of literary and cultural Disability Studies. While disability scholars within the social sciences were principally busy in exposing social and institutional prejudices that created a disabling atmosphere and disempowered disabled people, these foundational texts sought to understand the social meaning of disabled identity by associating them with the systems of language and culture that produced them in the first place.

Davis's critical examination of the representation of disability in the 19th-century novel, for example, poignantly reveals that disability in this body of literature is never depicted as an autonomous mode of being. It always makes an appearance within the narrative as a 'deficit'—a lack that symbolically represents that which the normal body is not. As disability to Davis is a form of negative difference discursively constituted in opposition to the idea of the normal body, he suggests that any critical engagement with literary representations of disability must first concern itself with the idea of the normal body—which Davis calls normalcy:

> To understand the disabled body, one must return to the concept of the norm, the normal body. So much of writing about disability has focused on the disabled person as the object of study … but … would like to focus not so much on the construction of disability as on the construction of normalcy. I do this because the 'problem' is not the person with disabilities; the problem is the way that normalcy is constructed to create the 'problem' of the disabled person. (2013)

By dwelling on the inescapable presence of the idea of the normal body and its centrality in representations of disability, Davis brings to bear upon the field of literary and cultural disability study a methodological orientation that had already become commonplace in academic enquires about race. Much of scholarship on race during the late 1980s and early 1990s, instead of focusing on the person of colour, had turned its attention to the ideological category of whiteness to understand the problematics of colour. Davis draws heavily upon this methodology and outlines his concept of normalcy, which in time would become a core critical term that shaped the growth and development of Literary and Cultural Disability Studies.

Even Garland-Thomson, while exploring the figure of the disabled body in American literature and culture, focuses on the power of the normal and conceptualises disability subjectivity as deviating from this norm. She coins the term 'normate' to designate the 'veiled subject position of the cultural self, the figure outlined by the array of deviant others whose marked bodies shore up the normate's boundaries' (1997). Her reading of the 18th-century American freak show, the 19th-century sentimental novel by white women and the 20th-century novel of empowerment by black female authors reveals that the figure of the disabled body in these narratives merely functions as the image of the other in relation to which the normative American self has been defined. If disability is a deviant form of subjectivity, then the normative American self is the norm from which it deviates. As a result, Garland-Thomson notes, disability is 'not so much a property of bodies as a product of cultural rules about what bodies should be or do' (ibid.).

At the heart of these academic investments on the 'notions of cultural rules' and 'deviation from the norm' lies an implicit interrogation of power. While the concept of normalcy, to Davis, is a statistical artefact that allows people in positions of power (the non-disabled in this case) to classify and categorise their 'other' (the disabled body) as deviants, Garland-Thomson's neologism of the normate evokes the 'constructed identity of those who, by way of the bodily configurations and cultural capital they assume, can step into a position of authority and wield the power it grants them' (1997). Both in their own respective ways deconstruct the idea of the norm, the hegemony of normalcy in the case of Davis and the idea of the normate in that of Garland-Thomson, and demand a shift to a 'vision of the body changeable, unperfectable, unruly and untidy' (Davis 1999). Predictably, the academic focus of subsequent scholars in the field was on critically engaging with the idea of the norm and tracing the proliferation of its hegemony in and through literary representations of disability.

Davis and Garland-Thomson, in this way, seek to unravel the complexity of identity formation within the narratives of bodily difference through a systematic interrogation of the normative conventions of disability representations within the context of social relations of power. They push Disability Studies beyond purely sociological, economic and rights-based perspectives to critically unpack the various literary and cultural discursive processes through which disabled people are categorically othered. The novel becomes one such literary discursive process that interests most disability scholars around the time Davis and Garland-Thomson are writing. The question that needs to be asked, especially regarding the novel, then, is whether literature becomes an exclusive proliferator of non-disabled ideology. Davis's position on the subject is quite clear and somewhat troubling. To him, the novel as a literary form symbolically reproduces and promotes the hegemony of normalcy:

> I am not saying that novels embody the prejudices of society towards people with disabilities. That is clearly a truism. Rather, I am asserting that the very structures on which the novel rests tend to be normative, ideologically emphasizing the universal quality of the central character whose normativity encourages us to identify with him or her. Furthermore, the novel's goal is to reproduce, on some level, the semiologically normative signs surrounding the reader, that paradoxically help the reader to read those signs in the world as well as the text. (2006)

Literature has indeed played an instrumental role in enforcing and reinforcing the hegemony of normalcy. It has also ceaselessly produced and disseminated damaging myths about disability. Davis, in *Enforcing Normalcy*, systematically documents the above and mercilessly exposes the enforced systems of aesthetic expression and social exclusion that had, in the 19th century, systematically denigrated the identity of disabled people in literary narratives. The academic merit of such a seminal contribution to the growth and evolution of literary and cultural Disability Studies is undeniable. But, by reducing the 19th-century novel to being mere proliferators of non-disabled ideology, Davis has simply overlooked the wide range of diverse political possibilities that the novel as a literary form could offer and has failed to 'acknowledge the potentially diverse range of forms of novels themselves and the agency of critics in bringing different critical models of reading to a particular text' (Hall 2016). Predictably, during the late 1990s, literary and cultural Disability Studies was also characterised by attempts to move beyond hegemonic notions of normative narratives of disability and search for an alternative site of resistance to the dominant mode of representing and reading disability. Garland-Thomson, for example, finds in the sexually attractive black American woman amputee from Toni Morrison's Sula, Eva Peace, a character that defies conventional representations of a disabled woman's sexuality, thus, disrupting the dominant protocols of disability representation.

The first decade of the 21st century, however, saw the discipline of literary and cultural disability move beyond debates about disempowering and/or empowering narratives of disability. This period witnessed growing recognition, within the field, that even reading a text from a disability perspective would effectively disrupt the dominant assumptions and critique the hegemonic ideologies of disability. This recognition resulted in a substantive shift in the critical focus of the discipline from the texts themselves to the reading practices brought to bear upon them, helping literary and cultural Disability Studies to push the discipline forward towards embracing methodologically rigorous reading practices that could radically reconfigure normative conceptions of disabled subjectivity and the relation of power between the disabled body and non-disabled world in complex ways. In *Aesthetic Nervousness*, for example, Ato Quayson outlines one such theoretical formulation. His reading strategy is methodologically oriented towards locating, within the literary texts, moments of 'aesthetic nervousness' which occur 'when the dominant protocols of representation within the literary text are short-circuited in relation to disability' (Quayson 2007). 'The primary level in which it may be discerned,' he argues, 'is in the interaction between a disabled and nondisabled character' (ibid.). This encounter, he further notes, is disempowering from the perspective of the non-disabled subject. The encounter with the disabled body provides this subject with a shocking reminder of the uneasy table upon which normalcy rests and, by extension, of the various contingencies to which the non-disabled person is subjected. For this reason, this encounter between the two characters, Quayson argues, constitutes a primary scene of extreme anxiety. It is this extreme anxiety that is augmented and refracted 'across other levels of the text such as the disposition of symbols and motifs, the overall narrative or dramatic perspective, the constitution and reversals of plot structure, and so on' (ibid.).

Though Quayson recognises that the interaction between the disabled body and the non-disabled one is an integral part of a felt structure of power, there is, in *Aesthetic Nervousness*, an explicit interrogation of this power. There is also an ethical core to the concept, as it could deeply influence and problematise biases, prejudices and social attitudes to disability, including the reader's inherent biases and predilections, which form the filter of aesthetic nervousness through which a particular representation of disability is viewed.

The relationship between the aesthetic, political and ethical aspects of disability representation is an ongoing major concern in Literary and Cultural Disability Studies. Theories of disability that lay emphasis on reading practices, however, have their limitations. Critics are quick to point out that an over-emphasis on the text and reading strategies would easily distract the scholar from the materially embodied experience of disablement. In response to such criticism, Tobin Siebers continues to advocate the need to meditate on the processes of reading. 'Oppression,' Siebers argues, 'is driven not by individual, unconscious syndromes but by social ideologies that are embodied, and precisely because ideologies are embodied, their effects are readable, and must be read' (2008). In *Disability Theory* and *Disability Aesthetics*, while dwelling on the impact of disability embodiment on the processes of aesthetics, he suggests that the processes of writing and reading are necessarily materially embodied. Attention to disabled embodiment would, therefore, substantively alter our understanding of literature. Even a casual look at the discrete grammatical conventions of sign language would substantiate Siebers's argument as they have deeply influenced the narrative style of speech and hearing-impaired people and the way they read the text. This subtle interweaving of the material, textual and cultural aspects of representation, therefore, offers radical conceptions of disability and its representations.

Recent scholarship in the field of literary and cultural Disability Studies has been largely informed by the affective turn in cultural theory, debates about the metaphoricity and materiality of disability and discussions about the intersectionality that Disability Studies shares with Marxism, feminism, queer theory, post-colonialism and Dalit studies. All these concerns have rejuvenated the discipline and imparted to it fresh critical energy that has opened the discipline to new challenges. Some of these challenges are explored through the critical introductions to the stories collected in this volume. Many of them document and expose the various forms of oppression and discrimination that disabled people routinely face in their day-to-day existence. While some of them proliferate the hegemony of normalcy, others locate alternative figures and sites of resistance.

The Archive

Before a detailed delineation of these academic methodologies, it is imperative to point out that, quite like all other similar modes of scholarship, Literary and Cultural Disability Studies inherently depends on the presence of a pool of narratives that reflect the existence (objective and subjective) of the disabled human being to both themselves and the world. These narratives, in a sense, reveal, rather explicitly (read politically), the existential conditions of an entire community of people who have been forced into the margins by the exigencies of normalcy. Any academic exercise within and as Literary and Cultural Disability Studies becomes, therefore, a 'reading' of these revelations. Such epistemological interactions both acknowledge these narratives (and by extension the lives they represent) and brings back into critical light an existence that has been denied its humanity either as an individual being or a social entity. This does not mean that all narratives concerning disability are narratives of freedom and written by a disabled writer. In fact, there are, in absolute terms, *more* narratives, produced by the abled world, which seek to re-establish the norm and disallow the disabled human their due. But, it is in critically engaging with even these latter kinds of narratives that Literary and Cultural Disability Studies is able to win back the spaces that the abled world (even though the narratives under question) seek to take away. Thus, disability stories become a strong structural base to support the theoretical methodologies, of people like Daivs, Garland-Thomson, Seibers to stand on.

The problem, however, rears its ugly head in and as an absence of such narratives in either absolute terms or in the consciousness of scholars in the field. In a sense, without the base of stories that can re-present the disabled life, any Literary or Cultural scholarship superstructure tends to fall flat on its face. While the West, with its intensive rigour in the field, has been able to amass a pool of such stories, India (and Indian academia) still lacks behind. One of the reasons is that Literary and Cultural Disability Studies has been all but absent in Indian academia is this gaping void. The research scholar invoked at the beginning of this introduction stands as a shouting example of this absence. She was unable to instinctively recollect the titles of disability stories she had already read because, for her, these stories were not narratives about a systemic predicament but stories about particular individuals—Subha, Kumu and so on. But everything said and done, while it is easy to find faults in individual scholars for not recognising disability as a collective and social problem, the root of this issue, in truth, lies in the absence of a corpus that can, in its singular unity, explicitly reveal this social modality of disability. In other words, to expect everyone to automatically know about this problematic would be unfair if those who are in a position to create this knowledge do not do so. There is, therefore, an ever-increasing need to represent disability in fiction not merely as an experience exclusive to a particular individual but also as a shared experience of a collective—as a community experience with profound social, cultural and political significance. This can happen only through the creation of an archival singularity. It is here and against this absence that the current anthology seeks to step up and intervene as it aims to create an archive of disability-centric short stories from across the nation and translated from different languages. This would, the editors of the volume believe, not only create the requisite knowledge base, thus filling an erstwhile gap in it but also, in being an archive, as Marlene Manoff, quoting Derrida, writes, 'affirms the past, present, and future; it preserves the records of the past and it embodies the promise of the present to the future' (2004).

As a small additional note, there is a need to say here that this embodiment of the 'promise of the present to the future' is not innocent. It comes attendant with questions of power. As Derrida writes, '[t]here is no political power without control of the archive' (1995). To make this point somewhat more apparent, there is a need to think about the canon and the canonical. In their introduction to their book *What Makes It Pop*, Dutta and Bhattacharjee show how the canon, at its ontological level, is an act of judgement. Any formation that tends towards its situation as the canonical always happens through an explicit judgement; a verdict that always chooses one over the other (Dutta and Bhattacharjee 2020). The issue, in such a scenario, is who or what chooses. The answer is simple: society does. But, within this simple answer of the social lies a complicated network of subjectivities in and of power that governs and/or make this society. This automatically means that these subjectivities always judge towards the formation of the canon in such a way that their being-in-power is always left unchallenged. To do so, these subjectivities in power would not only have to ensure the creation of specific archives towards canonisation but also enforce the suppression of others: at times into a forgotten oblivion. In the case of disability, this network is made up of the able-bodied. In other words, it is the abled who have, especially in academic circles, so far adjudicated the production and collation of discourses and knowledge systems to always be in their favour. This has, in effect, relegated not just the academic study of disability, but even the simple consciousness of its narratives to a comfortable forgetfulness. The aforementioned absence, then, is verily created. To produce an archive of disability narratives in such a scenario is then to rightfully take back what has been denied and put a strong opposition to the forces of canon formation. This anthology, then, seeks to make a dent in the way the abled world seeks to repress disability discourse and disability narratives. Forgetting is not an option. There is, in this way, a political charge to the current work as well. These are not just stories. They represent, often through their broken problematic and questionable movements, an idea and a state of being: an idea that threads into the existential realities of millions of lives and one that has, so far, been judged as irrelevant and forgettable. This is an archive that, finally, having been so, can, henceforth, provide a disability scholar with enough material to embark on multiple kinds of academic endeavours and produce literary historiographical discourses of the Indian short story from a disability perspective; especially considering the fact that the stories collected in this volume provide a rich insight into the various modes through which a nondisabled consciousness apprehends a disabled person and attaches 'value' to them.

Having thus shown the necessity of narratives for Literary and Cultural scholarship to begin from and the central structure of the current volume towards the fulfilling of that need, it behoves here to point out that the book does not end simply at the collection of narratives. There is a conscious attempt here to present one of the key methodologies which have (as already mentioned above) influenced the academic engagement with disability-centric stories: that of the effect that disability has on the abled world. This would, in a sense, allow, on one hand, new entrants into the field of Literary and Cultural Disability Studies, to find in the following pages an introduction to the key debates of affectations that define Disability Studies today. On the other hand, those who are already researching in the field will find new perspectives to this approach to the study of disability.

Disability and Its Affect

To begin thinking about this affectation, however, requires, at this juncture, a revisitation of the central precepts of Disability Studies. As already noted, one of the most important achievements of Disability Studies (where Disability Studies is a system of generating and modulating knowledge of and about the life of the disabled body) has been the distancing of the phenomenon of disability from medical discourses. Over the years, the proponents of this mode of evaluation have impressed upon the fact that even though 'impairment' happens on and of the body, it is society's inability to create a world where all forms of bodies can (co)exist that 'disables' that impaired body. Disability is thus not something that needs to be treated or cured medically, for it is moored inside the crisscrossing matrices of society, culture, tradition and history. This does not mean that an individual with an impairment does not have the right to seek the removal of their impairment. But, for those who do not or cannot take a medical recourse, the infrastructures of society should not disable their access to an equitable existence that non-impaired bodies have. Nevertheless, while 'impairment' is, in this way, set up to denote a difference in physiological makeup (and not debility), 'disability' gets associated with the failure of society to take into accord the aforementioned difference. This is an important distinction for it not only changes the way disability has been seen historically but also reveals the locus of either of these frameworks. Impairment, on one hand, in being figured on a specific place of a specific body, gets rooted to a spatial cite, while, on the other, disability, owing to the figuration of the society in its ontological makeup, finds being as a transitional evaluation. It is this moment of transition implicit in the conceptual paradigm of disability that becomes rather central towards a delineation of the structures of affectation that disability generates in both the disabled body and the abled one. The current section, then, seeks to look at this phenomenon in detail and show how affect ties into this issue of the transitional and, subsequently, acquires political dimensions as well.

Lennard Davis's concept of the temporarily abled-bodied becomes, perhaps, a good place to begin interrogation of the aforementioned temporality quite well. In his seminal essay 'Crips Strike Back', Davis outlines how all abled-bodies are merely temporarily so. Accidents, old age and/or disease inevitably end up impairing presently abled bodies and marking them out as 'disabled' sometime in the future. This temporariness, as Davis further notes, reveals the 'shaky footing on which normalcy rests' (1999), thus, threatening to destabilise and deconstruct a world which, based on a spectre of the normalcy of the abled, seeks to disable and marginalise the corporeally different (thus 'disabling' them). For Davis, and, by extension, the project of Disability Studies itself, the revealing of this temporariness, hence, becomes rather important as it becomes catalytic towards the presentation of the futility of categorisations founded on feigned bodily normalcy and naturalness. But there is another aspect to this temporariness that stands to make an equally vital revelatory change in the way the corporeal 'ability' of the human is evaluated: a change in the comprehension of disability itself. This new kind of revealing rests on the moment of transformation: the moment in which a body moves from an abled framework to a disabled one. In other words, if all abled bodies are temporarily abled, they will, inevitably, become disabled. The temporal space in which a body is disabled, therefore, necessarily follows a time when it was not disabled. Disability, then, as it sets in, comes at the cusp of being non-impaired and impaired: rendering disability, itself, both as a phenomenon and an event. While, as a phenomenon, 'disability' seemingly stays with the body throughout that body's life, as an event, disability marks that moment of transition that sets in impairment and (subsequently brought in by societal constructions) phenomenal disability. Consider, for example, a body A that has recently lost its sight. That the body has 'lost' its sight betrays the fact that it once had it. In becoming disabled, thus, A has transitioned from one state of being to another. In such a case, any evaluation towards the management of A's disability, either by A itself or anyone else (abled or disabled), will always take into account both what was and what is. A's rehabilitation post impairment, institutional or individual, for example, will necessarily take into account both the states of being or run the risk of failure. A's disability is, therefore, not just that it cannot see any more but that it once could and now cannot. The movement, generated through a time frame, in this way, becomes rather crucial towards the comprehension of disability. Davis's use of temporariness, after all, finds its etymological roots in the Latin *tempus*: time.

An important note of caution needs to be struck here. The use of either Davis's concept of the temporarily abled-bodied or the example of body A leaves out a large chunk of the disabled population: those who are born disabled. Having said that, this apparent exclusion does not mean that disability cannot be seen as an event in the lives of the people who are disabled by birth. To find a more holistic comprehension of the aforementioned complex nature of disability, there is then a need to fine-tune the inclusion of temporality within disability. This can be done by looking at the framework from within which either of these presentations works. In other words, while Davis's concept, and subsequently A's example, make manifest the equation of disability as an event as well as a phenomenon, they have to be seen as an instance, albeit infinitely repeatable, of a Platonic form: a form that can be better understood by going back, once again, to that moment of transition. In the case of adventitious disability, since this is a case that already has been spoken about, this moment is manifested by a temporality: a differentiation between two states of being separated along the temporal axis of existence. The question, however, that needs to be asked is what are these two states of being. While these states have been demarcated by 'non-impaired' and 'impaired', there is a necessity to see this demarcation contemporaneous and coterminous with the structure of ability. Consider then, in such cases, the conceptualisation of the 'non-impaired' body. It is a body that has the ability to do all things that the majority of human beings have been witnessed doing. The 'impaired' body, on the other hand, fails to do or act in one or more ways as the majority. The transition, thus, happens from a state where the body *can* do a thing to a state where it *cannot*. In such a transition, the earlier body, in a society that necessitates presentations of the 'natural' in terms of its ability to do things that the majority of the people are able to do, becomes but a representation of a state of being that should ideally be (because it's natural and is how the majority are). The transformation, thus, is not just from an abled entity to a disabled one but, more importantly, from a body that should be (or should have been) to a body that should not be. It is this distinction, this differentiation of two states that constitutes the Platonic form or the framework. What matters more than the transition itself, in a sense, are the two states of existence that are differentiated by that transition. Disability as an event, hence, is not just about a transition but the simultaneous comprehension of the body within the dual frameworks of the ideal and problematic; of the proper and the flawed and of the normal and the deviant. The disabled self is, in essence, both. In the case of adventitious disability, this differentiation is quite concretely present on a temporal framework. However, in those who are born disabled, this duality operates in more abstract a background. For the latter, the transition is not an actual movement from a state of existence to another but a becoming: a becoming that navigates the dualities that frame the lives of all disabled humans. So, against body A is body B which is born blind. Though this blindness does not necessitate a looking back (in the strictness terms), rehabilitation for body B still takes into account what it should have been. Disability as an event, in this way, ensures that the impaired are not seen as simply those humans who cannot do an act in the present but also those who should have been able to do that act ideally. Both these notions of the disabled body go hand in hand. The present volume has exemplary stories for both these types of bodies: 'Khitin Babu', 'That Woman' and 'Breath' for type A and 'Vishakha', 'Subha' and 'Gungiya' for type B immediately come to mind.

At this juncture of the argument, there is a pressing need to confess that though this consideration of disability seems rather obvious, it has hidden nuances. For one, a body can always be unable to do a certain thing or act in a certain way. But that (for the lack of a better word) disability need not accompany the enforcement of a parallel notion that that body *should have been* able to do the thing it cannot. For example, if a child is unable to carry a heavy bag up ten flights of stairs, there is no compulsion that they should have been able to carry it up. However, if the same child (in a different situation) is unable to go up even a single flight of stairs because they are wheelchair-bound, they are immediately judged to be failing at a thing they should have otherwise done. The should-ness that accompanies the duality is important. It is based on, as already mentioned before, what the majority of the human population can do. In any case, one of the major implications of this duality is its rather immediate and automatic creation of systems of normalisation. On the one hand, the bodies that are able to do what they are expected to become normal and the ones that are not able to do the things that they should have been able to, on the other, become nothing but abnormal. For another, insofar as the abled-bodied is concerned, this duality is embedded within the psychological makeup of the disabled self as well. The abled world, lost in its notions of normalcy, is sure of the fact that the disabled humans view their selves within the dualities of should-ness as well; that there is a strong desire in the disabled subjectivity to reacquire that lost ideal; and that they can only always try and move towards the ideal and never achieve it. What these two points reveal, thus, is a lack; an absence or a void. However, this lack isn't just in the form of a loss of an appendage or a sense but a deeper and a more existential lack: a normal, once again, always desired but unachievable. That this grafting of their own concept of the disabled identity on the disabled body is, once again, enforcement of normalcy and a mere abled fantasy towards the fulfilment of their own emotional and political motivations does not need reiteration; especially because one cannot forget the involvement of society in disability. As a note of caution, this does not necessarily mean that they have failed in normalising this graft either. Finding themselves inside social spaces and thus badgered constantly and consistently with their apparent lack over centuries, the disabled 'identity' has, understandably, come to believe in the un-ideal nature of their being as well. This has, if nothing else, allowed the abled world to continue with its project of normalcy.

An immediate modality of this complication of normalcy is found alongside and along with the event that is disability feature in the form of the affectations in the mind-space of an abled body when it comes across a disabled body in the world. Before talking about this affectation, however, it is necessary to take a slight detour and speak about the concept of affect in itself. This interrogation would, in effect, put the larger question of the affect that disability and the disabled body generate especially in and through its form of the event. But, to talk about affect presents an immediate problem. It is impossible to think explicitly about affect, let alone talk or write about it, because it is a feeling and, thus, somewhat outside the bounds of language. The only possibility is to think about it in conjunctions or presentations that are perhaps as abstract. Affect, thus, is a framework-of-evaluation (and not just evaluation): something that is an automated response to a 'worldly' interaction encoded into the minds of all human beings (the reasons for such codifications could be many: beginning with a person's interpellation in a 'normal' system of being to explicit indoctrinations) and not, generally, a consciously assessed method of interrogation of the object or body that the person in question comes into contact with. There is, then, as Brian Massumi writes, an intensity of feeling attached to affect (Massumi 2015). This is a rather Wordsworthian intensity that has the power to propel the affected human into particular states of being. To have a happy affect off a certain person, object or happening does not simply mean that the affected person is simply happy at having witnessed that person, object or happening. There is something more; something that is indescribable but has enough force to fundamentally alter that person's existence, even if temporarily. But, all this does not mean that the witnessed person, object or happening is in stasis. It too has an energy of its own. It has, in literal terms, 'affect'. If affectation is thought of as an action, it is an action that happens entirely *in* the subject even as it originated outside it. There is, hence, a symbiosis between the human affected and the person, object or happening affecting which gives rise to that moment of affectation. In essence, the framework of evaluation that affect is necessitates the inclusion of both the subject and the object. Thinking on similar lines, Massumi too writes that

> Although affect is all about intensities of feeling, the feeling process cannot be characterised as exclusively subjective or objective: the encounters through which it passes strike the body as immediately as they stir the mind. It involves subjective qualities as directly as the objects provoking them, or with which they move. It concerns desire as much as what is imperatively given; freedom as much as constraint.... This is complicated by the fact that although affect's openness is unconfinable in the interiority of a subject, to take one of the concepts in need of restaging, it is at the same time formative of subjects. Although affect fundamentally concerns relations in an encounter, it is at the same time positively productive of the individualities in relation. In its transversality, affect is strangely polyvalent. (2015)

For Massumi, then, moments of affectation are not just mental phenomena restricted inside the individuated mind of the affected subject but an 'encounter' between the subject and the object. This encounter, further, is not in isolation for it is 'positively productive of the individualities in relation' as well. This implies that affectations propagate; they move beyond that simple encounter to become a part of the larger fabric of existence. But, in founding future encounters, or at least becoming a part of them, affectations also invoke encounters past. For how can they not? Both the subject and the object are a part of a world: where the World is not just planet Earth but all the multiple strands of existential conditions that interact and interconnect—including (though not limited to) history, tradition, society, culture and economics in all their complexities—to make the planet the space that it is for the affected subject and the affecting object existing in it. Both the subject and the object, thus, *become* in their worlds. This means that the encounter that Massumi speaks about is also a synthesis where the subject, as it exists in a world, comes into contact with the object, as it, in its way, exists in its world. This, in turn, means that the World cannot be taken out of the equation of affectations. The repercussion of this inclusion, thus, stands out in the following ways: a subject cannot be affected by an object in the same way as another subject, two different objects, however seemingly similar, cannot affect the same object in the same way, and, finally, how a subject is affected by an object (or how, concomitantly, how an object affects a subject) depends on the worlds that they are in. A painting, for example, can neither affect all its viewers in the same way nor enforce affectations when there is none. Similarly, a viewer can be affected by a painting in a completely different way than another viewer or not be affected at all. What effectively decides the fruition of affectation in this synthesis is the world (or the world)—

which, once again, include to a large extent, history, tradition, society, culture and economy. It is impossible to say what the conditions for a successful affectation are. That's where, perhaps, the mystery about affect lies. In any case, successful affectations stamp, as it were, the worldly conditions that make the 'encounter' of affect a success. This is what allows Massumi's production of the subject. Herein also lies the political dimension of affect: for it brings out, through its happening, the conditions of the world as the subject finds itself in it.

It is this 'political' characteristic of affect that becomes quite crucial towards the interrogation of the way the disabled body and disability affect the abled world. While, as already mentioned above, it is not always possible to figure the worldly conditions that generate successful moments or encounters of affectation, in the case of disability, the reason is not as hidden. The only catalytic requirement for the affectations of disability is its presence as an event. In other words, the dualities of the ideal and problematic; of the proper and the flawed or of the normal and the deviant that the disabled identity is evaluated within, invokes in the abled body 'emotions' that inevitably, as Bill Hughes, in his essay 'Fear, Pity and Disgust', notes, take an 'affective turn' (2012). The worlds required for this affective turn are brought in via the should-ness of the disabled body and the figuration of the naturally 'abled' physiognomy within that should-ness. These two worlds, in effect, encounter and create not only a moment of affectation but also a framework for all such future encounters. Before delineating these frameworks, however, there is a need here for a small example to show how the dual of the disabled body figures in these moments of affectation. Of late, a new genre of films has cropped up over public streaming platforms and mobile applications. The concept is simple. Anyone can download and install any such application on their mobile phones (TikTok being one of the more famous ones, not least because of its controversial ban by the Indian government) and shoot a short, 10–25 seconds-long video with pre-programmed dubbing, and publish it on the internet. It is available for anyone and everyone to watch. What has been strange, however, is the inclusion of blind characters in such videos. The word inclusion here is slightly misleading, for these videos do not deploy blindness for any political manoeuvres. The only reason for such portrayals, played, undoubtedly, by abled bodies, is the affect it generates among the other characters. The stories, themselves, tend to take different routes but the end is always the same: a deep-seated pity for the blind. In one, for example, a blind boy is walking with (one can presume) his significant other when he bumps into another girl. This second girl, angry at being hit, turns to slap the boy but the first girl puts herself in front and gets slapped. In another video, a blind boy is sitting under a tree when a girl, apparently tired, comes and sits next to him. The two start speaking. Long story short, the second half of this video reveals that the girl was the one who used to be blind. The boy (now blind), having met her, falls in love with her and decides to donate his eyes to the girl. So now while she can see, he cannot.[1] In either of these videos (and other videos like these), the idea is simple. The blind can only be pitied. In the first video here, for instance, the girl fundamentally believes that the blind boy is unable to solve the problems of his life and thus needs her to take care of them. She pities him and believes that the right thing to do is to step in and save him. Similarly, in the second video, the boy thinks that the only way to express his love is to give away his own eyes because blindness is a pitiable condition (since everything said and done, the girl does get 'better' because of his 'charity'). This is an ignominy that he would happily tolerate for her. The reason that pity is thus evoked is because the able-bodied characters are always evaluating their disabled partners as bodies that should have been similar to their own. In this lacking to be the ideal, the disabled characters are not just suffering their disability but also, in the eyes of the abled characters, always limiting towards the ideal. As a side note, the fact that these videos are made by able-bodied people goes to prove that they cannot think of the blind as bodies who are complete in themselves; who are not suffering and who should not be pitied.

Pity, however, is only one of the frameworks through which the abled world is affected by the disabled body. Bill Hughes adds two more: fear and disgust. For Hughes, these three emotions—of fear, pity and disgust—are the major 'building blocks of the emotional infrastructure of ableism' (Hughes 2012). All these three emotive frameworks, which take the 'affective turn' (as shown in the case of pity), find roots in the event that is disability through its association with the worlds in which both the disabled and the abled bodies exist. A closer look at how Hughes delineates these affectations shall reveal that at the heart of these three frameworks, there lies an impregnable existence of this duality of disability (where the body is once again both the ideal and the problematic). Firstly, the fear that the abled world feels when it comes across the disabled body is a result of the comprehension of their frailty. Such an (to go back to Massumi's

1 The first video can be found at: https://www.youtube.com/watch?v=VLeShOUqC8U and the second at https://www.youtube.com/watch?v=pyj86XcczTw&t=645s

term) encounter challenges 'the stable view of [the] embodied self that is characteristic of non-disabled identity' (Hughes 2012). When the abled body, in a sense, encounters a disabled one, it recognises the fact that there has been a transition in that body from the body it should have been to what it is. But, this is also the body that should never have been. The abled body suddenly realises that the disabled human manifests the body that should never have been. In this manifestation, there lies, for the abled body, a very real possibility that their ideal body can, and as Davis says will, turn into the unideal one. This evokes nothing but fear. Quoting Margrit Shildrick, Hughes says that the abled world harbours for itself the 'fantasy' of an 'invulnerable body' which is shattered the moment a disabled body comes in front of it (2012). This fantasy is shattered simply because the disabled body harbours the reality of the transition; or through the transition, the reality of the duality. The 'normal' world can, as much as it wants, classify the disabled body as unideal but it never removes the facticity of its existence. This, then, becomes a threat. To be feared and thus segregated away into safe institutional spaces (safe for the abled). The second framework, pity, has already been spoken about. The only thing that needs to be added is that there is always a necessary hierarchy implied in feelings of pity. Hughes, thus, notes that '[the] object of compassion and pity … is always the victim, the other whose shoes one does not want to be in … [the] charitable attachment to the disabled body other is saturated with selfishness because it sustains one's sense of ontological security and wholeness' (2012). This ontological security that evokes pity is, as shown before, another by-product of the disabled body being an entity it should never have. For the unideal, is just that: a thing that lacks, that wishes to be the ideal like the normal and that can only be commiserated. Thirdly, and finally, disgust 'stems from the fear of the messiness of our own intrinsic, organic human constitution' that hits against the modern human moralities that vie for a sanitised and clean existence (Hughes 2012). The disabled body displays and, therefore, reminds the abled that their 'normal' body is, as Hughes says, messy, slimy and leaky as well. This reminder is, first and foremost, against the cultural sensibilities that make up the ideal world and ideal body of the abled human. For them, these displays of viscera should be kept where they are meant to be—inside and hidden. Secondly, in being thus reminded of their viscera, the ideal that abled live in tends to be deconstructed. But this is a breakdown that the abled world can tolerate especially since this would inevitably create a problem vis-à-vis the disabled body's current existence, thus, in turn, challenging the political supremacy that the abled world enjoys via their normalcy. Disgust, thus, re-enforces the disability duality and keeps them in their undesired position of an absence.

As a final note, four things need to be said with respect to the frameworks that Hughes offers. Firstly, none of them is merely emotions. They are, for the lack of a better word, affectations. They are, in the moment of their happening, quite intense. Fear, pity and disgust against the disabled body have the power to move the affected into action or inaction against the body that affected them. The very fact that people have been making the micro-videos as mentioned above stand a testament to this. Secondly, none of these is restricted to the individual. True to the kind of effect, as Massumi shows, that affect has, the three create subjectivities via societal modulations. Fear ensures that society always imprisons the disabled body in correction houses, hospitals, asylums or special schools. Pity engages and encourages society to keep the disabled body as always those who lack and desire the ideal body and life. Disgust not only creates a cultural imaginary of the disabled body as unclean and uncouth but also allows society to maintain distance from them lest their leakiness is contagious (leading a full circle back to fear). Thirdly, fear, pity and disgust are not the only ways disability affects. Obviously, there are other ways. An abled body can, for example, always be indifferent to a disabled one. The problem of disability will, in any case whatsoever, keep on existing for as long as the disabled body affect the abled, it would mean that they two are not the same. There will always, in a sense, be a strange relationship between them where difference would always lead to a hierarchy. For, in the passivity of being the affected party, the abled world finds the possibility of an active response against the 'object' that affected them. This disabled object, on the other, will always affect the subject (for, as already mentioned, the conditions for affectations are always already met by the two entities being abled and the disabled bodies), thus, never finding even an iota of say in this relationship. Finally, and this is a point that concerns this entire section, it is impossible to find any temporal linearity in the way normalcy is constructed on the basis of ability (or the lack thereof) and the way disability affects. In other words, neither does the creation of normalcy precede the fear, pity and/or disgust the abled world feels against the disabled body nor does it succeed it. Perhaps there would have been a clear movement between the two when the problem of disability began (disability and not impairment). But, in today's age, the two feed into each other, bolstering the other and ensuring the retention of political autonomy at the hands of the abled. The question, therefore, is not which came first but, now that both normalcy and the affectation of disability are encoded inside the matrix of human existence, what is next?

The Anthology

With this anthology, then, an attempt has been made to bring together various narratives from across state/linguistic borders of the country and create an epistemological ground for the interrogation of these narratives. Put together, this anthology illuminates the various cultural and ideological processes through which the disabled subjectivity and selfhood affects the world of the abled and, in process, is discursively constituted and negotiated. Thus, some of the questions that the volume seeks to answer are: What do the representations of disability tell us about the culture that they affect and in which they are produced? What are the principal themes they draw upon? What are the implications of these narratives on questions related to the agency of disabled people? How do they shape the world disabled people inhabit? Do these representations cement longstanding normative, social and cultural conceptions of disability, or do they open up new discursive spaces from where these conceptions can be interrogated and problematised? In short, what are the cumulative effects of these representations on the way the world understands, responds to and is affected by disability and disabled people?

These questions, and their answers, undoubtedly relay a sense of what is at stake in narratives of disability that emerge on the contested margins of a predominantly ableist nation. This is what, perhaps, drives this book's desire to not only create an archive but also critically locate each story in this archive within its discursive spaces. Towards the same, then, each story anthologised here, is prefaced with an editors' introduction that seeks to present not only a critical entry into that particular story for the reader but also a nuanced reading of that story. The intention, here, is of questioning the very basis of these representations in ways that they become, at times questionable, and others, quite innovative, aesthetic responses to disability and disabled people. The attempt, through each story, is to expose the politics and short circuit the underlined logic of these representations and show, wherever necessary, possible ways by which the disabled body can be represented to the Indian imaginary.

Works Cited

Berube, Michael. 1997. 'The Cultural Re-presentation of People with Disabilities Affects Us All'. Available at: https://www.chronicle.com/article/on-the-cultural-representation-of-people-with-disabilities/ (Accessed on 13 October 2021).

———. 1996. *Life As We Know It: A Father, A Family, an Exceptional Child*. New York: Pantheon.

Bowe, Frank. 1978. *Handicapping America*. New York: Harper and Rowe.

Charlton, J.I. 1998. *Nothing about Us without Us: Disability Oppression and Empowerment*. Berkeley, CA: University of California Press.

Davis, Lennard J. 1999. 'Crips Strike Back: The Rise of Disability Studies'. *American Literary History*, 11(3): 500–512.

———. 1995. *Enforcing Normalcy: Disability, Deafness, and the Body*. London and New York: Verso.

———. 2013. *The Disability Studies Reader*. New York and London: Routledge.

———. 2006. 'Constructing Normalcy: The Bell Curve, the Novel, and the Invention of the Disabled Body in the Nineteenth Century'. In *The Disability Studies Reader*, edited by Lennard J. Davis, 3–16. New York: Routledge.

Derrida, Jacques. 1995. *Archive Fever: A Freudian Impression*. Translated by Eric Prenowitz. Chicago and London: Chicago University Press.

Dutta, Srinjoyee and Ritwick Bhattacharjee. 2020. *What Makes It Pop? Introduction to Studies in Popular Fiction*. New Delhi: Worldview.

Finkelstein, Vic. 1980. *Attitudes and Disabled People: Issues for Discussion*. New York: World Rehabilitation Fund.

Foucault, Michel. 1976. *The Birth of the Clinic*. London: Tavistock.

———. 1977. *Discipline and Punish*. Harmondsworth, London: Peregrine.

Garland-Thomson, Rosemarie. 1997. *Extraordinary Bodies: Figuring Physical Disability in American Culture and Literature*. New York: Columbia University Press.

Goodley, Dan. 2012. 'The Psychology of Disability'. In *Routledge Handbook of Disability Studies*, edited by Nick Watson, Alan Roulstone and Carol Thomas, 310–323. London and New York: Routledge.

Hahn, Harlan. 1988. 'Can Disability Be Beautiful?'. *Social Policy*, 18: 26–31.

Hall, Alice. 2016. *Literature and Disability*. London and New York: Routledge.

Hughes, Bill. 2012. 'Fear, Pity and Disgust: Emotions and the Non-Disabled Imaginary'. In *Routledge Handbook of Disability Studies*, edited by Nick Watson, Alan Roulstone and Carol Thomas, 67–77. London and New York: Routledge.

Lane, Harlan. 1992. *The Mask of Benevolence: Disabling the Deaf Community*. New York: Knopf.

Manoff, Marlene. 'Theories of the Archive from Across the Disciplines'. *Libraries and the Academy*, 4(1): 9–25.

Massumi, Brian. 2015. *The Politics of Affect*. UK: Polity Press.

Mitchell, David, and Snyder, Sharon. 2012. 'Minority Model: From Liberal to Neoliberal Futures of Disability'. In *Routledge Handbook of Disability Studies*, edited by Nick Watson, Alan Roulstone and Carol Thomas, 42–50. London and New York: Routledge.

Oliver, Michael. 1990. *The Politics of Disablement*. Basingstoke: Macmillan.

Quayson, Ato. 2007. *Aesthetic Nervousness: Disability and the Crisis of Representation*. Columbia: Columbia University Press.

Sati, Someshwar and G.J.V. Prasad. 2019. *Disability in Translation: The Indian Experience*. New Delhi: Routledge.

Siebers, Tobin. 2008. *Disability Theory*. Ann Arbor: University of Michigan Press.

———. 2010. *Disability Aesthetics*. Ann Arbor: University of Michigan Press.

Shakespeare, Tom. 2006. *Disability Rights and Wrongs*. London and New York: Routledge.

Shapiro, James. 1993. *No Pity. People with Disabilities Forging a New Civil Rights Movement*. New York: Times Books.

VISHAKHA

By Medha Trivedi

Introduction

By Editors

In Lewis Carroll's *Alice's Adventures in Wonderland*, there is a longish episode where Alice, having eaten an unclaimed piece of cake, begins to grow in size. She keeps on growing till she is, quite literally, stuck inside the house she's in because the space inside cannot accommodate someone her size. At this point, rather angry and frustrated at being 'grown up' in a space that is actively restricting that growth, Alice declaims that she does not want to grow up anymore. While on the face of it, Alice's declamation is against her literal size, there is another deeper meaning that Lewis Carroll wishes to present: that of the undesirability of adult life. Alice, in a sense, does not want to grow up—not only in size but also in age. This idea of the retention of a childlike state, in fact, continues throughout the book and spills over, as a more central argument, into its sequel *Through the Looking-Glass* as well. In the second book, for example, Carroll shows his derision against the adult world in the prelude poem of the novel where he warns Alice Liddell (for whom Carroll writes these stories) to never let her childishness be taken over by the incursions of the systems and institutions of the 'adult' world lest she die a 'melancholy maiden' (Carroll 1965). Obviously, Carroll does not mean that people should find a way to always remain a child. Rather, he wants to bring to notice the myriad methods and processes of stigmatisation that the adult world partakes in to ensure placements and continuations of hierarchies. Children or childlike states for Carroll do not participate in such structures that seek to marginalise entire categories of people. In other words, the adult world—in Carroll's conception—is classified by the mechanics of marginalisation where the world of children is bereft of such formulations. It is, understandably, not out of the blue that Carroll subscribes to such an idea. He was, after all, disabled and had to face marginalisation by the world. Natasha Gilmore, for example, notes how he suffered from chronic migraines, epilepsy, partial deafness, stammering and ADHD (Attention-deficit/ hyperactive disorder) (Gilmore 2015). Combined, all of his ailments, never really allowed him to have a 'normal' relationship with most of his peers. The only meaningful relationships he could have, thus, were with children. It is because of this ease that he felt with children that he could write such a fantastic children's tale.

That Carroll's disability forced him to the edge of society is not surprising at all. Disability, physical or mental, has always been one of the most highly stigmatised human conditions. The adult world, characterised by stringent identity formations based on an ostensible 'normal' way of interacting with the environment, always chooses to revel in its normalcy and reclassify even the probability of heterogeneity as an impossibility. The reasons for these formulations are varied: ranging from the primacy that is afforded to temporal experience (where more a human lives, more they believe themselves to be the custodians of social, cultural, historical, economic institutions) to dogmatic entanglements with the prevalent social structures. What this results in, however, is the complete obfuscation of existences that, for one reason or another, seem different. For those like Carroll, whose misfit vis-à-vis the societal normative is quite apparent, the adult world has only disdain and disqualification. These people, the ones who are physically and/or mentally impaired, hence, become 'the disabled'; unable, as it were, to navigate the world in a fashion that human beings are 'meant' to. This, then, is the beginning of stigma: where the existence of those whose bodies do not function like that of the majority is simply discarded. After all, there is a telos to stigma: as it reveals procedural declassification levied against the different (from the majority). Arthur Kleinman and Rachel Hall-Clifford, in their presentation of stigma as a social, cultural and moral process, quote Goffman and write something quite similar to this argument when they say that '[the] modern idea of stigma … [is] a process based on the social construction of identity. Persons who become associated with a stigmatised condition thus pass from a "normal" to a "discredited" or a "discreditable" social status' (Kleinman and Hall-Clifford 2009).

The implication of the entanglement between stigma and identity is quite serious. As shown above, social identities (of the self) formed by the adult world are always stringent and unchanging. There is no account of possibilities of flux when it comes to their being in society. This obviously doesn't mean that identities and identifications do not change. Take, for example, Lennard Davis's concept of the temporarily able-bodied, which reveals the ever-present possibility of an able body to become a disabled one. The manifestation of this possibility necessitates a contemporaneous change in the identity of that body, thus, proving the fluidity of self. But changes of this kind are never considered a true possibility by the adult world; especially when it pertains to their ability to act as per the demands of a normative model of behaviour and conduct. The adult world, rather, chooses to believe that identities are always final because it allows them comfort and, through it, grants them (social) power. After all, the continuance of power requires dogma; an orthodoxy, as it were, of being. Fluctuating identities would mean fluctuating power positions, thus, wrenching away control from the hands of those who wish to retain the aforementioned comfortable and 'normal' positions. The able-bodied world, for example, does not want to give up its control of infrastructural decision-making because it would, then, require them to get used to a world where architectures of navigations inconvenience them. It is, after all, easier to simply project a presentation on screen rather than figure out methods that would enable blind audiences to access the content the same way sighted ones do. Nevertheless, this belief in the unchanging form of social identity inevitably leads to a contemporaneous rigidity in the manner the 'other' identities are 'dealt' with. This ensures the facticity and finality of stigma itself, thus, turning it into something natural; something that needs to be. Why should one consider creating an accessible presentation if the normal existence is a sighted condition and blindness is merely a deviancy? It is natural for the presentation, in such a case, to simply be visual because one can only cater to normalcy. Towards the same, Kleinman and Hall-Clifford write how stigma is internalised and shapes individual behaviour. This, for them, is distributed through propagations of 'social, economic, and political power' (2009), thereby, ensuring continuances of stigma.

The methodologies of the promulgation of stigma, especially against the disabled body, is brought out quite well by Medha Trivedi in her Gujrati short story 'Vishakha'. The narrative of 'Vishakha' revolves around the eponymous character who, after a failed marriage, is left alone by her husband to take care of their mentally challenged daughter Chandudi. From the beginning, Vishakha's relatives and neighbours advise her to get rid of the little girl as she would be nothing but trouble. For them, a mentally challenged human being is fundamentally incapable of living as a human and, as such, has no right to grow up in a 'normal' family (of able-bodied people) of a 'normal' world. It is necessary for such people, they say, to be shipped off to special care houses and schools where they will grow up among their own kind and not disturb the world and its ways. Vishakha, however, does not listen to anyone and chooses to nurse her daughter herself. However, when Chandudi is old enough to go to school, the only option that is open for Vishakha is to send her to a special boarding institute. Distraught that she will have to spend most of her time without her daughter, Vishakha decides to take her out shopping a day before Chandudi is supposed to go away. From the moment they step out of their house, however, Vishakha is chastised by everyone for taking Chandudi out of the confines of the 'comfort' of her home. Her taxi driver, for example, repeatedly counsels Vishakha to go back because, for him, a mentally challenged girl cannot navigate the world in any meaningful way.

As if this were not enough, the shopkeeper to whom Vishakha takes Chandudi to buy new dresses refuses to serve them and calls Chandudi an abomination that will curse his shop and sales. Vishakha breaks down at this comment and shouts out and asks the shopkeeper how could such a little girl be a curse? The shopkeeper, of course, does not have an answer to her question but still banishes them from his shop. This is the world of the adult where the mentally challenged Chandudi has no place. Both she and Vishakha, by the virtue of being the mother of a disabled daughter, are stigmatised and forced to come face to face with an assumed unnaturalness of Chandudi's existence. Everyone, from Vishkha's relatives to the shopkeeper, is tied up within the concreteness of their own abled identities to even allow a possibility of Chandudi's normalcy. She is, for them, nothing but disabled, different and discredited.

Opposed to this world of adults, however, is the world of children. Unlike the former, the latter is marked by nothing but possibilities. In this existence of the child, identities are in flux, thus, allowing them to be whatever they want. Lewis Carroll's fascination with the state of the child finds its bearings within the contours of this infinite possibility. In *Through the Looking-Glass*, for example, he shows how Alice can become comfortable in impossible situations by simply believing them to be possible ones. For Alice, who imagines five impossible things on a daily basis, nothing is outside the realm of the possible; thus, fundamentally disallowing her to form any singular stringent identity. The entire novel, in fact, is about how she wants to change her social self from that of a pawn to that of a queen. For her, the world not only allows such a change but, in fact, thrives on it. This is the state that Carroll wishes Alice Liddell to hold on to; to find an existential connection to her childish self which asked for nothing but nonsense on the day Carroll went boating with her (and her sisters) and narrated the beginnings of *Alice's Adventures in Wonderland*. In fact, that boating memory is quite precious for Carroll as it is one of the rare times he felt included. None of the children had any problems with the different kinds of disabilities he was, even then, suffering from. In fact, it made him feel 'golden' to be with them (Carroll 1965). Stigma, after all, as shown above, is a phenomenon of the adult world, where social existence becomes far more important than individual ones. For the child, the socially stigmatised condition does not even exist. Even Trivedi's story shows that. At the end, when Vishakha is returning home, Pankti, a young child from the neighbourhood, stops her and asks her if she can come with her to play with Chandudi. Pankti's earnest and quite innocent desire to interact with Chandudi is set in and as a sharp contrast against the manner the adult world reacts to the mentally challenged girl. Pankti is able to do, with a single question, what the entire adult world could not: restore Chandudi's humanity. The story, thus, ends with also restoring the child's name back to Chanda from its mutilated form Chandudi and asserts the power that children like Pankti have in (re)making the world into a better place.

Works Cited

Carroll, Lewis. 1965. *Alice in Wonderland and Through the Looking Glass*. London: Peal Press.

Gilmore, Natasha. 2015. '10 Random Facts About Lewis Carroll'. *Publishers Weekly*. Available at: https://www.publishersweekly.com/pw/by-topic/childrens/childrens-authors/article/65414-10-random-facts-about-lewis-carroll.html#:~:text=Carroll%20suffered%20from%20chronic%20migraines,12%20works%20of%20literary%20fiction (accessed on 10 October 2020)

Kleinaman, Arthur and Rachel Hall-Clifford. 2009. 'Stigma: A Social, Cultural and Moral Process'. *Journal of Epidemiology and Community Health*, 63(6): 418–441.

Vishakha[1]

Translated from Gujarati by Nilufer E. Bharucha

Vishakha stood up although there was no real reason to do so. She opened the door and, standing in the middle of it, started looking out. In this opening, there was as much space as there could be between being and not being. If you looked inside, you would feel the sheer chill, the cold in which life had become frozen. If you took a step outside, there was the burning heat and searing wind. These days, she heard a lot of sounds—sounds of the changing days, sounds of the changing seasons, sounds of clouds splintering, sounds of a gang of children going to school or a lonesome man walking by. If, in the middle of the afternoon, she heard the bell of the peddler's cart, she would start and rush to the door. The shriek which would have otherwise escaped from her was suppressed under these sounds. The anguish in that shriek would then plunge right down as though from a great height and whirl and bubble around. It would be heard first by her before it could be heard outside and gradually subside within her. After that, everything fell silent until the next shriek tried to find its way out.

She came inside the house. Chandudi was still innocently asleep, imprisoned in the emotionless unconscious inside her. To helplessly observe this unconsciousness was the punishment she had to endure. She smoothed back the strands of hair that kept falling on Chandudi's forehead, blown there by the fan. She was as fair and white as alabaster. She had been named after much thought. Shweta, Poonam, Shashi, Chandra, Chanda … she couldn't remember how, within two years, she had become Chandudi from Chanda. Just like a block of ice, which may be like water, but in which nothing could grow. She would lie motionless for hours together, without consciousness of hunger or thirst. If you forced her to eat, she would spit out everything from the corners of her mouth, making you wonder if she would survive. But she teethed on time, and with that began the intense hunger. Her eyes would roll around and whatever she found would go into her mouth. Then she learned to move a little, only at the age of five did she finally start walking. The succinct result of all the reports was the same: mental retardation. Her body seemed to have no relationship with those reports and had started fulfilling its duties quite faithfully. Thick black hair, an aquiline nose, finely shaped lips—how lovely she looked when she was asleep! Leena had scolded her—what's the use of such beauty without

1 Translated with permission. All rights reserved with the copyright owners.

any sensibility? Now don't become sentimental and weak—I'll make an appointment, you just be ready for it. She wiped with her saree's pallu, the dried grains of rice and dal from Chandudi's fingers. Even her clothes had been soiled, so what was the point of tying a bib around her neck? She removed it.

All around the spot where she had seated Chandudi, littered outside her plate were mashed lumps of rice and dal. The glass of water had been overturned; the spilt water was turning red with the sweet peppermint ball melting in it. The rice and dal were spread out right till the very edge of the verandah.

She collapsed right there on the steps ... 'Will you be able to bear this?' Leena had asked her this question. Vishakha, this body is like an animal, it won't listen to anyone. It will become maddened by thirst and ferocious with hunger. At such times, it cannot think of anything else. It will demand it's due. Be warned, Vishakha, that sometimes ugliness itself becomes a blessing. How long will you keep nurturing this invisible ocean you can only imagine in the sound inside a shell? Wipe it out, rub it out forever. What should she wipe out? The lines that are drawn on the slate of nine months? It was because of Chandudi's life, her very existence, that she could not wipe away the memory of that first meeting ... I do not believe in bringing a stranger into my house and then tying her down with the bonds of responsibilities. I have no faith in such useless relationships. I am just helpless before my mother's stubbornness.... Mother's stubbornness? Don't you have any desires of your own? The big toe which had been circling the floor had stopped suddenly. The small pieces of stones in the mosaic tiles seemed to have lodged in her eyes. She raised her eyes but there was only nothingness before her. After he left, she had spoken about this to the family. 'Aah! Is this what he said to you?' They said and laughed. He was a distant relative of her brother's wife, so how would she pay attention to anything she had to say? It was true that he was an only child, a scientist, one with a long list of foreign degrees after his name. After the death of his father, he had given up a highly paid job and returned to India to look after his sick mother. My dear girl, once he realises he is a married man, his foreign ideas will, by and by, get wiped out. He has no vices like drinking or gambling, does he? How I wish he did have such vices! The screech which had been caught in her throat could have then been let loose.

The wind blew hard and the door which had been left open started banging. The clothes which were drying in the yard flew up all at once. Will there be a shower? She quickly started removing the clothes from the line. The hissing wind rekindled the fire that had been turned into ashes. It was as if life had re-started with the falling of the raindrops. Hours turned into days and days into nights. She would become restless and ask his mother—Was he always like this? If he gets lost in some work, he loses sense of time. You have to get used to this. So, like an old newspaper, she found herself pushed into the drawers of routine without ever having been read.

She heard Chandudi's animal-like whimpering and immediately went back into the house. Chandudi was sitting up in bed with her head tilted to the right side. Hearing her, she raised her eyes, looked at her from its corners and was happy. She started beating the bed with both her hands. This is the way she showed that she was either happy or had recognised her. 'Get up my child', she said and hugged her. 'I have prepared your favourite *kheer* today, but I'll give it to you only on the condition that you will do what I say. What you have to do is quickly swallow the medicine I give you. Agreed?' Chandudi nodded her head in acceptance of this condition. She took Chandudi's hand into her own—'Look, do you remember what Leena maasi says? She says that I should send you to a school. Not forever, of course. You can come home in the holidays. Chandudi, you'll learn so many new things there and become so clever. But how shall I live without my Chandudi? So I said to her....' Who knows how much of this Chandudi understood? Even if she did not understand anything, she would still keep on babbling. Apart from Chandudi, who else was there in the house that she could talk to? Within two months of his leaving, his mother had passed away. Vishakha had never missed him as much as she was missing him today. That day, in the morning, she had lit the fire in the hot-water storage tank and become busy with other work when the whole house had filled with smoke. She had gone into the courtyard and found him sitting there shredding papers from old files and feeding them to the fire. When she had gone up to him, he had said, 'Vishakha, there is no point in keeping these old things now.' Then he had locked himself up in his room the whole day. When he had come out in the evening, he had happily held court. Friends, family, neighbours had all clustered around him. He had entertained all of them with interesting stories of his life in the foreign land—where the row of tiled houses ended was a church at the very corner of the street and after that a bakery. Sitting on the doorstep of the church could be seen a black woman. Her face was half hidden by her curly hair. She would take out a hat from her belongings and put it in front of her. Then she would spend the day turning the pages of her Bible. Just as the church clock struck seven in the evening, the aroma of baking would waft out from the bakery. The black woman would then do the drugs she had bought with the coins collected in her hat. I would finish my work in the house and then, enjoying the fragrance of the cakes, would go out for a walk. The striking of 7 o'clock, the aroma of the cakes, was a common experience between me and the black woman. There was nothing new in this. But this experience would create a sense of bonding between me and that country, those people. You may call what happened either the beginning or the end. But, whatever it may be, it was rather strange. That evening, as the clock struck 7, the aroma started floating out from the bakery and I as usual set out for my walk. But that corner outside the church was without the presence of the black woman. I was a little surprised. I passed the bakery which was situated after the church. The baker beckoned me over and held out a plate with a piece of cake on it. He held my eyes with his own and said, 'She could not balance her life properly.' I was turning away without touching the piece of cake when the baker laughed, 'Her being or not being there will trouble you.' I had become so used to seeing this black woman outside the church that I now found the empty corner rather upsetting. So I started filling it up with metaphysical fantasies. But I could find no solutions. This made me restless. The corner without the black woman would create an uproar in the blood flowing through me and make me extremely worried. At the end of each day, I would become restless. I couldn't concentrate on any work. That which was once so distant, which had nothing to do with me, had now become very close to me. I wanted to get away from such intimacy but how does one do this if one had in the first place not built a close relationship? I had then realised that there is a certain mystery even in logic. It had become essential for me to find out what this mystery was and to get to the bottom of it. But living as I did, in this material world, I couldn't reach the ultimate truth hidden in such matters. These last few sentences had been addressed to her. This is all that Vishakha had been able to understand at that time. Then, from a village in a Himalayan valley or the banks of a sacred river, she would receive a scrap of a message that said, 'I am fine.' After that, there was no news from him. Who knows how this part of Vishakha, which had been dead for so long, had today shaken off its dust and come alive again?

Exile was written in Ram's destiny and for her was destined the responsibility of raising that which had been created out of a very slight relationship and which had no real consciousness of existing or not existing. He had left behind for her all his earnings and she supplemented this by coaching children. At such times, she would have someone or the other coming in and looking after Chandudi. There was this college student who had for the last three to four months been babysitting Chandudi. He would also help her out with some housework. Today, when she returned home, she had found Chandudi's hands soiled with sticky sweet peppermint juice—her cheeks were also full of it and her lips reddened by it.... A horrified screech escaped her, whatever came to hand first was hurled at the boy, who tucked in his tail and fled for his life.

The phone was ringing, Vishakha somehow dragged herself to it and took Leena's call. After two days, they had to register her in the school. What Leena said was reasonable. Chandudi and she had to struggle with society and with their conditions. Chandudi had to wage a war with her own body—a body that kept moving all the time and was out of her control. Even the simplest task was difficult for Chandudi. This is what she resented. She had to change the sheets. She held Chandudi by her shoulders and tried to lift her. Chandudi started waving her hands at her and her head started shaking more than ever. Saliva started dripping from her mouth.... 'My good girl, you shouldn't worry your mother. Come, we have just a little more to do, then my Chandudi can sit down comfortably with me and have her meal, listen to stories.... You'll do this won't you?' It was as if Vishakha was trying to convince herself rather than Chandudi that all would be well.

The clouds which had been gathering since the day before had by now come down in a shower. The dusty trees were washed clean and looked like good little children who had been bathed by their mother. Birds were circling in the sky like so many flowers unfurling their petals in the morning. The sky was witnessing their flight. This quiet morning had spread its magic all around. A beautiful day had dawned. She looked at Chandudi who was trying to hold on to the pencil stub that kept slipping out of her hand. She was unaware of the change that was about to take over her life. Within a few days, just like any other child, Chandudi, too, would go to school. Just like that empty corner, her house too was going to be empty of Chandudi, but she could fill this empty house with very solid reasons for emptying it in the first place. She had to capture the time that had rushed ahead and left her Chandudi behind and, by doing so, she hoped that Chandudi would be able to lead a normal life. After all, Vishakha was Chandudi's mother. She had to fulfil her duty of putting a blank slate in those hands which were waving around in frantic protest and lead her towards normalcy.

Medicines, massage, hot water compresses, measured food, diapers ... had Chandudi's infancy been lost in such a routine? Had her Chandudi remained unaware of her infancy? She came to a decision. She combed Chandudi's hair in the latest fashion followed by girls of her age. She made her put on a new dress. She took with her all that she would need for her.... 'Look, Chandudi, we shall have a lot of fun today. We'll do some shopping for you. We'll have a picnic. We'll go to the seafront. We'll go roam around till we get tired....' Saying this, she caught hold of Chandudi's hand and opened the door but Chandudi was unwilling to step out, she made little sounds deep in her throat and wound herself around her mother.... 'My dear Chandudi, just look out a little, see what a beautiful day it is! How could Chandudi stay inside the house on such a lovely day?' She pushed Chandudi out gently and shut the door. Seeing her struggling, the neighbour who was passing by said, 'Are you taking Chandudi to the doctor?' 'No, we are going out to have some fun.' The man was surprised, 'Out to have fun? You'll be able to take better care of her inside the house. What will Chandudi understand of such an outing?' She gave him no reply... 'Chandudi, we are getting late now!' The man sighed impatiently and said goodbye to them. Chandudi kept clinging to her on the main road. Vishakha rented a taxi for the whole day. 'Where do you want to go? The hospital?' 'No, take me to some readymade-garment shop.' The taxi driver cast a look at Chandudi. Her head was turned to one side. Her hands were slapping against one another in some kind of protest. From a mouth full of drool came soft sounds. Shopping in such circumstances! Not just the taxi driver but passersby on the road were looking curiously at Chandudi. Today, however, she was not going to give up. After getting into the taxi, Chandudi calmed down a bit but she still kept holding on tightly to Vishakha. After some time, she started looking with interest at the passing scenes. The taxi halted in front of a shop on a crowded road. The road was full of the hustle and bustle of the constant movement of people and vehicles. Vishakha tried to open the taxi door. Chandudi, however, did not want to leave this secure space. She was so frightened that her whole body started trembling. Vishakha somehow managed to get Chandudi out of the taxi and into the shop. But Chandudi now clung tightly to Vishkha and started shouting. Seeing this, one of the shoppers felt sorry for her and asked, 'Why are you torturing the poor thing like this?' The shopkeeper was beginning to get angry, 'Madam, why have you brought her here?' 'No, no, she's just a little frightened she'll calm down in a moment. Show me some dresses for her.' The shopkeeper then angrily said, 'We don't have anything for her! Bringing this inauspicious sinful thing here early in the morning will drive my customers away!' 'Inauspicious? Sinful?' Vishakha couldn't understand what was being said. 'What sin could such an innocent child have committed?' She too like Chandudi wanted to screech. 'You are calling her physical disabilities sinful! She has two ears, eyes, a nose and hands and legs just like you. She too is a human being. She is a part of society and who is going to sit in judgement on what is or what is not beautiful.' However, the narrow-minded shopkeeper was hardly going to understand her. 'Come, Chandudi, those who don't want Chandudi, Chandudi too doesn't want them!'

She caught hold of her hand and left the shop. Chandudi was now absolutely quiet, it was as if she had understood all that had happened. She started walking quietly beside her. The taxi driver was about to say something but she stopped him and said he should take them back home. She shouldn't have taken Chandudi outside the house. Whom had she been trying to introduce to Chandudi? There was only disappointment and contempt for Chandudi here. In such a situation, she did not need education as much as an understanding of her existence and self-respect. They had reached their house. She helped Chandudi alight from the taxi, paid the driver and was just going to open the door when she heard a sweet voice—'Aunty, can I come to your house to play with Chanda didi? My Mummy has gone out.' Her hand froze right there. She looked behind her. It was little Pankti from next door who had asked this question. She blinked away the tears which had been about to spill out of her eyes…. 'Yes, come in. Chandudi … no Chanda too would like to play with you, won't you, Chanda?'

LOHINI SAGAI

(The Ties of Blood)

By Ishwar Petlikar

Introduction

By Editors

While, in Medha Trivedi's short story, young Pankti's desire to play with Chandudi revives hope in the heart of Vishakha, it does not erase the fact that Vishakha sees no choice but to send Chandudi to a 'special' school. Quite obviously, this is not a school that would allow Chandudi even a semblance of inclusion. By its very conception, this is a school that is meant to keep children like her away from a society that does not want her. In fact, the entire effort on Vishakha's part to show Chandudi as much of the world as possible before she goes to her 'school' betrays even Vishakha's knowledge of the true nature of this institution her daughter is being sent to. Everything said and done, such schools and establishments are physical manifestations of the abled world's desire to segregate the 'deviant' and spare themselves interaction with them. They are, after all, as the cloth-house shopkeeper does not fail to remind Vishakha, inauspicious, and the farther the disabled humans are from them, the better. No wonder then that, Liat Ben-Moshe, quoting Harriet McBryde Johnson, calls these institutions, designed to 'contain', 'educate' and/or 'treat' the impaired, the 'disability gulag' (Ben-Moshe 2013). They are, in definite terms, quite like prisons; keeping the disabled bodies in their destined place and, in process, becoming an expression of the policies of eugenics that the abled world deploys for the maintenance of its normalcy. That Vishakha is constantly pestered with advice to keep Chandudi inside her house, away from the world, stands testament to such desires of segregation. Further, it is important to note here that throughout Trivedi's story, Vishakha has always been resistant to the idea of sending her daughter away. In fact, Vishakha accepts it only because her family and friends keep on telling her that it is the best course of option; not perhaps for Chandudi, but Vishakha. This constant 'advice', in favour of putting Chandudi in a special school, thus becomes symptomatic of an ontological need that the abled world feels to stay away from the disabled one.

Having said that, behind Vishakha's acceptance of the 'special' school also lies the politics of knowledge dissemination. It is possible, to a certain extent, to understand Vishakha's desire to educate her child (even if that 'education' imparts a mandate about the normalcy of ability). This entanglement with child education, at least ostensibly, reduces the degree of the presentation of the prison-like nature of this separation. Ishwar Petlikar's Gujarati short story 'Lohini Sagai' (translated as 'The Ties of Blood'), however, reveals the true nature behind not only these institutions but also the reasons behind such institutionalisations. In fact, the very first line of the story relates a call to admit Mangu, the mentally disabled daughter of Amratkaki, to the mental asylum. As the story progresses, the narrative shows Amratkaki struggling between her able-bodied sons and daughter constantly badgering her to take Mangu to the hospital and her mother's desire to take care of her daughter at home. But, her desire does not deter the able-bodied world from enlisting the 'positives' of institutionalising Mangu. There is then, in Mangu's life, to use Ben-Moshe's phrase, "the institution yet to come': a looming presence in the lives of all people with disabilities, even those who do not reside in them (for the time being)' (Ben-Moshe 2013). Quite naturally, the inevitability of this 'looming presence' is made even more real when Amratkaki too gives in. Witnessing the success of hospitalisation in the form of the cure of Kusum's (a girl from the neighbourhood) 'madness', Amratkaki finally agrees to send Mangu to a mental asylum. However, on the day of Mangu's admission, Amratkaki realises that, despite all the sweet words said in her presence, Mangu is not in a place that would take care of her as her mother would. The story, therefore, ends with another 'tragedy' when guilty over her abandonment of her child, Amratkaki too loses her sanity.

A few major implications vis-à-vis the abled world's treatment of the disabled body lie behind this entire narrative. The first is the insistence on finding a cure. Amratkaki leaves no stone unturned to try and 'fix' her daughter. In fact, the only reason that forces her to agree to Mangu's hospitalisation is Kusum's treatment. There is, hence, in the discourse of the abled, a necessity to bring the impaired over to their side of normalcy. The only way to believe that is possible lies in being normal and like the majority. The second implication follows from the failure of finding a treatment. The abled world, upon realising the impossibility of 're-turning' the disabled humans to their normal state, necessitates their removal from the normal world. Amratkaki's abled children constantly telling her to remove Mangu from the house is, in fact, a rather stark example of this. In fact, after the initial exhilaration of the possibility of a cure ends, Amratkaki too justifies Mangu's admission by telling herself that the hospital will take care of her when, after Amratkaki's death, nobody else would. There is, in a sense, a reluctance by the abled world to provide the infrastructure, which is important for the survival of the disabled body. The only option left is the 'disability gulag'. There is, as Ben-Moshe adds, an interconnectedness between institutionalisation and imprisonment not only in form but also 'their logic, historical enactment and social effects' (Ben-Moshe 2013). This then, effectively, leads to the third implication: that of the necessity of the segregation of the disabled body, not because it would help them (help, if any, is merely coincidental) but because it would allow the abled world to live in 'peace'. Like prisons incarcerate criminals not (necessarily) to rehabilitate, but to keep them apart from the rest of society, institutions, like the one Mangu and Chandudi are sent to, segregate for the sake of the segregation. This allows the abled world to distance themselves from not only the aberrations of normalcy but also the fearful reminders of their fragility. Ben-Moshe thus notes how the abled world, afraid of 'the disability yet to come', projects their anxiety onto the disabled body in the form of 'the institution yet to come' (Ben-Moshe 2013). Fear of becoming disabled, after all, as Bill Hughes suggests as well, drives most policies of eugenics.

Outside of the push towards institutionalisation, or perhaps to hurry the disabled self into it, one of the first targets that this fear finds is the mother of the impaired. Alongside the politics of gender at work, in finding a target in the mother, what is added on in such an attack is the hypocrisy of ability. On the one hand, there is, as Marsha Saxton notes, an illusion that the abled world sells where it assures that the 'burden' of mothering a disabled child can be 'alleviated by medical science' (2013). While Saxton goes on to speak about selective abortion to create, as it were, the desired normal human being, the only recourse that the abled is left with, in the absence of such elective abortion, is medical institutionalisation. Amratkaki, being constantly badgered by everyone in her family to seek medical help, despite knowing that Mangu cannot be 'cured', is, in essence, an exemplification of this need to resort to corrective medicine. It is, at the end of the day, Amratkaki's responsibility to 'take care' of the disabled child she has birthed without bothering the rest of the abled world. Since, however, it is impossible for Amratkaki to sever her ties with her sons, daughter and their families, it is best that she 'takes care' of the problem of the disabled child by sending her away to a medical facility. After all, in the abled world's mind, the logical frameworks of science that support such facilities also make them infallible. On the other hand, the abled world does not pull punches in blaming the mother for failing to either give birth to a normal child or, subsequently, taking care of it, as a mother should. The world, in a sense, as Saxton points out, through its sexist and able-ist tendencies, denounces the mother as incompetent thus making them 'feel guilty about their decisions' (Saxton 2013). At the beginning of Petlikar's story, Amratkaki's refusal to let Mangu go to a hospital stems from this guilt. She replies to each request by saying that if Mangu's mother fails to take care of her and sends her to a hospital, how would the hospital do it? This catch-22 situation comes back to haunt her when, on the way to the hospital, the people sitting with her (admittedly, strangers) accuse her of having failed as a mother and shipping her daughter off to a hospital to be locked up. This is an accusation that never really leaves Amratkaki and becomes a rather potent force, changing into her guilt, to turn her 'mad' as well.

It is difficult to reconcile these opposing instincts that the abled world harbours. But, perhaps, there's no need to. In remaining such, this dichotomy lays bare not just the hypocrisy of the abled world but also the baselessness of their demands. If fear, in a sense, is what propels the abled to seek the disabled body's incarceration, it is this demand for incarceration that gives rise to the fear in the first place. What remains then is normalcy deconstructed and a hope that perhaps, in its breakdown, also lies salvation. That, by the end of Petlikar's story, Amratkaki's son comes to his 'senses' and decides to get his sister back and take care of her is a direction towards that hope. While the story never shows Mangu's fate, one can, once again, hope that the son sticks to his words and takes at least a step forward towards the dismantling of normalcy that forced him to put his sister behind 'bars' and break his mother's heart.

Works Cited

Ben-Moshe. 2013. '"The Institution Yet to Come": Analyzing Incarceration Through a Disability Lens'. In *The Disability Studies Reader*, edited by Lennard J. Davis, 132–145. New York: Routledge.

Hughes, Bill. 2012. 'Fear, Pity and Disgust: Emotions and the Non-Disabled Imaginary'. In *Routledge Handbook of Disability Studies*, edited by Nick Watson, Alan Roulstone and Carol Thomas, 67–77. London and New York: Routledge.

Saxton, Marsha. 2013. 'Disability Rights and Selective Abortion'. In *The Disability Studies Reader*, edited by Lennard J. Davis, 87–99. New York: Routledge

The Ties of Blood[1]

Translated from Gujarati by Shilpa Das

When people advised Amratkaki to admit Mangu to a mental hospital, her eyes welled up with tears and she told everyone the same thing: 'If as a mother I cannot be a caregiver to her, how can I expect the people in the hospital to look after her with love and affection? Putting her in the hospital would be similar to deserting one's infirm or disabled cattle in a panjrapol or animal shelter.' When Amratkaki's angst became common knowledge, no one broached the topic again. When people saw for themselves how she brought up, cared for and indulged her daughter—whose hearing was impaired and who was mentally disabled from the time of her birth—they praised her, saying that only Amratkaki can raise a 'mad' daughter. Had Mangu been born in another home, she would probably have starved to death a long time ago and if, perchance, she had lived, she would never have been so stout.

Besides Mangu, Amratkaki had three other children: two sons and a daughter. The sons had finished their studies and were working in the city. The daughter was married and lived in her marital home. Amratkaki poured all her motherly love on Mangu as if she had forgotten her other children. Now and then, during holidays, when her sons arrived from the city, her home would resound with the laughter of her grandchildren. And yet, Amratkaki never seemed overjoyed to see them. She rarely carried them in her arms, played with them or pampered them like a grandmother. This did not bother the sons but both her daughters-in-law were incensed. This was their sole complaint to their husbands: she does not like her sons' children one bit and clutches her mad diamond close to her chest. Their complaint about Amratkaki's injustice to their children was quite unfounded for she behaved in the same detached manner with her daughter's children. While the daughters-in-law only grumbled to their husbands, the daughter would openly tell her mother off, 'By needlessly pampering Mangu, you have made her more insane than she otherwise would have been. With proper training, even cattle understand where they can answer nature's call and where they can't. Why can't a 12-year-old girl have that kind of toileting sense? She is dumb and not deaf that she can't do as asked. If she persists with this behaviour and makes a mistake, two tight slaps will ensure she doesn't make this mistake again.'

1 Translated with permission.

Before the daughter could say anything further, hot tears rolled down Amratkaki's cheeks. The daughter would regret her harsh words for a moment but relentlessly carry on with what was on her mind: 'You think you are looking after your daughter and making her happy, but, in reality, you are doing her a bad turn. You are not going to be around forever. When she falls to the lot of my sisters-in-law, they are not going to be tolerant about her toilet habits, and then she will be truly unhappy.' She would pause awhile and then continue in a low tone, 'As the saying goes, a mother will never have the heart to do something that can cause her child discomfort or pain. If she is not meant to improve in the hospital, she won't. But it will be enough if she acquires some sense of dressing and proper toilet habits. Otherwise, God has blessed my brothers by giving them plenty and my sisters-in-law are not so mean as to not give her food.' Other people in the village could never say the kind of things her daughter said when Amratkaki compared the hospital to an animal shelter. Nonetheless, they thought, 'Perhaps the hospital is like an animal shelter but if Mangu dies there, it will be blessed relief for both the family and her.' Amratkaki too felt that Mangu's death would bring in much relief, but only if it were brought about by a natural cause. She could not bear the thought of deliberately pushing her daughter to her death through neglect. She'd say, 'Everyone is selfish in their relationships with others. A true relationship is based on selflessness. What's the point of showering my love on my prosperous sons and my well-settled and happily married daughter? Only if I can be a mother to Mangu in the true sense will I be true to our ties of blood, our lohini sagai.' Sending Mangu to the mental hospital was but hastening her death and, so, Amratkaki did not heed the remonstrations of either her sons or the married daughter.

The sons understood their mother's sentiments and never brought up the matter. They felt there was no point in being anxious about Mangu's well-being. After all, three specialist white doctors had diagnosed that Mangu could never be cured. Their only regret was that Mangu hadn't been placed under a doctor's or a trained nurse's supervision to be adequately toilet-trained and to acquire some sense of socially appropriate dressing. They could not have made alternative arrangements at home for Mangu and ended up maintaining a steadfast silence on the subject.

Despite it all, Amratkaki persisted with several treatments for Mangu as per her faith. Since word got around, different kinds of alternative healers landed up at her home uninvited. Vendors of herbs such as shilajit or condiments such as asafoetida claimed to have a cure for her mental condition. Amratkaki believed that one must try out a thousand cures for one to finally work. She listened attentively to all that these healers said and implemented their injunctions with great faith. No matter if others often found these treatments foolish to undertake. Now and then, astrologers and bhuvas or faith healers visited her home. One astrologer predicted that Mangu's stars would improve in the upcoming month of Magshar and she would recover fully. From then on, Amratkaki waited excitedly for the month of Magshar. Mangu would turn 15 that month. Amratkaki had married off her other daughter, Kamu, at the same age and so her mind of its own volition drifted towards thoughts of Mangu's marriage. 'Had Mangu been normal she would have been betrothed too by now. If she is going to be cured in the month of Magshar, her looks are such that any prospective bridegroom will immediately consent to marry her.' Her thoughts would drift towards planning Mangu's wedding as though Mangu were cured: 'At the time of Kamu's wedding, my sons were not so well-off. Today, they are both very prosperous and spend money lavishly, then why should I restrain myself from having a grand wedding for Mangu?'

On one occasion, Mangu went to the chowkdi or wash area outside their house to urinate. Amratkaki was thrilled to see this 'newfound development' in her and for days tediously mentioned to all and sundry, 'The astrologer's prediction will come true. This is the first time that Mangu went on her own to the chowkdi to urinate.' The listeners found this hard to believe, for, even as Amratkaki was speaking, Mangu could be seen sitting in the mud in clothes wet from answering nature's call and scraping at the wet mud with her fingers. When Amratkaki noticed her doing that, she gently admonished her as though talking to a normal daughter, 'Mangu, you must not do that, child.' If Mangu were to get up on a whim, Amratkaki picked this up, 'See, she understood what I asked her to do and got up like a good girl!'

Soon, Amratkaki's hope-filled month of Magshar arrived. There was no change in Mangu. But a girl from the village who studied in the girls' school of the city, Kusum, went mad. Just like Mangu, she lost all sense of personal hygiene and of properly answering nature's call. While Amratkaki was saddened to hear the news, she felt gratified too. 'If a perfectly normal girl can go mad and lose her sense of personal hygiene, then what's unusual about poor Mangu, mad from birth, not having such a sense?'

When Amratkaki learnt that Kusum was to be admitted to the mental hospital, she felt sad; had Kusum's mother been alive, she'd never have allowed for such a thing. It is not for nothing that people say one is forlorn without one's mother. She shuddered as a mental image of Mangu's brothers leaving her at the hospital flashed before her eyes.

After a month, the news came that Kusum was now fine. She was no longer tied up at the hospital but roamed freely about without creating any nuisance. She had regained full toileting sense. The only trace of her former condition was that she kept singing all day. The doctors had assured the family that she would stop doing that too the following month. Kusum did indeed recover fully next month. The doctors advised another month's stay in the hospital and, thus, she stayed on for the third month. When Kusum returned, the entire village flocked to see her. Foremost among the visitors was Amratkaki. Everyone who saw Kusum's recovery advised Amratkaki, 'Kaki! Put Mangu in the hospital at least once. She will surely turn around.'

For the first time in her life, Amratkaki did not oppose this good counsel. She mutely listened to their string of advice. The next day, she invited Kusum home, sat her down and asked about the hospital. When she heard what Kusum had to say, her misgiving, that a hospital would never be able to care for a child if the mother herself could not, melted away. She began to have some faith in the hospital when Kusum added that the doctors and nurses there did not react adversely in any way even when any of the mad patients misbehaved with them. A new hope was kindled in her now. 'Who knows if Mangu is destined to be cured in a hospital? I have already tried out so many different treatments to cure her. Where's the harm in trying out one more? If there's no improvement in her condition, one can always bring her back anyway.' Finally, Amratkaki decided to put Mangu under institutional care in the hospital. She had someone write a letter to her elder son, asking him to come home. But, from the time she made up her mind, she simply could not sleep at night. The entire situation seemed oppressive to her, as though she was just giving up after resisting the move for so long. The reason for sending Mangu to the hospital was indeed borne of her newfound faith in it, but, deep down, she knew she had another reason for doing so which was gnawing away at her.

Mangu was growing up while she herself was growing old. It was clear that her daughters-in-law would not step into her caregiving role. So far, neither of them had asked Amratkaki to move in with her. Times were such that in every household, sons were under their wives' control. So, she had no expectations of her sons. Given that situation, whether Mangu recovered by god's grace or not, if she were to get adjusted to life in the hospital, then she would be able to die in peace with the assurance that her daughter was being looked after well if only by strangers. With that thought, Amratkaki shed copious tears. Her heart cried out in pain, 'You may give any excuse for doing this but the root problem is that you yourself are tired of your daughter!' Amratkaki woke up startled from her sleep, 'Am I tired of her?' and her heart vehemently replied, 'Not once. A thousand times!'

Amratkaki felt she'd made a huge mistake and been too hasty in dashing off the letter to her son. What was the big hurry to push Mangu away in the dead of winter? 'All night I keep covering her with her quilt. In the hospital, who will bother to do that every time she throws it off in her sleep? It would be better to take her there in summer....' But her son came home as soon as he received her letter. He even managed to get the magistrate's order permitting Mangu to be admitted to the hospital. The day to take Mangu there came upon them within a week. Amratkaki was convinced that her son was in a hurry to push his sister to the hospital and relieve himself of a burden. Why else would he show up at her door so soon after receiving her letter? Why would he use his influence to quickly arrange for a doctor and a magistrate? She had been considering taking Mangu to the hospital only in summer. But she could not utter a word to her son. 'He may have taken leave from his office with great difficulty; has already carried out the admission procedures of the hospital, and now if I ask him to defer taking Mangu there, he might feel I have nothing better to do than waste his time.'

Amratkaki could not sleep at all the night before Mangu was to go to the hospital. In the morning, she felt it would be better if she did not accompany Mangu. She would not be able to bear it when the authorities at the hospital separated her from her daughter. At the same time, she could not rest assured without seeing for herself what kind of facilities the hospital would offer her daughter. She had to go. And yet, when she stepped out of her home with Mangu, she felt as if the weight of the whole world was pressing in on her. Tears coursed down her face. She could not take her eyes off Mangu. Mangu was staring fixedly at the colours of her new dress. As if pleased, she looked at Amratkaki and gave a broad smile. Amratkaki's heart sank. She thought of how even cattle protest when a new master tries taking them away. Mangu had not even sensed she was being taken away from her home to a new place. With that thought, Amratkaki collapsed at the threshold of her home. Her heart cried out, 'A mentally disabled girl has no one in the world. Even her mother can desert her!' Her son was choked with emotion too. He could not even look at his mother. The greater their delay, the lesser was the time to catch the train. The bullocks yoked to the cart in the street outside the house seemed restless to move. Without meeting his mother's eyes, the son staggered to his feet, 'We are late. We should leave now.' And as he stepped out into the street, he wiped his eyes with the hem of his dhoti.

The neighbour's wife took Mangu by the hand and led her out. Other women tried to help Amratkaki to her feet. Finally, with a long sigh of resignation, and supporting her knees with her hands, Amratkaki stood up. Two people had to hold and hoist her onto the cart. Upon learning that Mangu was mad and was being taken to the mental hospital, the other passengers seized the chance to amuse themselves. 'If you put such a healthy girl in the hospital, within a month she will wither away. It's enough if they manage to survive some way or the other like cattle over there ... An old woman from our village has been left there by her sons. It's been five years now but there's been no improvement in her condition. When people from the village visit her, she falls at their feet and pleads to be taken back home. But, the less said of today's sons the better! How can one expect them to look after their mother? As such the sons are not bad, it's the modern-day daughters-in-law ... you know how they are. They want to strut about in their lives free of restrictions and do not want an additional person at home.... Doesn't this girl have a mother?' To Amratkaki, this wounding remark was unbearable. Her eyes brimmed with tears. Her throat choked. Oh, the shame of it! Her head bent down of its own will and affirmed she was the mother. 'My God! If you, her mother, can push her away, what can one expect of the hospital authorities!' Had Amratkaki been travelling alone or not feared her son's ire, she would have immediately returned home with Mangu. But, there was no other option now so, with a heavy heart and legs that felt like lead, she entered the hospital.

It was the time for visitors, so patients and their relatives were sitting about in groups in the central room. Some were eating the food their families had brought. Some were having fruit. A woman was sitting with her mad husband, telling him about their children and other news from home. A mad woman was fighting with her husband who was visiting her and was complaining about the attendants in the ward, 'These cows do not give me proper clothes to wear, good food or hair oil.' Amratkaki looked at the attendants. The woman's attendant smiled and said, 'From now on, I shall give you everything. Your husband has brought you delicious-looking food. Why don't you have some now?' The woman hissed, 'I haven't brushed my teeth. I haven't even washed my face.' To Amratkaki it looked as though she had. Yet, without the slightest irritation, the attendant fetched a pot of water and had her wash her face. She then wiped the woman's face with a napkin. Amratkaki heaved a huge sigh of relief. The attendants seemed to be caring enough.

Soon, the doctor and the matron of the women's ward arrived. Amratkaki's son extended the magistrate's order to them. In a voice loud enough for his mother to hear and feel at peace with, he asked them to conduct the treatment of his sister well. The matron replied, 'Please do not worry on that account....' Amratkaki broke in, 'Bon! We are worried because she is totally mad. If she is not fed by hand, she will not eat...' she trailed off, overwhelmed with emotion. The attendants rushed to her side. One said, 'Ba! Do not get anxious. We will push the morsel into her mouth.' In a miserable tone, Amratkaki said, 'That's exactly what I want to say, sister. She does not have proper toilet sense either. Please watch out if she wets her bed at night. Else she will keep sleeping on the wet sheets and catch a chill.' Another attendant replied, 'We check their beds four to five times at night.' To which Amratkaki responded, 'She cannot sleep if the light is on.' 'We give sleeping pills to those who cannot sleep.' 'Please ensure that rowdy inmates do not beat her up.' 'We keep the mischievous ones separate. At night, they are made to sleep apart in separate rooms.'

When the visitors left, the patients would be taken to the inner quarters. At such times, when the door was a little ajar, Amratkaki seized the opportunity to peep in and catch a glimpse of the living arrangements. She espied three or four women with unkempt hair and dishevelled clothes roaming about inside. One of them looked at Amratkaki, beat her chest and rolled her eyes, wildly startling her. She wanted to look at the living quarters and requested the matron, 'I would like to see the room Mangu is to live in.' The matron refused, 'Our rules do not permit anyone to go into the inner quarters where the rooms are.' Mangu, looking at this new world, wide-eyed, suddenly leapt to Amratkaki's side. Amratkaki lovingly put her hand on Mangu's head and was about to use her daily endearment 'beta' when her voice cracked and the word turned into a long death wail. The lamentation rang through the entire hospital. Tears flowed down the son's cheeks like a stream. Even the doctors, matron and attendants, who were used to witnessing such scenes, had heavy hearts that day. It was as if the walls also trembled for the very first time with the agony of a mad loved one.

An attendant tried to draw Mangu's attention towards her by waving a napkin in the air, 'Here! Do you want this?' Mangu suddenly left her mother's side to grab the napkin. Letting her hold the napkin for some time, the attendant caressed her hand and sweetly said, 'You will live with me, won't you sister? I shall give you tasty food and new clothes.' Mangu was staring at her, so, taking advantage of the moment, the attendant held her hand and ushered her in. The half-open door seemed to swallow Mangu. 'Mangu ... Mangu....' Amratkaki's moans were heart-rending. The doctor pointed at her son and consoled her, 'Mother! Consider me your son. Believe that you are leaving your daughter with your son and not in a hospital.'

The elderly matron, widowed at a very young age and working with the ill ever since, comforted her, saying, 'Until today you were her only mother. Today onwards I too am her mother.' Amratkaki sobbed and said, 'She does not have the sense that even mute cattle have. Till today I have never kept her away from me. Kusum came to your hospital, recovered and returned, so I gathered the courage to….' Her voice quavered. 'Soon, your daughter too will become normal like Kusum.' Amratkaki calmed down, but she kept steadily looking at the closed door as though she could see Mangu right through it. And then, as though Mangu reminded her, she said, 'She does not eat dry chapattis. In the evening, please give her chapattis mashed in milk. You could also mash in dal if you don't have milk.' The matron could not bear to look at the anguish in Amratkaki's eyes, so, with downcast eyes, she agreed. Amratkaki continued, 'She loves eating curd. It may not be possible for you to give her curd daily, but try giving her once every second or third day. We shall bear the additional expenses incurred for that. We shall also generously tip her attendant if she looks after Mangu well.'

Amratkaki and her son stepped out of the hospital with grief-stricken faces. Quietly, they left the place in a horse-cart. Just as she boarded the train, Amratkaki remembered something. She had forgotten to ask whether the hospital authorities gave the inmates cots to sleep on. Mangu had never slept on the floor. She would be uncomfortable doing that. Had she been allowed to go in and inspect the arrangements, she would have noticed that the cot was missing and would surely have made it a point to entrust Mangu to them with this information. The people in the hospital seemed a caring lot. They seemed to be good. Of that, she had felt sure. But, they had not allowed her to go in. She wondered whether they forbade her because the conditions inside were not fit to be seen. The half-open door seemed to prove that and also the mad woman who was wandering inside like a demon possessed. Not to forget the other famished-looking mad women she had spotted inside in utter disarray. Amratkaki felt she heard Mangu crying at not seeing her. Her tears streamed down once more. The woman sitting next to her asked, 'Ba, why are you crying? Has someone died?'

When they returned home close to 11 that night, the neighbour who was Amratkaki's cousin was up waiting for them. She had their dinner ready, but neither of them felt like eating. Their mood was as grave as though a dear one had died and the neighbour could not insist the way one cannot utter a word in the presence of the recently bereaved. There was but one refrain in Amratkaki's heart. What must Mangu be doing now? She kept worrying about her every second: 'How cold must it be? Have they covered her with a warm blanket? Have they changed her skirt and bedsheet if she has wet the bed?' As if Mangu could hear her, she mumbled, 'Child! Don't wet the bed. Don't throw away the blanket.' Earlier, every night at bedtime, she used to say this to Mangu. Yet Mangu had never followed what she instructed. When she wet her bed at night, Amratkaki would change her skirt and the bedding. Although Mangu was a grown-up girl, she would make her sleep next to herself so that Mangu would not have to lie on a wet mattress at night. Amratkaki missed her daughter's presence next to her on the bed. She thought, 'She is used to sleeping with me. Has she been able to sleep by herself?' She felt as though Mangu was desperately looking for her. She beat her forehead on the frame of the cot and sobbed, 'I am her mother, and yet I pushed her away from me!'

Even the son who was in the outer room could not sleep. He was not so attached to Mangu as his mother was but the grief coiled tight in his chest felt oppressive. The tears that ran down his cheeks were in tandem with his mother's sobs. If he was in such a state, what must his mother be feeling? For the first time in his life, the son could feel the agony tearing his mother apart. He thought, 'I must do something to relieve my mother's torment. What use is my life if I cannot do this much for her?' He took a silent oath, 'As long as I am alive, I shall look after Mangu well. If my wife refuses to clean her when she wets herself, then I shall take that task upon myself.' Having made that decision, the load on his chest lifted and he felt much lighter. Had Amratkaki sobbed once more, the son would have rushed to her the same instant and assuaged her grief by informing her of his decision. But it seemed to him that she had calmed down and fallen asleep so he decided to speak to her the next morning, closed his eyes and fell fast asleep.

At dawn, when the melodious sound of bells and valonaa, churning pots, rang through the village, a piercing cry suddenly rent the air. Amratkaki was screaming, 'Come here quickly everyone! Oh, they have killed my Mangu…!' The son leapt up from his cot. The neighbours dashed in. The bells and churning rods halted mid-air. Anyone who heard the scream ran in and halted on their tracks, jumping out of their skin: Amratkaki had joined ranks with Mangu!

PANGU

(Handicapped)

By Kalindi Charan Panigrahi

Introduction

By Editors

In her seminal essay 'What Is Disability Studies?' on the delineation of the scope of disability studies, Simi Linton presents an example of the golfer Casey Martin (Linton 2005). Suffering from Klippel-Trénaunay Syndrome, Martin needed the use of a golf cart to travel across the course and had petitioned the Professional Golfers' Association (PGA) for the same. The PGA, however, had rejected his plea, citing existing rules of the game and, thus, effectively disallowing him to continue playing. Martin, not one to take such an exclusion sitting down, took his plea to the Supreme Court which, after long deliberation, sided with Martin and allowed him the use of the cart. The most significant result of this entire episode, Linton argues, was both a discursive and constitutive renegotiation of the idea of golf (ibid.). A large part of the able-bodied world did not welcome this decision because they thought that allowing Martin to ride a cart between holes somehow destroyed the sport of golf. While Linton uses this example to display how disability studies, as a mode of enquiry, raises questions against structures that marginalise, such questioning does not negate the truth of Martin's exclusion from playing the sport. In fact, not only was Martin sidelined because of his disability before the verdict but, even after, he was not seen 'able' enough to conform to the rules of the game. Casey Martin is not an exception to the rule but a rather striking archetype displaying how society, with its stringent and apparently non-negotiable rules, always seeks to exclude the corporeally different. The reasons for this exclusion are multifarious: ranging from a fear that the abled world feels of the disabled body to a reluctance in giving up the comfort of the status quo. Whatever the reason is, this 'trope of human disqualification' (Kafer and Kim 2018) mars the life of the disabled human from birth to death. All processes of stigmatisation of the corporeally different, therefore, are singularly constructed for and towards disqualifying them from not only participating in the actions of the world but also being humans. The 'normal' way to do things, in a sense then, is a way that fundamentally disallows a good large chunk of the human population whose only fault is that they, perhaps, remind the other half of their frailty. Weakness is to be always abhorred and a sense of faux strength preserved. It's not, as Linton writes, that the disabled body doesn't fit into society. It is society that has moulded itself to not allow the disabled being to fit.

The Odiya writer Kalindi Charan Panigrahi's short story 'Pangu' is an excellent representation of this exclusionist nature of the 'normal' world.

It's a story about an unnamed character, called only the Handicapped throughout, who, because of his multiple disabilities, is treated by his family and neighbours as a venomous snake. From the day he is born, the narrative tells its readers, he has invited anger and scorn. His mother, ashamed of birthing, as the neighbours say, a monkey, wishes for nothing but his death. As he grows up, he is confined to a room and frequently beaten at even the most inconsequential of slights on his part. In fact, he is beaten so much that, by the time he reaches adulthood, he comes to think of his beating as a natural part of his life. Even at a formal level of the story, the third-person narrator does not fail to show how natural Handicapped's exclusion and stigmatisation is. Using, at multiple times, quite heavy sarcasm, the chronicler shows how Handicapped's family never realises that what they are doing to their disabled son is even potentially wrong. At the structural level of the narrative, there is, in a sense, a presentation of a paradox between the social and educational standing of Handicapped's family and the treatment they eke out to him. Not only is the family proud of its upper-caste heritage but has, across sons, produced people dextrous at different professions: from philosophers to lawyers. Yet, when Handicapped's pet blind bitch disrupts a religious ceremony, he is first (literally) kicked out of the house and then, even when brought back (after the youngest daughter-in-law's defiance for his safety), is kept outside the house like something dangerous. It is in this rather absurd intersection of the station and 'education' of the family with Handicapped's treatment that the true nature of the family's brutality and Handicapped's disqualification comes to the fore. The narrative's delineation of the irrationality of Handicapped's treatment is further heightened by its refusal to acknowledge the latter's identity and existence as anything but Handicapped. That the story chooses to call him Handicapped throughout shows how, when concerned with this being, the only thing that matters for the world is his disability. He has no identity beyond or outside his disability; subsumed within which exclusion is the only possibility. Expectedly enough, when he drowns, nobody notices. There's only the blind bitch, his lifelong companion, who wades in after him to try and save him.

But, the 'trope of human disqualification' (Kafer and Kim 2018) as levied against the disabled body is not necessarily one which demeans them. There is always the possibility of an elevation; of rendering the disabled body as something more than human. In this latter process, the likelihood of even the most 'normal' activity is thought of as an impossible thing for the disabled being. Therefore, when the disabled subject is able to do it, they are rendered superhuman. No consideration is paid, here, to the fact that what disables is not the impaired person's ability to do that 'miraculous' thing, but society's insistence on creating infrastructures (physical or otherwise) that never allow the inclusion of this community. The disavowal of the disabled body, then, as Dan Goodley shows, happens through the simultaneous upholding of two opposing views where the disabling culture 'reacts to disabled people in contradictory ways: as appalling/appealing, fear/fascination, hate/love, genocide/paternalism' (2011). Since the disabled body, more often than not, ends up doing acts that the abled world does not really want them to, they become, especially in those moments, the 'desired other' (ibid.). They represent a drive of superhuman achievement that warrants nothing but admiration. But, what needs to be kept in mind here is that what is lost in the disabled body's either subhuman existence or superhuman being is their humanity. They are, in a sense, always disavowed from being humans. Panigrahi's story, unsurprisingly then, begins by showing how Handicapped's birth is greeted with both mirth and hatred. At the very beginning, the story, in this way, shows the two movements of disavowal that Handicapped is made to go through in his life. True enough, while most of his family abhors him, the family's youngest daughter-in-law shows nothing but adoration. When Handicapped's elder brother lunges at him to beat him, the youngest daughter-in-law stands in the way, thus, stopping a possible fatal beating. When Handicapped is thrown out of the house, she breaks the rules of the zenana and follows after him to take care of him. Finally, in the end, she is the only one whose heart is broken when he dies. Obviously, there is nothing wrong with the kind of affinity the two of them share. However, between the rest of the family and the youngest daughter-in-law, what the narrative shows are the two ways in which the impaired are treated: either as inhuman or as creatures of admiration. Interaction between humans is never one-dimensional. It is a collection of different feelings that one feels for the other at different times. But, the youngest daughter in law in 'Pangu' is never shown to feel anything but admiration for Handicapped. What is even more problematic is how this affinity between the two is used to explain the youngest daughter-in-law's marginalised status in terms of his disability. It's as if the story is saying that the attraction (platonic by all means) between the two of them renders her as 'disabled' as he is. Herein lies the fault line of the story which, in its choice of the way of presentation, disavows the disabled body as something that other marginalised identities can become (often aspire to). Disability, however, cannot be, as Kafer and Kim remind, the 'master trope of human disqualification' for it takes away the particular history and being of the impaired human.

Works Cited

Goodley, Dan. 2011. *Disability Studies: An Interdisciplinary Introduction*. London: Sage Publications.

Kafer, Alison and Eunjung Kim. 2018. 'Disability and the Edges of Intersectionality'. In *The Cambridge Companion to Literature and Disability*, edited by Clare Barker and Stuart Murray, 241–268. United Kingdom and New York: Cambridge University Press.

Linton, Simi. 2005. 'What Is Disability Studies?'. *PMLA* 120(2): 518–522.

Handicapped[1]

Translated from Odia by Subhendu Mund

When you first looked at him, the amount of mirth evoked was not less than that of hatred. The right eyeball looked as if someone had put it upside down while the left one seemed to have turned halfway aside. As a result, he could see only one-fourth of what he would have with both eyes. The upper lip was torn into two and they joined at the nose in such a way that two of his teeth saw the light of day. It appeared as if the man was grinning all the time with the help of his two teeth. But, if you looked at him from one side, the deformity of his face was not that obvious—what you could see, however, was his unequal and imbalanced pair of legs. His waist was higher on one side and lower on the other. The hands were thin and curved. They appeared to be able to do nothing more than supply food to his mouth. The hunch on his back was so huge that it appeared as if the almighty had put a heavy weight and sewed it up on his back.

Since the day he was born, he had invited anger and scorn from everyone—parents, relatives and neighbours. Friends in the neighbourhood said that the daughter-in-law of the house has given birth to a monkey. Some even said it was a snake or a frog. His mother could not lift her face before others in embarrassment and desolation. Why is he alive? Why doesn't he die? That is all his mother could think. His father did not see him as an asset for his old age. He knew that his son would only be a burden to him. So he joined others in saying that he should be buried alive. Some educated but unemployed young men gained fame by writing about this weird figure of a man in weekly newspapers. One wrote: 'It is a living joke of Biswakarma, the god. He has constructed this man with whatever was broken, damaged and useless in his workshop. He is lame, hunchback, blind, hare-lipped and can hardly speak or hear. It appears from his body language that he can hear but one can't be sure whether he has heard something right because he is mute.' Someone else wrote: 'One can speculate on the shape and character of mythical characters like Astabakra and Jada Bharata by observing his activities.'

Despite the hatred and sarcasm of the world, the man kept growing slowly and steadily. The world had nothing to do with his life or death. But, he kept trying to ensure that others felt his presence intimately.

1 The editors and authors have made all attempts to contact the copyright holders.

Some people try to live with as little interaction with the world as possible. Their life is simple. But there are others, just the opposite. They become happy by living intimately with the world and sharing the joy and sorrow of others. The creature we are talking about belongs to the latter category. He would join a group while they were in conversation even though he could not speak. He would get into the houses of the neighbourhood and try to know how they were doing and try to win them over. Unfortunately, however, he could not enjoy a congenial relationship anywhere. His deformity allowed him to go anywhere he wanted. He was a good plaything even to the young women who were never seen by the sun. Those women, who hide in a corner when they see even a cat or a dog from their in-law's place, came out to the open to frolic with him. Someone would ask him about his marriage. Someone would pour hot rice water on his face out of love. Someone else would pour oil on his dry hair.

When he was home, he was a burden to his family. When he came out, he was in a pageant. Street urchins would chase him and throw dust, straw, sticks at him. Street dogs encircled him and started to bark. Maybe they were all curious about his abnormal existence. Children cried in fear and hid their faces in the laps of their mothers when they saw him. Sometimes he got angry and mocked them, spat at them or threw stones. When in agony, he cried; when in joy, he laughed. But there was hardly any difference between his crying and laughing because the distortion of his face was no less when he was laughing or crying. So it is not surprising for people to suspect his feelings.

In spite of being the subject of ridicule and getting the same kind of treatment in joy and sorrow since his childhood, the man was always inclined to have the exhilaration and vitality of a normal human being. Everyone called him Handicapped because of his natural constitution. It appeared from his body that the maker of the universe did not intend him to be useful for any work: good or bad. But, it appeared from his activities that he was eager to do something for others, to be useful to them.

Whenever a neighbour fell ill or there was any suffering, he would be ready to sit beside them or do something. But nobody wanted him around for any service; his presence was considered inauspicious. For his unsolicited service, one would chastise him while another would give him a handful of puffed rice and ask him to leave.

The members of his family kept silent when he was chastised by some outsider. No one seemed to bother where he was or what he was doing. But, whenever he reminded his presence in his family by some action, they used canes and hands on him as a potter would do to give proper shape to the pot. After receiving the blows, it was difficult to guess from his face whether he was laughing or crying, but the sounds he created did not arouse their pity—it made their irritation and hatred twofold.

Once, when his elder brother asked for oil for his bath, Handicapped rushed in with his funny gait with the oil pot. He had taken hardly two uneven steps when the unruly pot fell from his hand. Who wouldn't be angry? In no time, the anger of the big brother was realised on the face and the back of Handicapped. Another time, when he was massaging his elder brother's feet, two streams of saliva fell from his mouth and rolled down his brother's feet. Could any brother put up with such a nuisance?

His nuisance gradually increased. Soon it was transferred from human beings to birds and animals. A cat was writhing when some vehicle had smoothly run over one of its legs. The scavenger should have taken it away in his garbage cart with whatever was left of its life. But this fellow picked it up and brought it home to start tending its wound. A half-blind and lame bitch was beaten black and blue while invading someone's kitchen because she was hungry. This guy rescued her as well, brought her home and gave her rice to eat. Could his parents put up with such nuisance done by their son who couldn't earn a paisa? Parents don't give birth to a child only to sit and eat throughout their life. So, his punishments increased in proportion with his mischief. But he gradually became adept at being beaten. He would accept slaps and blows unflinchingly but did not abandon the cat and bitch.

The cat, with a tinkling bell tied around its neck, followed him wherever he went. The bitch joined them as well, her body unsteady owing to her dried-up tail dangling behind her. Handicapped would move along caressing one and carrying the other. How long such misconduct could be tolerated? Especially for the kind of family they were: a family of Vedic Brahmins respected by the people of four neighbouring districts. This family had produced so many degree-holding pandits in vyakarana, vedanta, kavya and nyaya who were illumining the world with their fame. This was also the family where the living deities Lakshmi-Narayan were enshrined and worshipped in 16 ways in 16 hours!

We cannot say whether Handicapped understood why he was being thrashed by human society. But he became so used to thrashing that he would sit down quietly without shouting or resisting once the thrashing would begin. Like a bag of cotton. The sankhya-vyakarana-expert brothers would secure their scholastic pride as well as the sanctity of Lakshmi-Narayana by felling on him like a sack, and kicking and boxing it.

There was of course another helpless, powerless creature who would stifle her cry of sympathy under her veil in the dark corner of the kitchen. Nobody knew that; nobody understood. Handicapped had found her as the only oasis in the Sahara of the human world. But what was in her power? She was a girl of 14 or 15 years of age. Her matriculation-failed husband worked elsewhere. Her father was busy earning money by usury. She had no brother. When she was only two, her mother had died after giving birth to a son. The eight or nine years of her life she had spent with her brother were the happiest of her life. Then she had lost that as well. She had to bear the sorrow of separation from her brother when she came to her in-laws' place after marriage. She had no one else here or at her parental place. Her husband Ashirvad had stayed at home for only four or five days in total after their wedding. During that period, she had neither seen him nor had he seen her face. But she looked like an idol of gold.

In the entire human world, she alone was Handicapped's friend. But she was not any abler than him in any way. Like Handicapped, she had eyes but could not see; she had ears but could not hear; she had a mouth but could not speak; she had feet but could not walk. She kept sitting silently behind the doors of the kitchen. If somebody from the neighbourhood came to see the new bride, her mother-in-law would raise the sari-end hiding her face. She would close her eyes and, with great difficulty, show her fair and rounded face like a tortoise taking out its neck. She was the daughter of a big man. As she had no brother, there was an expectation of getting a lot of dowry from the heirless family. But why should the elder sisters-in-law care? After all, she was the youngest, and she had to massage everyone's legs, do all the work, right or wrong, listen to everyone else—she could see everything, hear everything, but was not allowed to speak. She could not walk straight before the others. All the others in the family were her elders. She might have come from a rich family, but it was her duty to obey them for she was a woman. Her elder sisters-in-law had done so; everyone in this world obeyed these rules. Innocently, she too obeyed. When she was sitting, they called her an ant-hill; if she slept, she was called a pounding log; when she was just standing, she was called a ladder-to-heaven! She listened without saying anything.

It was, hence, just natural for her to have an affinity with Handicapped. Although she had no deformity in her hands, legs or other limbs, she was prohibited from using them. However, there was a difference between their persecutors. For one it was the human being and for the other it was destiny. Handicapped did not at all like the demeanour of his youngest sister-in-law. He found it very odd. So he asked her making signs why she did not speak out though she could. She had a beautiful pair of legs—why didn't she walk? Why should she hide her beautiful face? He pointed at his own limbs, indicating, 'I am Handicapped. You are not. Why can't you?'

Handicapped was the only one allowed to speak to the youngest daughter-in-law. But, there was no way he could get a response from her. She did not need to hear much, though she listened a lot from everyone in the house. She needed to speak. But it seemed only Handicapped was meant to listen to her. She spoke to him during the couple of hours that she got after toiling the whole day and listening to everybody. She would tell him about a kitten she had rescued from a tomcat, and how it walked, ate, etc. Then she would tell about her younger brother: how he loved her and picked ripe berries for her. And about her mother—but she did not remember much about her. She left her when she was only two. While telling about her, drops of tears would flow out of her dark eyes. He would raise his crooked hand and wipe it out with her sari-end. The lame cat would be purring nearby. But the half-blind bitch was not allowed in. She would be tied to a bamboo pole in the open shed in the backyard.

The mischief of the bitch was the most intolerable. This wretched creature would howl at the exact moment when an offering to Lakshmi-Narayan was being placed. Or, her howls would be heard by the erudite father-son-duo when they would be halfway through their lunch.

As Handicapped grew, his haughtiness and disobedience decreased to a great extent. Gradually, he became afraid of human beings. He looked upon them as superior to himself. He did not find any similarity with them. He had no right to offer help when they needed it or express joy over their happiness. Whenever he tried to do so, he was rewarded with thrashing. So, it was improper on his part to consider himself equal to them. Consequently, he too became apathetic towards them. His only asylum was with the youngest sister-in-law, the half-blind bitch and the lame cat. His father would look upon him as a cursed creature in previous birth and took him to the idols of Lakshmi-Narayan and forced his forehead below their pedestal. But the insolent Handicapped would either spit or heave his feet towards the deities. He would then be properly thrashed and finally returned to the youngest sister-in-law.

The poor sister-in-law would wipe him clean with a wet towel and apply oil to the wounds while drops of her tears doused the bald head of Handicapped. When the brothers of the elder daughters-in-law came and talked with their sisters, the youngest one would start gossiping with Handicapped and the lame cat. When his elder brother got mad with him because of some wrongdoing and came to beat him, he would run and hide behind her. How can one elder brother-in-law enter the room where the wife of his younger brother was there?

Everyone in the family refused to spare rice for the half-blind bitch. Handicapped would go to her and pour down half of his food before her. Then one day there was no more food for him. The eldest daughter-in-law went to her mother-in-law and whispered in her ear: 'Go and see what your brother-in-law-loving youngest daughter-in-law has done! You had ordered that Handicapped should not get his food. Go and see now. And you blame us that we are unmannerly to the youngest one.' The eldest was the right hand of the mother-in-law. The old lady went and saw bowls of rice before Handicapped as well as the bitch. Infuriated, she said, 'Hello, daughter-of-the-big-house! Do you think food is cheap in our house?' The youngest one was engrossed in watching Handicapped eat. Startled, she put the sari-end on her head and stared at her mother-in-law.

The youngest sister-in-law, the half-blind bitch and the lame cat grew in age along with Handicapped. Simultaneously, the world also kept growing. But time did not have any effect on the size of Handicapped, the half-blind bitch and the lame cat: as if they belonged to an eternal family of Handicappeds.

Handicapped found refuge in his youngest sister-in-law but would hide from others in fear. When upset by something at home or outside, he would cuddle in his sister-in-law's lap in fear—as if he was her pet. The mother-in-law and the other daughters-in-law did not appreciate this congeniality between them. The sisters-in-law would jeer at them; and, as the youngest one spent so much time with Handicapped and neglect household chores, the mother-in-law would shout at her. But they could not live without each other. The love she cherished for her brother was replicated in her heart for him. Whenever there was any cruelty bestowed on Handicapped, his silent suffering would echo in the heart of this voiceless woman. Who else can understand this voiceless message but the mute god who bears the injustice and affliction of the world silently?

It did not appear as if Handicapped's faculties grew with age. He became more dependent on the youngest sister-in-law. On her part, she defied everybody; and despite being admonished by her father-in-law and the brothers-in-law, she would never leave Handicapped's side. There was no one else in the family with whom she could, at least, have the practice of talking, or clearly look at a face, however distorted, without covering her face. Thus, it was impossible on her part to live without Handicapped.

Those days everyone was busy with the elaborate preparations of the puja. The house was thronging with the coming, going and eating of so many people. While Handicapped's mother was carrying the offerings to the deities, the half-blind bitch, who had unleashed herself as the knot of her leash had loosened, came rushing towards her. Apprehending an ensuing problem, Handicapped tried to chase the bitch and stop her. But, before he could do so, the bitch had already sprung up to the offering and polluted it. The old woman started howling. The eldest son, who was making arrangements for the puja, came running. He saw the plate of offerings lying on the floor. The bitch was happily slurping away the food items meant for the offering. When Handicapped saw his elder brother, he hurtled towards the kitchen. The elder brother chased him, roaring in anger. Everyone in the house was looking on—speechless. Nobody thought Handicapped would be able to save his life that day. Seeing the elder brother's anger, everyone stood aside. But his running feet stopped near the entrance to the kitchen. The youngest sister-in-law; who, on hearing his voice, would cover her face by her sari-end and hide in some corner, stood obstructing him at the doorway.

The elder brother stopped but his fiery anger was doubled after facing obstruction. His mother came to him and touched his lips: 'Don't beat him, please! He is as such a wretched fellow.' But the elder brother would not listen. He insisted that there would neither be any puja nor would he have food until Handicapped was driven out of the house.

It was a difficult situation. But there was no way out. Handicapped was dragged out. He had clutched his sister-in-law's sari-end so hard that it tore when he was dragged, but nobody could open his fist. The elder brother dragged Handicapped out of the house. Eyes glaring, he made it clear to his younger brother that his life would not be spared if he dared to come back home. Handicapped limped out. The lame cat jumped unto his hump. The half-blind bitch went along circling his legs around him. Handicapped knew his brother was very angry, so he went away without looking back. He did not know how long he kept walking. When his feet became tired, he sat down under a big banyan tree. The sun was leaning towards the west. Innumerable birds came flying from distant villages and assembled over the tree. Tired as he was, Handicapped fell asleep holding the cat and the bitch in his lap in that desolate place under the boundless blue sky.

No change was seen in the pandit family in the absence of Handicapped. But, the youngest daughter-in-law did not have a morsel of food that night. The mother-in-law kept shouting for some time but in vain. She slept beside her, but in the morning she did not see her. She thought the girl might be doing household chores, but she was not there. She looked for her in the front of the house, in the backyard, everywhere, but couldn't find her anywhere. Where did she go?

The brothers-in-law wrapped fine chaddars on their rounded tummies and started looking out for their sister-in-law. The married woman of the house had left! What a shame! Dharma, family prestige, social standing—everything was lost! Could they ever walk raising their heads?

Looking for her, they reached the tree under which Handicapped had taken rest last night. They saw a strange sight there. The youngest daughter-in-law had placed an earthen pot on two stones and was cooking rice. With a knife, Handicapped was chopping some vegetables while the bitch and the cat sat beside him. What would the pandits say to anybody in that wilderness? They fetched a cart from the village nearby and brought back the youngest daughter-in-law home. They had no other option but to bring back Handicapped, the bitch and the cat as well.

But the demeanour of the youngest daughter-in-law enhanced their anger rather than pacify them. Handicapped, the protagonist of all the drama, became the object of all that anger. He was brought back home for the sake of the youngest daughter-in-law but more stringent rules were made for him. He was made to live in an open shed with his bitch and cat. He would be supplied with his food and drinks there. He was prohibited from entering the home.

Handicapped did not know the meaning of insult. He would bloom in joy when, once in a while, during a day, his youngest sister-in-law—who was his dearest friend and who, for him, was like the only source of water for a thirsty one—would come to his shed. There was no beauty in his smile and his crying was extremely hideous. Nevertheless, the childlike language of his heart was reflected as happiness or sorrow on his face when he did not see his youngest sister-in-law, the only goddess he worshipped. His lone eye would express the yearning of his heart. None else but that kindly mother figure longing for her brother empathised with him. The youngest daughter-in-law had been forbidden from going near Handicapped. As he was in the backyard, at times she could go there. But she was scared and had to be very cautious. Hell would break loose if her mother-in-law or the sisters-in-law saw her there.

Being thus free from her loving control, Handicapped gradually became more rebellious. He became more intimate with his cat and dog. He would make them sit near him and feed them. A Brahmin sharing his meal with a cat and a dog! Whatever happened to charity, piety and gods? Trouncing on him increased every day. No way could he run to his youngest sister-in-law anymore. So, like a motionless sack of things, he would silently bear all the torture inflicted by the humans. Just as the innumerable birds and animals have to bear torture without any fault. Only one mute creature would sulk, weep and go without food. But nobody took that seriously.

As he had neither solace nor attraction in his family, Handicapped became more intimate with the outer world. He was indifferent to summer, rain or winter season as he always remained in bare body. Even during a violent rainstorm, he would be seen moving like a dancing buffoon exposing his hairless head to the sky. When one's bone marrow was frozen in the sharp cold, he would be seen getting up early in the morning and, with or without any reason, would traverse two miles up and down baring his black body in the grey fog. Nobody seemed to be curious about this or ever asked him anything. Initially, maybe, he was an object of curiosity but, in course of time, people became used to his nature and became indifferent towards him.

On one rainy day, Handicapped set out somewhere in bare body. The sun was yet to rise. It was drizzling after a heavy pour. He just walked like that under the rain and above the water on the ground. He saw, at a little distance, the water of the overflowing pond was running in a stream below the mango tree. Below the tree, many crows were crowding over something. Handicapped went closer, adjusted his one eye and tried to focus on the object. He found a little myna chick being swayed away in the stream. The crows were hovering over it and were plucking its feathers. Handicapped never thought before doing anything. No one could say whether he had any such faculty because whatever he did was out of instinct like that of birds and animals.

When Handicapped saw the calamity of the chick, he jumped into the water. The lame bitch that was behind him also followed suit. The level of water increased from knee-deep to the waist. The chick was still five to six feet away. He progressed towards the chick with his crooked hand extended. The water rose to his chest now and his hunch was immersed in it. When the water touched his nose, he raised his head and kept moving towards the chick. Being free from the clouds now, the sky shone in golden splendour. The first rays of the morning fell like a benediction on his ugly face. A soft line of a smile was seen on his lips. He had never smiled like that before.

His uneven body had never allowed him to learn swimming. The chick was still a little away. Handicapped stretched his hand to catch it in one go but his feet slipped and his ugly body was buried in the deep waters. One who was hated and neglected all through his life went on his final journey similarly unseen by anyone.

A farmer saw this. He rushed and informed the pandit family. By the time people came and fished out his body from the waters, the sun had already traversed a good distance. He still had the chick clutched in his hand. The lame bitch, his companion for years, had also died with the end of Handicapped's cloth in her mouth.

The world gained or lost nothing with the sudden death of Handicapped. But the woman, an embodiment of love, who lived with the cat in her lap in a dark corner of the house and shed hot tears of anguish only she knew, in her tender and affectionate heart, what she had lost.

SUBHA

By Rabindranath Tagore

Introduction

By Editors

The desperate desire for the retention of the normal characterises the existence of most humans of the world; most because the normal is always only the realm of those who find themselves in it. It matters little to them if this normal is itself problematic or, for that matter, imaginary. In the face of possibilities of catastrophic alterations, these denizens of the normal cling to their constructed mechanised lives, hoping to remain shielded from inevitable transformation. This desperation, more often than not, manifests at the cost of the lives of those who find themselves either at the fringes or outside the normal. For the inclusion of these, the abnormal will always challenge the normal. These two are, in a sense, existential categorisations: with the normal feeding on the abnormal even as the former keeps on sustaining the latter. This normal is the abled world and their insistence on Casey Martin's 'unfair' usage of a golf cart to travel the course is symptomatic of the disease of the normal. His inclusion into a sphere of existence classified by the other 'normal' golfers bothers the abled world. In fact, as Bill Hughes observes, it makes them practically afraid that, with the inclusion of people like Martin, their cherished normalcy will break down (2012). The abled world, then, due to its desperation and fear, discards even the possibility of the merger of abnormality as illogicality because the abnormal does not fit into their constructed world. It is, after all, illogical for them that Martin should be allowed the use of a golf cart. Handicapped, from Panigrahi's story, has it even worse. He isn't just abnormal, but abhorrently so. The normal, upper-caste and highly educated people of his family cannot even fathom the possibility of accepting him as a human being because that would shatter their standing in the world. Therefore, his place is outside the house, in a menagerie, fated to exist like the beast he is made out to be. What is apparent in these two examples is what Tanya Titchkoksy calls the 'problem' of the disabled. For the abled (normal) world, 'disabled people are … "only relevant as problems"' (Titchkoksy 2000). Such an understanding, Titchkoksy cautions, is not 'simply because … bodies … give … trouble; [but] is presented to people through interaction, with social and physical environment, and through the social production of knowledge' (2000). This means that the problem of the disabled lies, technically, outside the body of the disabled, thus, necessitating a solution by those not afflicted by the problem. Obviously, that the disabled bodies are a problem means that they cannot, at an existential level, be someone who can be included within the realm of the normal, especially since the problem rears out of the 'interaction' that the abled and the disabled subjects have—a problem that is often, as Hughes too notes (2012), approached with fear, pity, charity and/or disgust.

Thus, the disabled bodies are cast out of the world: to live with the charity of the abled and never allowed a strong enough position to let them realise that since the problem is not their body, they too are, for the lack of a better word, normal. One such method of exclusion and disqualification is a profound silencing of the disabled body. Their voices are literally subdued and, even if heard, completely discarded. Such processes of silencing not only ensure that the disabled body is never able to speak loud enough to affirm their position as human beings but also keep them, perpetually, as a problem to be solved. It becomes easy, in such a case, to point out and say that, since the disabled subject cannot speak (either literally or metaphorically), the abled will, in their stead. The irony, rather obviously, is that it is not the disabled human who cannot speak but the abled world that does not want to hear. Rabindranath Tagore's short story 'Subha' shows a rather poignant example of this silencing. The story revolves around a young mute girl, ironically named (although not so by design) Subhashini—the one whose voice is melodious—as she negotiates a world that does not want to listen to her. Yes, she is mute and cannot speak, but the story tells its readers that she doesn't require sound to speak. Lacking the faculty of speech, she expresses through her eyes and face; a language that, the narrative says, is far better than any other: '[s]he, who can't express other than through the contours of her face, has a language in her eyes which is inconceivably vast and unfathomably profound—much like the clear sky, that theatre of the silent play of light and darkness' (79). But the world never cares enough to notice this language. Subha, a blemish on her mother's motherhood and a curse to her family, never warrants enough humanity to have people listen to her 'unconventional' speech. Even the local loafer, Pratap, the only human friend she has, keeps her close only because she can't make a sound and disturb him while he fishes. Try as much as Subha wants to make him look at her as someone useful, as someone who could help him, she always fails, ultimately taking recourse in a world of fantasy where her desires are fulfilled only as of the fantastic. By the end of the story, rather evidently and despite Subha's silent yet loud pleas, she is married off to a stranger who isn't even told about her disability. When he discovers her incompleteness, as it were, he too discards her and brings home another wife who 'could speak in a language he could understand' (83). Throughout her life, hence, Subha keeps on trying to make people listen to her even as nobody (quite adamantly) does. Since, further, nobody could 'hear' her (because they didn't want to), they categorise *her* as the mute one, thus, silencing her in quite definite terms. Once she is silenced, the abled world proceeds to decide her fate as it fits them: the parents retaining their social status by marrying her off and the husband securing his abled normalcy by remarrying. Thus, the 'problem' of Subha is resolved and the structures of normalcy persist intact.

Having said that, it would be somewhat unfair to say that no one in the world listens to what Subha has to say. She has two best friends—Shorboshee and Panguli—two mute cows who always know when she is coming to them, understanding 'her poignant silence better than any language' (80). Apart from the two cows, there is also a kitten and some goats who populate Subha's world as friends. This affinity that Subha, as a disabled, has with animals is quite interesting. In fact, it isn't just Subha. In Panigrahi's story, the multiply disabled Handicapped forges similar connections with animals as the blind cat and the lame bitch become his companions in misery. This affinity is interesting because it shows how easily the disabled body is pushed into the realm of nature. This realm of nature, full of trees, flowers and animals, is in stark contrast to the arena of culture, populated by humans. The latter always rejects and disqualifies the disabled body. The representations of disability in culture, however incorrect or unreal, encourage, in a sense, a particular kind of existence of the disabled self. Richard Dyer, saying something similar, writes that though 'reality is always more extensive and complicated than any system of representation can comprehend', the cultural representations of the disabled body are always real because they 'have real consequences for real people, not just in the way they are treated but in terms of the way representations delimit and enable what people can be in any given society' (1993). Obviously, the representations that are being spoken of here are not just artistic representations but the way the reality of the disabled body is re-presented to the world through culture. This representation has, as already shown above, always been in terms of the derogatory where the disabled body is nothing but the problem. In being the problems of culture, then, the disabled subjects never finds any kinship in it or inclusion. The realm of nature, however, is different. There the disabled bodies feel at home, in connection to other entities outside them, thus, recovering their lives from an abyss of loneliness. Both Subha and Handicapped are prime examples of this connection. One can, obviously, see the disabled body's affinity with nature in bestial terms: that the disabled subjects are so loathsome that they can never enter the cultural sphere and have to be, necessarily, pushed into a regressed state of the primitive. But, there is also another way to understand this relationship that the disabled bodies have with nature where, in rather Romantic terms, nature becomes a repository of all the things that culture denies them: things not only in material terms but also emotional. Handicapped finds himself at home, even outside his house, as long as his companions are with him. Subha, similarly, not only finds friendship with animals but is also able to converse with nature:

> And nature seemed to compensate her silence. It talked for her. The ripple of the river, the chatter of the crowds, the song of the boatman, the chirping of birds, and the rustle of leaves—sounds, vibrations and movements of the world all came together, and followed ceaselessly, one after another, like the waves of the sea, upon the ever-silent shores of her heart. (79)

The implication of this latter reading is quite profound. On one hand, it proves the abled world's insistence on their normalcy, where normalcy rests on the natural, the redundant. On the other hand, the disabled bodies become the natural ones, thus, asserting their normalcy. After all, if, as Lennard Davis says (1999), abled bodies are merely temporarily abled, then the natural is this 'disabled' form. Between these two points, finally, it is the arena of culture that is put into question as to the one that is, for the lack of a better word, unstable and 'unnatural'.

Works Cited

Davis, Lennard J. 1999. 'Crips Strike Back: The Rise of Disability Studies'. *American Literary History,* 11(3): 500–512.

Dyer, Richard. 1993. *The Matter of Images: Essays on Representations*. London: Routledge.

Hughes, Bill. 2012. 'Fear, Pity and Disgust: Emotions and the Non-Disabled Imaginary'. In *Routledge Handbook of Disability Studies*, edited by Nick Watson, Alan Roulstone and Carol Thomas, 67–77. London and New York: Routledge.

Titchkosky, Tanya. 2000. 'Disability Studies: The Old and the New'. *The Canadian Journal of Sociology,* 25(2): 197–224.

Subha

Translated from Bengali by Banibrata Mahanta

1

He named her Subhashini. How was he to know that she would be mute! Her two elder sisters were named Sukeshini and Suhashini, and the father, attracted to the appeal of rhyme, named the youngest one Subhashini. Now everyone calls her Subha.

The two elder daughters had been married off according to the ways of the world—suitable matches were sought and finalised, followed by considerable expenditure for the ceremony. Now, only the youngest one remained to be married, a silent weight reigning heavy on her parents' heart.

That a person who could not speak could have feelings was something few villagers seemed to understand. They discussed their apprehensions about Subha's future frequently, often in her presence. Subha felt troubled by their insistent and insensitive discussions about her future. From an early age, these discussions left her in no doubt that her birth was god's curse on her parents. As a result, she tried to remain hidden from the eyes of all. What a relief it would be for her parents if people forgot about her, she thought. But, can anyone forget grief? Try as she might, she was ever-present in her parents' minds. The mother, especially, looked at the daughter as a flaw in herself—a personal failing, a cause for shame. Banikantha seemed to love her more than his other daughters, but his wife considered Subha a blemish on her motherhood and remained resentful of her.

Subha had no speech; but she had beautiful eyes—large, dark and long-lashed, eloquent and expressive—and lips which quivered wordlessly at the slightest hint of any emotion, like the newborn leaves of a plant.

What we express through words is constructed, the result of conscious effort, not unlike the act of translation. It might not always be appropriate; it might be incorrect too at times. But eyes express directly. They are candid screens that directly reflect the soul, and feelings and emotions unfold and recede on them without the mediation of words, burning brightly on some occasions, wan like the dimming moonlight on some, flashing like frenzied lightning in all directions on others—they do not need any translation. She, who can't express other than through the contours of her face, has a language in her eyes which is inconceivably vast and unfathomably profound—much like the clear sky, that theatre of the silent play of light and darkness. Like vast, silent nature, wordless human beings too have a profound, cosmic depth. That is probably the reason that other children were scared and did not want to play with her. Wordless and companionless, she was like the silent depths of the dark night.

2

The village was called Chandipur. A small river flowed beside it; like the little girl in the story, its boundaries were defined. She worked tirelessly and continuously within the confines of her banks like an obedient daughter; she was related, in one way or the other, to every villager living on either bank. The high banks were lined with habitations and trees; and the river which sustained the village flowed in between, nimbly and cheerfully—moving, as it were, with a spring in her step, from one work to another.

Banikantha's house was right on the river bank. The fence, cowshed, the stacks of hay and the orchard with its numerous fruit trees defined his prosperity and attracted the attention of many a ferry-goer who travelled down the river. Did any of them notice the mute girl who inhabited this prosperous household? We don't know! But she did go and sit, silent, on the river bank whenever she got some time from her household chores. And nature seemed to compensate her silence. It talked for her. The ripple of the river, the chatter of the crowds, the song of the boatman, the chirping of birds and the rustle of leaves—sounds, vibrations and movements of the world all came together, and followed ceaselessly, one after another, like the waves of the sea, upon the ever-silent shores of her heart. Nature's various sounds and strange movements are the language of the mute too—an infinite extension of the silent language of Subha's large, long-lashed eyes. From the chirping grasslands to cosmic vacuum, there are only signs, gestures, songs, cries and sighs.

In the afternoon, when the boatmen and the fishermen left for lunch, the household folks had their siesta, birds stopped chirping, ferries stood still and the familiar, busy world suddenly fell silent, then, under the afternoon sky, both—silent nature and the silent girl—sat facing each other, one in the sunshine, the other under the shade of a small tree.

It is not that Subha did not have any intimate friends. There were two mute cows in the shed, Shorboshee and Panguli. They had never heard their names spoken by Subha, but they unfailingly recognised her footsteps—and they understood her poignant silence better than any language. More than the people around her, it was they who could understand Subha's wordless emotions and moods.

Subha would enter the cowshed, hold Shorboshee around the neck with both hands, caress her and rub her cheeks near her ears. Panguli would observe her and then lick her affectionately. Subha would visit the shed thrice daily; she would also come to the shed whenever she was distressed. When she was upset by harsh words at home, she would pay an unscheduled visit to her two mute friends, who had an inexplicable understanding of Subha's moods. One look at her gentle, grief-stricken eyes was enough for the two animals to understand her pain. They would come close to Subha, rub their horns on her arms and attempt to console her.

Besides, there were the goats and the kitten, but Subha was not as close to them as she was to Shorboshee and Panguli. However, they too were loyal to her—the kitten, especially. Snugly ensconcing herself in Subha's cosy lap any time of the day she wanted to, she would make it amply clear that it would be of great assistance in her sleep if Subha would caress her chest and back with her fingers.

3

Among the developed animals, Subha had one more companion, but what relation she shared with him is difficult to decide, as he could speak, and so they could not possibly communicate at the same level.

He was the Gosains' youngest son, Pratap, a worthless boy. His parents, having tried their best, had given up hope that he would ever do anything for the betterment of the family. While good-for-nothing people are a source of constant irritation to their immediate family, they are generally well-liked by those unrelated to them—as, not being bound by any specific duty, they become something of public property. Just as a town needs a few public gardens, similarly, a village needs a few worthless people. Whenever there is a person short in any activity—celebrations or amusement—these people are conveniently at hand to save the day.

Pratap's sole interest in life was angling, as it is probably the best way to while away time. In the afternoons, he was often found at the riverbank, fishing rod in hand. It was here that he often met Subha. Pratap was happy to have company, and happier to have a silent companion, as it suited him if he was not disturbed when fishing. He acknowledged this by showing Subha some extra affection—he called her Su.

Subha would sit under the tamarind tree as Pratap would cast a line. Subha prepared a paan for him every day, and Pratap would chew on it as he expectantly looked at his line. Sitting and watching Pratap for long periods, Subha would often yearn to be of some use to him—a slight bit of help somewhere, any small way in which she too could show her worth in this world. But there was nothing she could think of doing. Then she would pray to the almighty for powers which would help her perform astonishing deeds, so that Pratap, seeing her perform these miracles, would exclaim in wonder, 'Oh! I never even knew our Shubhi has such supernatural powers!'

What if Subha were a mermaid? She would gracefully emerge from the river, place an invaluable pearl on the river bank and disappear into its waters. Putting aside his petty fishing, Pratap would grab the pearl and, following her, dive into the river. He would swim down to the netherworld, and there he would see, residing within the silver palace, reclining on her golden bed—who else but our Banikantha's youngest daughter, Su, the one who is mute! Su, the lone princess of the silent, gem-studded subterranean realms of the universe.

Couldn't that have happened? Was that so impossible? Come to think of it, nothing is impossible. She, however, was not born to the royal family of the netherworld devoid of humans, but to Banikantha. And she was just not able to surprise Pratap, no matter how desperately she wanted to.

4

Subha was gradually growing up. She was starting to experience herself. Like a tumultuous tidal current urged forward by the full moon, an inexplicably new consciousness burst into her soul and inundated her. She agonised over it and questioned herself, unable to comprehend what was happening.

Unable to sleep, afraid of her own self, she surreptitiously opened her bedroom door one night, only to be confronted by an equally wakeful full moon shining over a sleeping world—like the mysteries of youth, its joys and its sorrows—drenching in its light the farthest stretches of loneliness and beyond, yet simmering and silent, unable to utter a word. And the anxious, yearning girl stood at the fringes of this anxious, desperate nature.

Weighed down by the responsibility of a girl of marriageable age, the parents too were anxious. And talks of the possibility of the parents being ostracised for not being able to fulfil their duty started doing rounds. Banikantha was a prosperous man, one who could afford to have fish and rice twice a day and, therefore, had no dearth of enemies.

A long discussion ensued between husband and wife, following which Banikantha went away for some days.

When he returned home, he announced, 'We will go to Calcutta.'

Preparations for the journey started in earnest. Sorrow enveloped Subha's heart, like fog on a winter morning. Like a mute animal that senses an unknown danger, she followed her parents around, looking at them with her large, dark eyes. She tried desperately to fathom what was afoot. But she got no answers from her parents.

One afternoon, Pratap, after casting a line in the river, casually mentioned to her, 'Su! I heard they've found a groom for you? You're getting married, are you? I hope you won't forget us.' And he went back to his fishing.

Subha looked at Pratap in agony, as a stricken doe looks at the hunter, the eyes saying, 'What harm did I do to you?' She did not sit under the tree that day. She went back home. Banikantha had just woken up from his afternoon nap and was lighting some tobacco. Subha came into the room, dropped near his feet, looked up at him and burst into tears. Tears rolled down Banikantha's cheeks too as he tried to console her.

The day before she was supposed to leave for Calcutta, Subha went to take leave of her childhood companions. She fed them with her own hands, hugged them, gazed at them; her eyes seemed to express everything she could not say. She looked at their faces one last time—and tears started trickling down her eyes.

It was a moon-lit night, the twelfth tithi of shuklapaksha. Subha, getting out of bed, went to the familiar riverbank, and lay down there—as if trying to embrace the earth, to encompass the immensity of Mother Nature in her outstretched arms and say, 'Please don't let me go, mother. Hold me tight in your arms as I am holding you.'

One day, while in Calcutta, Subha's mother dressed her up elaborately. She tied Subha's hair tightly in place with brocade ribbons and decked her with jewellery, managing to make Subha look quite different from how she usually looked. Tears rolled down Subha's cheeks. Her mother, anxious lest her daughter appear puffy-eyed, admonished her to stop crying. But when have tears obeyed scolding?

The groom came with his friends to check his bride-to-be. The bride's parents were tense and fidgety. God himself had condescended to come and select his sacrificial animal. The mother, anxious, scolded the daughter, asking her to stop crying as she was sent to be examined by the prospective groom, but it only served to double her tears.

After examining her for quite some time, the examiner said, 'Not bad.'

The girl's tears convinced him that the girl had a heart. He calculated that a heart that was distraught at the prospect of being separated from her parents today would be of service to him tomorrow. Like dust in an oyster's shell, tears only served to increase her value.

The wedding took place at a very auspicious moment according to the astrological calendar.

Having successfully delivered their mute daughter to unknown hands, Subha's parents went back to their village, with duties as parents of a daughter fulfilled—they had been successful in safeguarding their caste and saving themselves in their afterlife.

The groom worked in the west. He went back immediately after the wedding, taking his wife with him. Within a few weeks, everyone realised that the newly-wed bride could not speak. But nobody realised that it was not her fault. She had not duped anyone. Her eyes had expressed everything she wanted to say. Was it her fault that nobody understood their language? She looked all around to be understood, but those familiar faces who understood her language were not there anymore. An endless, inexpressible shriek welled up and kept reverberating within her heavy silent heart, but none, other than the omniscient, could ever hear it.

Her husband, more cautious now, examined with both eyes and ears, and this time brought home a bride who could speak in a language he could understand.

GUNGIYA

By Mahadevi Varma

Introduction

By Editors

Subhashini's fate, of first being forced into marriage through lies and deceit and then, upon the discovery of the 'treachery', being discarded for a 'complete' woman, lays bare an often-overlooked aspect of disability discourse at large: disabled women. While the study of disability seeks to figure out ways that would change the frameworks of normalcy, women seem to largely be absent from this discourse. There is, in a sense, an inherent and ironical normalisation of the disabled human as a male subject. This is a lacuna that is, and should be, rather concerning for the field of disability studies because women are affected by disability somewhat differently than men. Mary Jo Deegan, in fact, begins her seminal book, *Women and Disability: The Double Handicap,* by pointing this out. To her, there is a 'seriousness [in the form] of [a] lack of recognition of the special needs of women who have disabilities' and an unawareness of the 'unique issues' that women with disabilities deal with (1985). While, over the years, after the publication of Deegan's book, research has tried to fill this aforementioned omission, there remains an overshadowing of disabled women in favour of a generalisation of disability affectations. Writing almost 15 years after Deegan, Carol Thomas, for example, voices similar concerns as her predecessor does when she notes how 'the voices of disabled women are almost totally absent in sociological work' (1997). Since generalisations disallow presentations of specificities that make up that generalised demographic (thus creating the normal), indiscriminate allocations of policies towards the alleviation of (social) disability necessarily overlook the specific and 'unique' needs of disabled women. After all, it's not as if the outcomes of disabled women have changed for the better over the years. In fact, if nothing else, modernisation has failed to not only change social behaviour towards disabled women but has also not seen any significant positive development towards the provision of specific social infrastructure targeted for them. Take, for example, Mahadevi Varma's short story 'Gungiya'. Written almost a century after Tagore's 'Subha', and in a different cultural landscape, the central character of the story, Gungiya, mute like Subhashini, not only undergoes the same treatment as Tagore's protagonist does but is also treated as a disposable caregiver. Like Subha, Gungiya is first forcefully married off to preserve familial caste and then, upon the discovery of her disability, rejected by her in-laws for her younger sister. Later, when the sister dies, the husband dumps their son on Gungiya who, after growing up, once again rejects her love and care by automatically construing her as someone who has destroyed his life by being disabled. A note of caution needs to be struck here. The intention here is not to deny any changes that have happened over the new millennium for disabled women. The attempt, instead, is to show a historical negation that has led towards a normalisation of disability discourse for men and hint at the different 'unique' affectations that are peculiar to disabled women.

The immediate one is perhaps the one that both Subha and Gungiya suffer from: the rejection of disabled women as 'proper' and 'complete' mates for able-bodied men. This rejection stems, largely, from two different aspects. The first one is the general stigmatisation that disabled people are made to go through. They are, insofar as society is concerned, either accursed or incomplete. Whatever the case may be, it is impossible to have a 'normal' life with disabled people as partners. The second aspect, unlike the first one, concerns disabled women particularly. Owing to the general subaltern position that women occupy vis-à-vis men, impairment enforces in what Deegan calls the 'double handicap' (1985). What this means is that while disabled men still have some social power over abled women (even if not as much as abled men), disabled women have absolutely none. Therefore, while disabled men still have a possibility of finding acceptance by abled partners (Manik Bandyopadhyay's 'The Leprosy Patient's Wife', anthologised later in this collection, is a good example of this acceptance), women like Subha and Gungiya have nothing but rejections lined up for them. It is important to note here that the rejection of these two women happens before their husbands refuse to stay with them and subsequently find new wives. That both of their parents had to use deceit to get them married in the first place shows how both, the rejection of the disabled woman and the acknowledgement of that rejection, is coded into societal intellects. Both the sets of parents knew that their disabled daughters would be rejected by prospective grooms and thus had, in their minds, no option but to resort to deceit to send them off into their respective marriage disasters. The final rejection, by their grooms, is simply a manifestation of a presence that haunts the social psyche throughout. The subsequent selection (a very metered and careful selection, at that) by the grooms of abled wives is simply the final nail in the coffin.

The reason for the immediate rejection of women like Subha and Gungiya, however, is not just a result of Deegan's 'double handicap'. There also lies a physiological reason that, in fact, is a strong cause of the disablement of impaired women in the first place: that of motherhood. For disabled women, bearing children and raising them is not a concern separate from their disability. Carol Thomas, thus, writes that 'disabled women's desires, decisions and experiences of childbearing and parenting are interlaced with additional concerns stemming from the disablism they encounter, their personal experience of living with impairment per se, and their knowledge about the possible effects of reproduction on their bodies' (1997). Their disability (where disability is societal), in other words, decides for them if and how they should become mothers. Thomas's work, in fact, traces three different effects that govern the choices regarding motherhood that disabled women make: 'the women's engagement with the medical "risk" discourse; the pressure felt by disabled women to demonstrate that they are, or could be, "good enough mothers"; and their experiences of receiving unhelpful 'help' from health and social care workers' (1997). While each of these three affectations become equally important for the lived realities of disabled mothers, the immediacy of rejection that Subha and Gungiya go through, however, relies, for the most part on the first one. They are rejected, in other words, not only because they themselves are stigmatised but also because their partners do not find them capable enough to bear children because they present a 'risk' to, if not necessarily the life of the future child, then, surely, their normalcy. The two husbands work within a framework that always doubts if the impairment of the mother will pass on to the child and thus make the babies 'abnormal' as well (Thomas 1997). That is not a situation that is acceptable (as is clear from the fate of Chandudi in Medha Trivedi's story or Handicapped in Panigarhi's). Therefore, rejecting the possibility of such a risk is the only 'natural' response to disabled women and the possibility of their motherhood. It is in matters like these, matters which are specific to women that the necessity of the development of a heterogeneous disability discourse lies. Yes, disabled women do go through the same social exclusion and stigma that men do, but there are differences of framework that need to be taken care of. It is only in such considerations that there lies a possibility of, as Deegan notes, making appropriate changes to public policy, 'academic and professional rehabilitation communities' (Deegan 1985) and society at large in general.

Having said that, there is another issue that needs to find a delineation here. Gungiya's story, unlike Subha's, does not end with the rejection of her husband. She is replaced by her younger sister as her (ex) husband's wife. But, when the younger sister dies in childbirth, the (ex) husband, unable to raise the newborn by himself, goes back to Gungiya with a proposition to take her back if she agrees to take care of the child. While Gungiya turns down this proposition quite promptly, the audacity of the husband to present it reveals two fundamental problems. The first is the treatment of women as factories whose existence is secured and legitimised only in association with a man. It's not as if the husband wants to 'accept' Gungiya because he wants to. He proposes this because the acceptance is the payment he is willing to give to Gungiya for taking care of his child. After all, for the poor disabled woman, what can garner more importance than male acceptance and, from that, societal acceptance? The second, and perhaps the more important one insofar as the disabled Gungiya is concerned, the husband does not feel his lineage at 'risk' anymore. Now that an able-bodied woman has produced an able-bodied child, a large chunk of what stopped him from accepting Gungiya as a wife is gone. Further, being a disabled woman, Gungiya, for the husband is, what Deegan calls, 'roleless' (1985). Her inability to fit into any social role, due to her impairment, makes her, for the husband, somewhat of a free agent and in search of a role. He is, in other words, not only granting Gungiya social acceptance but also a place to fit into this society through acting out of a role that, otherwise, would not be available to her. That Gungiya refuses his proposition shows nothing but an immense strength on her part and an assertion that she will change the 'norms'. Sadly, however, it does not really pan out. First, the child, by being associated with a disabled caregiver, is ostracised and mocked by the world. Second, this marginalisation of the child prompts him to lay the blame for his misery on Gungiya and her disability. By the end of the story, the child, whom Gungiya raises despite economic and social hardships, accuses her of stealing him from his father and wishes her nothing but death. Even when he is proved wrong, he never apologises or accepts his foster mother. Finding the first chance, the son, like the rest of the world, rejects Gungiya and leaves for an unknown place.

Works Cited

Deegan, Mary Jo. 1985. *Women and Disability: The Double Handicap.* New York: Routledge. Reprint 2018.

Thomas, Carol. 1997. 'The Baby and the Bath Water: Disabled Women and Motherhood in Social Context'. *Sociology of Health and Illness,* (19)5: 622–643.

Gungiya[1]

Translated from Hindi by Shubhra Dubey

I may have written only a few myself but writing letters for others has become a duty for me. So, my reputation as a letter-writer-on-request is here to stay, be it the plains or the hills.

It started when, upon seeing me writing, a mother deeply upset at having been abandoned entreated me to compose a letter to the son who now lived overseas. Many others followed her and, soon enough, writing letters forced itself into the range of my daily duties.

There is an incalculable variety to the solicitors of these letters. The content of these letters too is so diverse that even an expert in the art of letter-writing will be awestruck. Since I am slower at letter-writing than an amateur rhymester composing poetry, my inadequacy at the task and the ignorance of the letter solicitors often leads to interesting situations.

They have so much to say that, when they begin saying it, their sentences lack coherence and emotions lack clarity. To stitch a cohesive narrative by putting their sentences in a graspable order, to help find continuity between these and their confused emotions and give all this the outward appearance of a letter is no small task. Any interruption on my part to seek clarification is taken to be a sign of ignorance. So, the whole exercise they assume is doomed to failure. Further, giving their narrative the contemporary format of a letter is difficult. Not only are they experts in the rustic style of writing but are staunch adherents to it. A letter is not a letter until it begins with salutations to Lord Ganesh or Lord Ram. The letter-writer is then regaled with all the stories from their past so that they cannot but be dumbstruck. It is assumed that what she should and should not include is not her decision to take. If she does take a few liberties here and there, they will entreat her to read out the letter after she has finished, leaving her more bewildered than before. Their stories have so many oral versions that the small portion that makes it to paper quickly informs them of its incompleteness almost immediately.

'There is no space left to write' is not a convincing argument for them. Eyes filled with dismay, they will point their wizened fingers in a blank corner of the page and entreat you to cram those discarded fragments in there, somewhere! All this is done in such a way that there is hardly any room to refuse. To leave out margins at the cost of

1 Translated with permission. All rights reserved with the copyright owners.

their story is wrong. Only when the entire sheet of paper is drenched in ink, and all alternatives have been exhausted that they resign and fall silent.

To understand the conundrum of the writer is not easy either. Ordinarily, the rural subject is more sentimental than the intellectual is. Just as a single feeling is brought up, a flood of emotions follows. Each component of the message evokes newer sentiments in them. But which emotion to emphasise in their story is difficult to decide for the writer. A father wishes to chastise his son living overseas, for his irresponsibility and profligacy. All too soon, the letter-writer can be a witness to the harsh words giving way to the moistness of tears in the span of a single sentence. When they look up, they will see that the countenance of the severe adjudicator has given way to that of a pitiable, weeping father. Which of these is true is difficult to say. Hence, which of these two sentiments should find its way on paper is even more challenging a task.

Their wretchedness frustrates me. At times, guilt overtakes me. Their ignorance is laughable at times, and annoying at others. Who is responsible for the hapless misery of a people so eager to express their sentiments and thoughts? How shameless are those who have managed to wrench the voices of such vast multitudes? Quite naturally, questions such as these come to mind.

Things were passing at their usual pace when, one day, Gungiya started pulling at the end of my aanchal. The appeal, as she explained through various gestures, was to write a letter. I was stunned. Is there no end to my tribulations? Write a letter for a mute person? How in the world will I understand what she wants me to write, and to whom?

Gungiya was unaware of the concerns that plagued me. All she could think of was the letter. It was beyond her that a learned person like me, one who had written so extensively on the sorrows of others, would not be able to find expression for her grief.

It took a while but I had become used to her stubborn presence. She could be spotted perched at the gate waiting for me to come back from work and to see me off the next day. She sat at a distance and watched me as I flailed about in the throes of writing. I had begun to get used to her as a mere spectator. So, when she became a letter-solicitor herself, I was understandably taken aback.

Gungiya has acquired this name because she cannot speak, her real name being Dhanpatiya. Her father Raghu Teli used to be a prosperous man. A couple of healthy oxen in the house helped grind the machine that pressed everything from mustard to castor for oil. The neighbouring villages used to swear by the superior products of his mill.

Hence, the birth of Gungiya, his first child, was celebrated with great splendour. The nagadawala came for his present, the domni's dance was rewarded with a chunari and innumerable canisters of ghee went into feeding the Teli community leaders.

The lactating mother was fed harira made of chironji and gond. The baby's skin was kneaded with oils and ointments until it glistened and glowed with good health. When the new mother and the child stepped out of the house for the first time after her birth, relatives and well-wishers summoned spirits to guard them against the evil eye.

At ten months, the chubby little Dhanpatiya could be seen tottering around the neighbourhood. But five years went by and not a single sound had burst from her throat. No sound of ma or dada, no tantrums for dudhu, no happa. All everyone heard were ululations of *aein-aein* as she tried to mimic the sound of words she heard around her.

The time at which other children begin to talk came and slipped by. A shadow fell over the parents' faces. Amulets and talismans, sorcery and various incantations were tried. Vows were taken, votives offered in exchange for the well-being of the child. A doctor was consulted. Diagnosis suggested that her condition is as natural as that of a crow's. Corrective surgery would have needed the kind of nerve and expenditure that Raghu could not afford. And, thus, Dhanpatiya began to grow up as Gungiya. That she was not deaf added to her woes. Not being able to speak perhaps isn't as painful when sound cannot be heard.

Her birth was followed by another daughter who was born, to the good fortune of dear ones, with speech.

What Gungiya lacked, she made up for in brains. Quick to learn and gifted with a photographic, razor-sharp memory she was unlikely to commit an error after the first instruction. Even before she was nine, she began to assist her mother in the chores at home.

And so, the need to get her married became even more urgent. To save the child from the horrific fate of a spinster, her parents did that which is the last resort of parents whose daughters are deemed unfit for matrimonial bliss: fraud. The father got the youngest daughter engaged with someone from a far-flung village. However, on the day of the wedding ceremony, Gungiya was made to sit in the mandap to complete what was left of the wedding ceremony.

Gungiya came face to face with her wretched circumstances only when, three–four years later, she was sent to live with her in-laws. As attempts to make her talk turned more and more aggressive and finally resulted in a high-pitched, guttural *aein-aein,* they flew into a rage. The deception had finally become known.

Her father has duped us! The girl is dumb! Seize all her jewellery! Many other such insults woke her up to the reality of who she was—something that Gungiya had not known in the warm comfort of her father's home.

Meekly, she begged at the feet of her mother-in-law who aimed a kick at her. She hid her face in those feet and wept. Not one heart broke. The daughter must pay for the father's deed, or how else would justice be served! Finally, she was packed off and dumped at her father's house.

Raghu had already begun to regret his actions. In order to atone for what he had done and to establish a truce, he promised to give the younger daughter in marriage. After testing her against all physical defects, an auspicious time was chosen and the wedding ceremony was completed. Gungiya broke down when she saw her husband and sister in the mandap. Older women in the village recall seeing Gungiya stuffing her aanchal into her mouth so as to not make a sound.

In stoic silence, after the sister left for her husband's home, she dedicated herself to serving her parents.

*

Years have passed since. Her parents have passed away, so have her in-laws. Gungiya's sister Rukiya gave birth to two children, neither of whom could survive beyond the age of three; perhaps she did not want to see the death of the third one and died as the baby was born. Unable to take care of the newborn, her husband came and, weeping, put the baby in Gungiya's lap.

Noone but she knows what she saw in the quiet, twinkling eyes of that baby. She could not find the courage to return it. Her face hardened when he hinted at taking her back to live with him and the suggestion died mid-sentence.

The people of the village were stunned to see the care and tenderness this voiceless mother was capable of. She sold one of the oxen to pay for two goats for the baby's milk. Clothes locked away in the closet were brought out to stitch dresses, caps. The silver in the house was beaten to make necklace, bangles, anklets and kardhan. On the day of his christening, she used up every penny of her savings to treat everyone and anyone who passed by.

Since the death of her parents, the business had been on a decline. As she remained occupied with the baby's needs, the coffer emptied, but Hulasi grew up. His father visited for the first few days, then got busy with his new domesticity—a new set of wife and children. Gungiya did not ask him for anything, nor did she compromise on Hulasi's upkeep or his ever-increasing demands.

Until they were both voiceless, the child and Gungiya communicated through signs and gestures. As he grew and developed, the child was surprised at his mother's silence, and slowly began to be embarrassed about it. It pained him when the village boys pointed and yelled 'dumb son of dumb mother' to tease him. Sometimes he got provoked, at other times he would cry. Gungiya would hear the commotion and chase the boys with reprimanding sounds of *aein-aein*. This usually resulted in more yells of Gungiya Mausi, Gungiya Mausi as the boys dispersed.

Gungiya would take Hulasi in her lap and bring him inside the house. She would stroke his hair lovingly and feed him homemade sweets and gesticulate at him trying to explain the situation. Instead of calming him, these actions would aggravate him even further. Sometimes, he would press past her and lie prostrate on the ground, howling. At others, he would twist and pull at her aanchal and demanded to know why she was the only mother in the whole village who would not speak to her son. What was she supposed to say? She was no less a mother when it came to love and care, but how was she to explain her impairment to him?

As Hulasi grew, he started stitching together the story of his life—some truth, some lies. Gungiya could not add anything to it, so she remained undefended in these narratives. Gungiya wanted to avenge the insult she felt at the hands of a sister who stole her husband and children from her! Out of revenge, she had snatched Hulasi away from the care of the father! There has got to be more to the affection she displays towards him! Talks like these slowly but certainly started to eat away at his insides.

As her struggles remained unsung, the small chance that Gungiya had at happiness had begun to come under attack by forces that lay beyond her. Who would tell her child of his abandonment by his own father, the neglect that Hulasi had been subjected to, of the tactics of the stepmother to shut him out in order to protect the interest of her own children?

It was beyond him to understand the depth of her love for him. A love that was not innate but benevolent.

One day, when he finally asked her why she stole him from her father, it was as if she had been pierced through by a poisoned arrow. Her eyes widened in horror as the boy struggled to interpret her frantic attempts to explain the dejection that had collected at the corners of her mouth.

When she tried to find out his whereabouts, it turned out that the father had been hired in a factory. He had left for Kanpur with the family.

She sold a few precious bangles to arrange for Hulasi to go to Kanpur. New clothes were bought for him. Toys made of wood and clay were bought and arranged carefully in a bundle made of cloth. Homemade sweets were packed carefully, an earthen pot of ghee too was added to the pile.

A wise man from the village was coaxed and cajoled into accompanying the boy to the big city. Fearful of any misfortune that might befall the boy in the distant land, an auspicious date was decided upon for them to leave. She walked three miles to see Hulasi and the wise uncle off on the train. Heartbroken, she could barely walk on her way back. She would stand in the sun, or sit in the shade of the tree, laugh and sometimes cry as she stumbled home and threw herself at the holy pot of tulsi and lay there until the next morning. For days, she remained there, paralysed with grief.

On the day she decided to step out of the house, she opened the door and saw a tiny dusty figure in the distance walking dejectedly towards her, closely followed by someone else. She ran, uttering loud, painful sobs and pressed Hulasi to her chest.

The outcome of the journey was for everyone to see. They had roamed around the city for two days before they ran into Hulasi's father. He lived with his wife and four children in a grimy back alley in two rented, dark-as-prison-cell rooms. His eyes had lit up at the sign of the son long-forgotten but lost their sparkle when they caught his wife's. The two of them argued all through the night.

In the morning, the father requested the wise old uncle to take the child away. While Hulasi would inherit all the property at his maternal home, his four children only had him, the father reasoned. Hulasi had a stepmother in his maternal house and he would have a stepmother in his father's. It was only right that he stayed with Gungiya and learnt to run the daily business his maternal grandparents had left him. When he grew up a little, the eldest stepbrother would be sent over in Hulasi's care. His stepmother wanted to return to the village too but Gungiya would not like it. But she was not going to live forever, would she! When she was gone, Hulasi, his father and the rest of the family would take care of her business.

Neither earnest appeals from the elderly uncle nor Hulasi's supplications were enough to thaw the cold formality in his tone. Eventually, the two visitors ran out of ideas and like two defeated soldiers trudged back home. Hulasi's stepmother had presumed the ghee and sweets were presents for the family. She had already distributed the clothes and toys among her children. Hulasi had returned to Gungiya a poor, desolate boy. She took it upon herself to heal his innocent broken heart with all the love she could muster. Steadily, the pile of his favourite things grew; but the crack that had appeared in his tender little heart was not to be healed with toys.

We spend our entire lives trying to achieve the impossible. And so Hulasi longed for his father, sisters and brothers. No, he was not merely a sentinel to their fortune, he told himself. It pained him that he could only be reunited with his family after Gungiya's death.

And so, two more years passed. Hulasi had just begun to assist Gungiya in the work at home when Hulasi's utter misfortune summoned, as if by magic, a baba. He arrived in the village one morning, flanked by two or three shishyas. He said he was merely passing by and was there to spend a month. Eventually, the baba put up a shelter in a mango orchard nearby, claiming to be waiting for the end of the monsoon.

The arrival of saints and babas is a great occasion for the people in any village. Somebody presented him with a pot of milk, someone else brought ghee. Someone donated a ripened jackfruit, another sent jaggery. Old and mature rice, ground white flour would be left at his doorstep. One person would send a batch of pancakes and another fed him kheer-puris. Even so, these were not meant to be selfless acts. The donors expected to be rewarded with divine blessings. Some needed a son for old age, others needed more money than they had. One wanted to get the better of a relative. Another person wanted to get rid of their sibling and wanted voodoo for the same. Somebody came in search of a charm to hypnotise. Someone else wanted to free their land from mortgage without wanting to pay the amount. One person wanted to extract their jewellery from a bad loan. One pleaded to be rid of bad health without having to take the necessary medicines. And soon enough, their hands folded respectfully and nursing suitable, but mostly unsuitable, wishes devotees could be seen standing in long lines outside his tenement.

It seemed that Babaji was born to prove spiritual quest as a mere pipe dream. His body looked shrivelled as a pile of dried tobacco leaves. He would apply ash all over his body, wear fake hair tied up in a bun and recline on a seat to conduct meetings with the public. A tender glance here, a casual healing touch over there. He would gesture towards them, beat his tongs ferociously, would express his displeasure where necessary and try to lull the crowd. A pinch of holy ash would be given as prasad. The people would return home neither fully supplicated nor, thanks to the prasad, empty-handed.

Those who felt neglected would double their efforts to get him to respond to their solicitations. Those who were satisfied with the attention would multiply the number of presents to keep the status quo.

Women solicitors were likely to get more attention than the rest. When women came with their problems of childlessness and defiant, belligerent husbands, his marijuana-induced sunset-red eyes would become even redder.

Three-four adolescent disciples would be at his beck and call all through the day. They would be clad in loincloth; some had shaved their heads, some wore wigs—tilted and slipping off the crown more often than not. One of them couldn't help but taste a bit of the prasad before serving it to baba, another would take a drag before passing the chillum. Baba also came to be surrounded by the curious village boys. This is how Hulasi began to visit the camp regularly.

Facial expressions, body language, general behaviour were enough for Babaji's clairvoyant powers. It is difficult to say how much he had come to know of Hulasi, but one day seeing him for (apparently) the first time he exclaimed, 'Aha! You have what it takes to be a great man young one! You have that glow … here, come here … show me your palm.'

As prey is drawn to a predator mistaking it for a flower, such was the attraction of Babaji. Hulasi could never quite extricate himself from the pull.

Gungiya too had sent jaggery, oil and sweets to the camp, but these were not meant as part of any transaction for her. She neither had the voice nor the inclination to ask about the mysteries of life. Naturally, she became concerned when Hulasi began to haunt the camp so much. She would call him, sometimes drag him home. But he would invariably return to the camp the next day. Very soon, she ran out of all options and begged at Babaji's feet for the life of her only son.

It could have been a pity, or it might have been done in jest but it is true that he told Hulasi to return home and never come back again. Thus, he washed his hands off the entire case. Hulasi was never seen going back there again. There were only a few days left to the end of chaturmas when one day the mango orchard was found deserted. Babaji had probably left in the night. When she found the bed in which Hulasi slept to be empty, Gungiya went into deep shock. She checked every nook and corner of the village and walked miles in search of the Babaji, but neither he nor Hulasi had left any trail. Days later, it came to light that a group of holy men had boarded a train at a station some five miles away. This was all that could ever be found about the entire scandal.

The people of the village chuckled. They teased 'Where is Babaji, Gungiya?'; others laughed, 'Aye Gungiya, see? A telegram from Hulasi!' Insults were heaped, 'This is exactly what you deserve, going around pretending to be a mother to someone else's son!'

But she did not know what to do except wait for her child to return. She would carefully examine the faces of the village boys. She would buy new toys and pack them away along with Hulasi's things. On seeing new clothes, she would get something stitched for him and keep it in the wooden trunk. She would buy his favourite sweets and keep them on the slab in the kitchen. She would open the main gate in the middle of the night so she wouldn't miss the sound of his footsteps. She was sure he would come back to her. But Hulasi had left never to return.

When I saw Gungiya for the first time, 12 or 13 years had passed since Hulasi's disappearance. He had been forgotten by all but his mute mausi.

Unexpectedly, one day, someone returning to the village after years told everyone that Hulasi served as a porter to a seth in Calcutta, that he had married and fathered quite a few children of his own.

Only the gentleman could tell how much of truth there was to this claim, but, for the villagers, the mirth received a fresh spurt. 'Arrey! Now that Hulasi is such a big man, he will take Gungiya back with him, she will travel in cars now.' Even as they laughed, Gungiya believed there to be some truth to these remarks.

Instead of anger for a son who had abandoned her and run away, the mother's heart felt a new surge of love for him. He must have seen such bad days, with no succour and with no one to look after his daily needs. That bunch of wayward babas must have fed him pig's meat in order to turn him into one. He might not have known how to return to his mausi. He must have taken to the first opportunity that showed itself, hence the job. How would he know that his amma was still alive and waiting for him back home? Upset, he must have been too ashamed to write to anyone else in the village. Who would remember him anyway? So, he must have waited for her to write to him instead. He would rush back home when he got her letter and would bring the wife too. The kids would demand to see their grandmother, wouldn't they? Submerged in these thoughts, she turned up at my doorstep with a request to write a letter to her son.

It was no simple task, completing that letter. After 'To the dearest Shree Hulasi Teli, your mother Gungiya sends infinite amounts of love and great fortitude', the writing came to a halt. 'It was very wrong of you to have run away', should I right that? Her severe expressions were answer enough. 'Whatever you did was right', should I write this? The shake of her head indicated a 'no'. 'Your mother has been waiting for your letter for the last 12 years now', should I write this instead? She nodded her approval. Like an amateur poet, learning to combine disjointed sentences, I somehow managed to finish the letter.

No one knew the address, so I wrote a glib 'To Shree Hulasideen Teli, Calcutta' and got rid of her. She went to post the letter herself. For me, though, it did not end there because Gungiya would chase me around with countless questions, signalling with her hands, wanting to know the probable fate of her letter, how a post office functions, etc.

One of my colleagues was in Calcutta for homoeopathic treatment for her ailments. I wrote to her about Gungiya's plight, requesting her to look for Hulasi. Her response, a week later, was full of ill-disguised insults. Without knowing the address, fantasising about finding a non-entity such as Hulasi in a sea of faces in Calcutta is a display of vacuous stupidity. Such naive individuals should not entangle themselves in the troubles of others. Her response vexed me, and justifiably so, especially when I had expected to hear the news of Hulasi.

A few days passed and Gungiya fell ill. It began with a high fever and deteriorated rapidly. Soon, she was bedridden and could not take care of the business. As her coughs got deadlier, the line of visitors and caregivers shrank to a sparse few. A distant relative would manage her cattle and his daughter would take care of the sick woman.

Every time I would visit her, she would forget all her ailments and, with frantic movements of her hands, she would enquire of the letter.

In the meantime, I received another message from my colleague in Calcutta. She informed me that, upon my request, she had entrusted the job to a servant named Harbhajan. Hulasi could not be traced but Harbhajan was visibly distressed when he heard of Gungiya's plight. He belonged to a village nearby. He too had run away from home some 12–13 years ago. His mother is no more, but he wants to support Gungiya in whichever way he can. He had put his third-division degree to use by writing a letter to her, offering her all sorts of support. That his employer send any help on his behalf was not acceptable to him as he wanted to send Gungiya his own hard-earned money. Hopefully, my colleague wrote, his zeal would not distress the sickly woman even further and would provide some succour to the parched soul of the mother.

A few days later, the letter and ten rupees were received. When told that it was from Calcutta, Gungiya assumed that the sender was Hulasi. I did not correct her. The letter did not carry any details of the sender nor the receiver. The letter contained what any son from the village would write to his mother—'*Maiya* I will be in your debt for this life and all life to come. You are everything to me. My mind was not working properly that I left a mother like you to come and suffer in this strange land. Very soon, I will come to pay respect at your feet. Just you wait till I get time off duty. You do not worry about yourself anymore. Your blessings are the umbrella that has saved me from the rainstorm of hardship. I will never face any problem till you are there. Your daughter-in-law and grandson hold you in great esteem and send you their respect.'

Gungiya held that letter in her emaciated fingers and pressed them to her wasted chest. A tear appeared at the corner of one eye and cut a path through her wrinkled skin, slid past the ear to collect in the folds of the grimy pillow underneath.

A month later, she was found lying crumpled in a pile of Hulasi's toys and clothes, dead. The ten rupees were found underneath the pillow where they had been left on the day they were received. I tried to inform Harbhajan but his employer never came this way, nor did he. To try to find him would be like looking for Hulasi in the great big city.

Imagination pales in comparison to the quaint people I have encountered and the stories I have heard of them; but the wonder and tenderness that Gungiya evokes in me are unparalleled. I did not stop writing letters. I used to write about others for inspiration. Now I read of others' lives to look for attributes as those of Gungiya. The heterogeneity of agyan far exceeds the quantity of gyan in the world. Perhaps, this is why to adequately write of moments that reflect the mysteries of life is no simple task.

I often wonder if that paragon of motherly care, the idol of human tragedy will lie unparalleled in my own creations.

KURAI PIRAVI

(Incomplete Being)

By T. Jayakanthan

Introduction

By Editors

Affectations of disability are never singularly experienced. Each impaired body, situated both in individual and cultural disablement, undergoes experiences that encompass most, if not all, forms of disabling institutions and machinations. In a sense, then, the outright demarcation of Chandudi from Trivedi's narrative as an accursed being; the societal exile, physical violation and emotional humiliation of Handicapped from Panigarhi's story; the establishment of religio-cultural fear of the impaired presented in 'Koobad' and the rejection that Subhashini and Gungiya face are not the only ways by which these characters are disabled. While each story chooses to locate its character within a particular form of disablement, it is imperative to realise that all these characters are affected by most other forms of disabling matrices as well. Neither Subha's nor Gungiya's rejection, for example, are affectations that are bereft of the belief of the accursed nature of the impaired. In the same way, the fear that cultural artefacts, especially religion, gives rise to ends up humiliating and making the world reject the Handicapped as well. There is, thus, through the institutionalisation of normative disabling structures, a formation of a culture of disability itself. It is this culture that constitutes the experiential realities of those who find themselves on the other side of normalcy. Each story, hence, chooses to highlight one such reality not because that's the only reality within which the respective character lives, but simply because each individual author believes that singularity to be of the utmost importance to their character while pushing the others into and as a constituent background.

T. Jayakanthan's 'Kurai Piravi' (translated as 'Incomplete Being') is perhaps somewhat of an aberration in this respect. Unlike the other stories, Jayakanthan, once again, knowingly or otherwise, is able to present a character who has, for the lack of a better word, a more real existence than any of the others in this collection so far. This is neither to deny nor to denigrate the real material problems that the bodies of the impaired characters of the other narratives and, by an extension, those people, in the lived real whom these characters re-present, undergo. Selvi, Jayakanthan's impaired character, however, brings about a change in perspective and allows a presentation of, somewhat ironically, the completeness of a disabled being. She is, in other words, a more realised representative of the impaired life not only for the ones in the lived real but also the characters of the other stories. These other characters become synecdochal of someone like Selvi, divulging the intricacies of the individual ways by which disablement takes root. Further, in terms of her impairment as well, Selvi occupies the entire formal range. She is both mentally and physically impaired: has the mind of a twelve-year-old, is anaemic, has disfigured teeth and a malformed face. This wide array of impairment renders her, for the rest of the world, 'incomplete'; as if human existence comes with a set configuration of being.

Selvi's introduction in the story is coupled with her rejection as an ayah for Balu, a baby boy, by the boy's father Rajaram. However, when Balu is afflicted with smallpox and Ranjitham, Selvi's sister and the new ayah, afraid to contract the disease herself, refuses to take care of the baby, Selvi steps in and, risking her own life (for, by the end of the narrative, she does contract pox), nurses Balu to health. There are two reasons why Selvi chooses to do what Ranjitham refuses to. Firstly, in Balu, Selvi finds not only acceptance but also her own temporal being. The first meeting that she had had with Balu had brought about a paradigm shift in the way she perceived being perceived. This shift, true to George Berkley's notion that the essence of existence lies in perception (1996), allowed Selvi to have the possibility of a 'normalcy', even if through Balu's life, that had been denied to her not only so far but also in the foreseeable future. It is Rajaram's refusal to keep her as an ayah for his son that, once again, disabled her and rendered her 'incomplete'. The little boy, however, even after her dismissal, retains an innocence that has the possibility of saving the disabling culture of the adults and redeem their stigmatising and marginalising tendencies. Much like Lewis Carroll's interaction with children and Pankti's desire to play with Chandudi (thus restoring her humanity), Balu's acceptance of Selvi not only shows the unnaturalness of disablement but also the inclusive world in which children live. After all, when Selvi asks Balu to describe her face, he does so with a beautiful smile. Secondly, the branding of her life as an incomplete one reinforces what Deegan calls the 'rolelessness' of a disabled woman (1985). The narrative, in fact, mentions in rather concrete terms that she is never going to get married. Thus, her disablement takes away even the possibility of a social role that she could enact. Further, this impossibility of becoming a wife necessarily translates into an impossibility of becoming a mother. For a society where women can have, primarily, only these two roles, Selvi is left bereft of even one. However, in imagining her entire life with Balu, Selvi regains her role in society. Even as an ayah, she begins to regard her life as having social meaning and inclusion as she imagines herself raising not only Balu but his children as well. This is an inclusion that, for Selvi, is something that deserves a rescue. Even if it means a threat to her own life. This, however, does not mean that Selvi is being selfish in nursing Balu to health (Selvi, as the narrative shows, is extremely kind). It is imperative that the relationship between her and Balu is not seen as simply an individual one. It is a relationship that exists within a socio-cultural framework. Their interactions are, therefore, both reflective and refractive of how Selvi is able to exist within this framework and not simply as an individuated entity alongside the child.

This social structure becomes all the more important because it is a system that does not, and will not, allow Selvi to live a dignified life. For example, while Balu, in his existential innocence, does not regard Selvi as someone aberrant, his father, entrenched deep within the cultural institutions of normalisation, sees Selvi as nothing but abhorrent. It is impossible, for him, that someone like her should watch over his child. She is, in his words, 'avalakshanam': ontologically unpleasing. Like Subha and Gungiya are rejected by their respective husbands (where this rejection is simply the inevitable manifestation of a societal refusal of the impaired), Selvi is rejected by Rajaram. Further, like in the case of the two husbands, Rajaram's dismissal of Selvi is not simply a personal choice. It is the product of a historical, cultural and traditional conjuration of the impaired as an 'inauspicious imp': a position where the cosmos, and the creator of that cosmos, is working towards the denial of the existence of the disabled human. Selvi is, after all, an incomplete being. If god was in her favour, Selvi would have been whole. How can a mere human, like Rajaram, then, have anything but abhorrence and fear in response to Selvi? This isn't a far call from the kind of religious fear within which Khalid Jawed's character, the Hunchback, locates his guilt. That Rajaram projects and transmits his fear onto his son proves not only the presence of this dread but its automatic perpetuation as well. For Rajaram, his fear is so natural that his son cannot be anything else but full of fear of the disfigured woman. Obviously, his son isn't and his wife points out as much. But, by that time it's too late and Selvi, having overheard Rajaram's rant and feeling humiliated, runs away. Rejected thus by the world of humans, Selvi, like Handicapped, moves back into the arms of nature and the natural and finds peace once again with the abandoned dog whose life she had saved a while ago.

Interestingly, in somewhat of a neat parallel to Gungiya's life, Rajaram has to not only accept Selvi when he finds himself helpless and unable to take care of his sick child but also help her out when she contracts the disease from the boy. This is an acceptance that lays bare the hypocrisy of normalcy. Both, Gungiya's (ex) husband and Rajaram believe in the normalcy of being only insofar as that normal allows a clean distance from the 'abnormal'. The moment either of them realises that it is only the 'disabled' who, ironically, has the ability to help them out of threatening situations, they change suddenly and accept the impaired. In other words, the disabled subjects are abhorrent only as long as they are not immediately useful for them. While this is, in itself, a problem, it also deconstructs the logic of normalcy for it lays bare the fact that there isn't a normal being. If the normal is not *the* normal and opposed to the abnormal come whatever may, the structural integrity of normalcy does not have the strength to stand on its conceptual presence. Rajamram's acceptance of Selvi is a revelation of not only the constructed nature of his normalcy but the very concept of normalcy as such. Further, this deconstruction of normalcy simultaneously dislocates ways in which impairment affects the sensibilities of the able-bodied. Bill Hughes classifies these affectations, rather neatly, as fear, pity and disgust (2012). In a sense, then, Rajaram's refusal to let Selvi be Balu's ayah is not because Selvi is abnormal or cursed by god, but because she invokes fear and disgust in Rajaram. It is he who is afraid of her and not the child. It is he, once again, who cannot help but puke when he looks at her face and not the child. In being thus destabilised, the normalcy of Rajaram gives a simultaneous way to the removal of such affectations as well. That said, there is a need to, in the end, also question the cost it takes to remove the stigmatising structurisation of normalcy. It is, after all, only when Selvi is herself sick, possibly mortally, that Rajaram discards the charade of normalcy.

Works Cited

Berkley, George. 1996. *Principals of Human Knowledge and Three Dialogues*. New York: Oxford University Press.

Deegan, Mary Jo. 1985. *Women and Disability: The Double Handicap*. New York: Routledge. Reprint 2018.

Hughes, Bill. 2012. 'Fear, Pity and Disgust: Emotions and the Non-Disabled Imaginary'. In *Routledge Handbook of Disability Studies*, edited by Nick Watson, Alan Roulstone and Carol Thomas, 67–77. London and New York: Routledge.

Incomplete Being[1]

Translated from Tamil by Hemachandran Karah

'Ranjitham, hurry up! You have to give Balu some gruel,' Pankajam will not let this commandment go unheard by her target. She has everything in her life: a man, reputation in the neighbourhood, material wherewithal and a dwelling to her name. But, what is the use? She is, after all, gripped by that female malady. Maternal guilt. What else can it be? In the five years of her married life, Pankajam has delivered four babies. While three have died postnatally, one has barely made it to her arms. She is pregnant, again, for the fifth time. The seventh month to be precise. Balu, who is still in the cradle, is very ill for the last two days or so. It all began with a raging fever. On the second day, Pankajam spotted a couple of ammai (pox) marks on his face. Then, they spread all over. Her husband Rajaram was certain that Balu would not survive this.

Pankajam finds it hard to pull up her own body. Doctors suspect tuberculosis. No doubt, she has been prohibited from giving any kind of care to Balu. The baby is kept safely in an outhouse, where he is taken good care of by Ranjitham. What about the cook? He is more of a wandering spirit! Nobody ever can afford to peruse him in human form. For example, he receives orders during coffee time. That's it. Food somehow will materialise for lunch. Since Ranjitham has not yet come, Pankajam decides to look after Balu. She approaches the cradle, now richly laden with neem leaves. There, in the outhouse, she picks up a hand-fan. It is already one, and there is still no trace of Ranjitham. Pankajam offers the child some gruel, water and some neem potion as well. She sits there savouring all the stolen moments. It is almost three now. She hears Rajaram sneak in from behind. 'What are you doing here? You should not stay here any longer.' Rajaram takes charge as his wife leaves the outhouse in total obedience.

Ranjitham lives in a neighbourhood slum. Her husband is a mason. Her elder sister, Selvi, who is not up to anything, in particular, is twenty and not yet married; will never be for sure. How can she? In mind, she is just a twelve-year-old. Her face throws up a different story altogether. It looks too old, perhaps thirty. Her body is anything but voluptuous. Its anaemic edges somehow appear held together by her tresses. Well, one may call them a rodent's tail. No less ghastly is her anterior teeth that do not budge. Her wedding prospects are not stunted by such aesthetic morbidities alone. It may have to do with her destiny tied to what

---

1 Translated with permission. All rights reserved with the copyright owners.

people call 'incomplete being'. Yes, to the mundane society, she seems somewhat less than a complete human form.

Selvi may be a four-feet of emaciation, but she has the rare capacity to offer herself as a whole to both less and greater lives. That black stray dog, for example, is so proud that Selvi treats him as a soulful follower. 'It is already five. Why are you not going to see Balu?' 'I will never,' replies Ranjitham. 'He is all taken over by mari atha. Every inch of his body is filled with pimples. Even his mother is keeping away. Why should I take the risk?' Selvi cannot hold herself together any longer. For a moment, she slips into a reverie duly entertained by Balu's caresses. Reveries don't last long. Do they? In fact, she hits hard on that terrifying, and yet not-so-distant, memory.

*

It was Selvi, and not her sister, who in the first place had been entrusted with the caregiving chore for Balu. Pankajam quickly began briefing her about terms of the job, timing, dos and don'ts, etc. Such a contractual verbalism did not in the least appeal to Selvi. Instead, she was engrossed by Balu's playful presence in his mom's lap. He stretched forward his tiny hands, and Selvi promptly picked up the signal. Off they went, swiftly across the garden, courtyard and the street front. They invented a universe that also included playthings, knickknacks and many other happy sundries.

Selvi and Balu finally reached that infamous outhouse. With newly discovered motherhood, Selvi gathered the courage to tell herself, 'I am no more an incomplete being.' The phrase reverberated, revitalising hitherto unknown inner frontiers. 'Ayah! Ayah!' That was unmistakably Balu's voice from the cradle. Selvi drew the child to her bosom. In a wholesome maternal journey, she was beginning to see far beyond. Balu would grow up. Then he would go to school. Of course, he would become a big man with an office of his own. Balu would get married one day. He would have a child who would, in turn, find a place in her lap. Thus unfolded Selvi's fictional empire in total violation of worldly logic.

'Who is that?' Selvi pointed a finger at a photograph in the corner. 'Amma and Appa,' exclaimed Balu with a loud cheer. 'What does Amma's face look like?' Balu twisted his face and made a sort of slurp with his nose. 'Enough, enough,' giggled Selvi. 'How is Appa's face?' They repeated themselves with full fervour all over again. 'Now tell me, how is Balu's face?' The child responded with wide-open eyes and a blossoming smile. 'Now, now tell me how is Ayah's face?' With all the delight in the world, the child snuggled into her lap and planted a kiss on Selvi's cheek. Rajaram sneaked in again. This time he was awestruck by the ongoing play between Balu and the new ayah. But the one who accepted the kiss was in a state of ekantha. She could not be any more stunted by an eternal curse of incompleteness. Now it was her turn to kiss Balu. Rajaram who, so far had seem transfixed, became violent and agitated. He chanced on her disfigured face. 'How can my priceless possession come into contact with that avalakshanam?' Such a question needed immediate clarification. And, hence, his impatient disappearance into his bedroom.

Pankajam was in a deep sleep for she remained undisturbed by the child's habitual crying. 'Who on earth brought such a misshapen creature?' Pankajam got up with a thud. 'How can you bring such an inauspicious imp to look after my son?' 'Are you talking about the new Ayah?' 'Ayah? My foot. I cannot help puking when I look at her face. I am damn sure the baby is frightened.' 'I am pretty sure not. The baby is quite fine with her. It is only you who have a problem with Selvi's appearance,' proclaimed Pankajam. Now they could hear the child weep very loudly. Rajaram walked out to see what was happening. He saw Selvi walk out of his bungalow. Little Balu was not willing to be left behind that way. He was all for that evil imp, and nobody else. 'Perhaps she heard my tantrum. My god, what an evil character I am.' The Rajarams instantly replaced Selvi with her sister Ranjitham. That black stray dog returned to Selvi yet again as her faithful companion.

*

It is six in the evening now. Rajaram is looking after the baby. He gives Balu some neem. Images of recurrent child deaths in the family strike him again like an axe. He weeps profusely inside. Balu is so weak. He cries bleakly too. 'My child is lying here like an orphan although my wife is around. What can we do with wealth when one's family is cursed with ill health?' Rajaram looks beyond. It is already dusk. 'Sami!' He hears a familiar voice in the dark. 'Is it Selvi?' 'Yes indeed, Sami. I come to look after Balu.' She is gently polished with turmeric. Her body, tresses, face and the rest look agreeable for now. She must have worked hard on it. But there is more to her make-believe appearance. She looks like someone seeking alms for survival. 'I heard that Balu is not well at all. Ranjitham is too scared to take care of him. If you permit, I can be with him all day and night until he is cured.' There is a quiver in her voice, although the plea stands clear and non-negotiable.

'He is your child. Go ahead as you wish.' Rajaram mutters these words as he slips away in guilt. Selvi stays awake all day and night, caring for the ailing child. The pimple marks begin drying up. They do not, however, fail to remind Rajaram about his rant about impish looks. A raging fever grips Selvi from nowhere. As the night approaches, she identifies a spot near the outhouse where she can rest. It is already way past dawn. Selvi does not wake up. Rajaram on his morning walk does not fail to notice her. 'Selvi! Selvi!' She does not respond to Rajaram. He gently lifts the sari around her face. It becomes obvious that Selvi is as much affected by smallpox. As expected, the doctor arrives. 'Sami, ammai is on me now. Please send me to the hospital.' The doctor agrees readily to Selvi's plea, for, small pox is a potential killer. The ambulance duly arrives. 'I told you not to get into this business.' Ranjitham is unable to control her grief, which now is on the verge of turning into a fury. Pankajam and Rajaram are as still as the dead. It is now time for Selvi to get into the ambulance.

Selvi finds it hard to get inside the car. She looks around eagerly. 'What do you want, Selvi? Don't hesitate to ask for anything,' reassures Rajaram. 'Balu … I want to see the child for a second.' Selvi's voice implores from within. Balu looks as puny as a dark speck. 'What does Amma's face look like?' By now, such rhetorical questions became somewhat like a private game between the two. Balu now twists his face. 'Appa's face?' The child repeats himself. 'Balu's face?' He responds again with a blossoming smile. 'Ayah's face?' Mustering all his might, the child bounces on Selvi for a hug. She quickly withdraws lest he will be infected again. 'Ranjitham, take care of the baby. I will be back soon, Amma.' Pankajam nods with a loud sob. The hospital car takes her away. Selvi's soulful follower does not fail her even now. The stray dog runs after the vehicle for as far as he can. Rajaram holds on to his chest, hoping to make sense of the inner uproar.

KOOBAD

(The Hunchback)

By Khalid Jawed

Introduction

By Editors

The entanglement of disability with the duality of nature and culture presents an interesting phenomenon. While human culture, through multiple representative methodologies, tries its utmost to oust disability as an 'unnatural' existence, the affinity that the disabled share with nature, as exemplified by Handicapped and Subha, prove the complete opposite. In fact, it is this cultural realm and its insistence on disqualifying the disabled that starts to fall apart at its seams as nature merges, rather easily, with and into the lives of the disabled. But, the inconsistencies do not stop here. While, on one hand, cultural artefacts vie to construct a world opposed to the natural setting in of impairment (in harmony with Davis's conceptualisation of the temporarily abled-bodied), on the other hand, it uses the same space of the natural to discard those who are, at least at that moment, disabled. This problematic relationship that the cultural articulation of disability shares with natural processes of existence puts into question every construct that humans have created for the disavowal and control of the disabled. For how can they stand on their own if, firstly, nature understandably sides with the 'disabled' and, secondly, they rely on shaky logical foundations for the processes of normalisation (where the normal is that which is the natural)? There is, rather obviously, a distinction between impairment and disability where the former is a bodily affliction while the latter a sociocultural one. Therefore, in the wake of the collapse of the cultural logic of disability, what breaks down along with it is this idea of the disabled that carries with it all prejudices, marginalisations, exclusions and disqualifications that society and culture have levied against it. Impairment, in sharp opposition, is rendered a natural process: something that can set on anyone at any time.

One such cultural artefact that is (and which desperately needs to be) threatened is religion and its exclusion of the disabled. Ontologically, religion requires a system of punishment to deter deviations from its dictates, and disability fits the bill perfectly. Being quite physical in nature, disability, for religion, becomes a phenomenon that, in literal terms, shows how 'painful' the wrath of god/desses can be. Thus, the disabled are not only turned into examples of sinners, of beings who are fundamentally wrong but are also excluded from the 'normal' world because of these sins and the punishments thereof. Take, for example, the perfect world in the Zoroastrian scripture Zend Avesta. This world, carefully designed by Yima, 'brings together all that is good in the world and leaves out all that is bad or evil' (Sati 2017). As such then, this is a world that is inhabited only by those who are whole and beautiful;

who are complete in every respect and have no negative being. In this perfect world, 'there [are] no humpbacked, none [bulge] forward ...; no impotent, no lunatic, no poverty, no lying; no meanness, no jealousy; no decayed tooth, no leprous to be confined, nor any of the brands wherewith Angra Mainyu stamps the bodies of mortals' (ibid.). Quite clearly, this is a world where the disabled are not allowed at all. They seem like blemishes that would destroy the purity of this society. Therefore, their exclusion is not only mandatory but a matter of immediacy. The implication of this exclusion, however, is far more insidious than it lets out at first. This segregation ensures obedience from the 'good' and 'abled' world by showing them the hideousness of the punishment for their deviancy: not only as and through their physical deformation and agony but also their assured disqualification from the world of perfection. The disabled, in a sense, are not only debarred but are done so after being turned into examples of everything bad.

The Zend Avesta is just an example of typological disqualification that pervades through all religions. Since it becomes important for religion to maintain orthodoxy and conformation through fear, the physical deviants become the best specimens of deviation. Interestingly, the maintenance of religion's hegemony is not restricted to the able-bodied. It's not as if the disabled are not modulated by such structures. After all, even as they are pushed outside cultural boundaries, they are still needed to be present so that the abled can look at them and fear. This fear is very similar to the one that Hughes point out: the fear that the abled will turn into the disabled. What is different is the space that this plays out in. In the kind that Hughes mentions, there is a sense of either inevitability or uncontrollability. However, religion ensures projections of feelings of control in the face of this fear. In other words, as long as people follow what it wishes to say, they will not become deviants. This religious fear, in turn, operates, often, through guilt. Each time someone deviates from the path that is set by the dictates of the god/dess, they feel guilt and fear in equal measure: guilt in the knowledge that they have done something wrong and fear in the expectation of retaliation. What is worse is that even the disabled, as long as they are functioning within the limits of religion, are not free from the guilt of having done something wrong. Since religion has drilled the wrongness of disability in the psyche of society, those who become disabled do not necessarily escape the system of religious causality. As Shilpaa Anand too observes, 'religions across the world have evaluated persons with impairment as blessed, cursed ... impure, polluted ... immoral, ominous ... reprobate ... and so on' (2013). Rather expectedly, then, Both Subha and Handicapped's births are seen as curses of heaven.

But, it is Khalid Jawed's character of the Hunchback, in his short story 'Koobad', through whom the religious guilt, which often haunts the disabled, is shown in excruciating details. The story follows the unnamed protagonist's journey to a mosque, to offer namaz during Eid, in the hope of getting redemption and forgiveness. This short journey becomes, for the protagonist, a painfully long one as he attempts to follow codes of conduct that his hunchbacked and deformed body simply does not allow him to do. Yet, he carries on as he wanders from one mosque to another, trying to find a place where he could offer his prayers and be free from his curse. He never really manages to and, by the end of the story, dies in front of a mosque at the graveyard. What is important, however, is his undeterred insistence on being blessed by god. He is assured that his painful condition, where most parts of his body do not function properly, is because of some mistake that he has done; perhaps in not believing in god for a long time. This conversion, from being an atheist into a theist, is quite important. Before, while he was in pain and misery, he never really felt guilty about it. In fact, he has, he is sure, forgiven everyone who has slighted him and humiliated him because of his condition: be it the women he liked (including his wife), his sons and even his molester. It is only with his attainment of religion that he is imbued with profound guilt about his situation. That somehow it is his fault that he is the way he is. So, making himself even more uncomfortable and ignoring the corporeal pain because of it, he seeks god's forgiveness. His redemption and the hope that he would finally be able to become a part of 'normal' society take him from one mosque to another. But, he is always late, to the point that, in the end, he escapes his mortal form trying to seek redemption. But, the story seems to say that there is no redemption for the likes of him. He can never be included and will, always, find only death even if he tries.

Works Cited

Anand, Shilpaa. 2013. 'Disability and Modernity: Bringing Disability Studies to Literary Research in India'. In *South Asia and Disability Studies: Redefining Boundaries and Extending Horizons*, edited by Maya Kalyanpur and Shridevi Rao. Peter Lang Publication Inc. 246–262.

Hughes, Bill. 2012. 'Fear, Pity and Disgust: Emotions and the Non-Disabled Imaginary'. In *Routledge Handbook of Disability Studies*, edited by Nick Watson, Alan Roulstone and Carol Thomas, 67–77. London and New York: Routledge.

Sati, Someshwar. 2017. 'The "Hallowed" Ways of Divinity: Ableist Constructions of Disability in Hindu Scriptures'. *Apperception*, 9: 41–50.

The Hunchback[1]

Translated from Urdu by Sania Hashmi

> The story may psychologically support the resolution but it does not logically justify it.
>
> – Braithwaite

> It is only in our mud-stained shoes that we can step onto the surface of heaven.
>
> – Rossovich

The heavy downpour the night before had left the roads treacherously slimy. The characteristic January cold was augmented by a hushed rainfall and roving hailstones. With his shoes threatening to give in to the mud, he kept adjusting his sherwani with every step, trying to stand as erect as possible. A velvet cap adorned his head. He was on his way to offer the Eid namaz. It wasn't easy for him to walk. While this was common for him during the winters, a stitch in the back in the previous month had worsened things that year. Perhaps if the sun had risen during the past few days, the pain could have been mitigated. But it was fog that dominated the sky, making even the city lights appear as distant and unapproachable as the stars. These menacing conditions had made life impossible for him. And whatever little spirit he still had left in him had been taken care of by his encounter with dysentery over the past couple of days. Even at this moment, the cramps were tugging away at his abdomen and his heels seemed to be on fire.

The previous night's rainfall had left the emaciated roads with umpteen puddles. He was cautiously hopping his way around them to avoid getting stains on his sherwani. Even if he bent just a little during the process, his spine would have given up on him, which is why he had no option but to maintain as erect a posture as possible while fighting the abhorrent puddles. The onlookers made no efforts to hide their amazement and intrigue at the sight. He had always walked with a bent back which didn't help the prominence of the hunch on his form. Or maybe it was because of his bizarrely long and slender legs. In comparison, the rest of his body was unusually heavy and, if one were to size him up, it would appear as if the disjunct upper body had just been

1 Translated with permission. All rights reserved with the copyright owners.

forcefully placed on those unpromising pair of legs. The sight of him walking straight provided a new diversion to the people.

Or maybe he was just looking ridiculous in his sherwani and orthodox shoes.

'The mosque is still a long way off,' he thought to his dismay. What was tugging away at his conscience, however, was the almost certain possibility that he had not been able to perform the vuzu correctly. The previous night, in the refuge of a fading candle, he had tried to memorise all the verses from the guidebook, and he had been successful to some extent. When he couldn't remember the many nuances of the vuzu, as he often did, he would return to the guide pages that he had earmarked. However, he still managed to forget quite a few details when he got down to cleansing himself for today's prayers. What made him more wretched still was the fact that, due to the crippling back pain and the bitter cold, he had not even been able to bathe properly. He had just poured some water over his legs while fatuously reciting the qalma. 'If the sun had come out, I could have bathed. Or if only there was someone who could have warmed up some water for me.'

The truth is that he lived a solitary life. He was now over sixty years old. His wife had died almost a decade ago. His two sons had left for foreign shores. And god knows what cardinal sins their father had committed that they had chosen to break all ties with him. When he was feeling better, he would somehow manage to prepare his own meals. At other times, he would just order food from the stall across the road. His humble pension was enough for him to at least afford a square meal. However, with the spine and dysentery making their presence felt, he pined for someone who could have at least heated some water for him. Oh and he could have even learnt the vuzu rituals from that person!

He thought himself incapable of seeking help from neighbours. Perhaps it was the sadism of his condition that condemned him to offer his Eid namaz without even a proper bath. This had been his life for as long as he could remember. The intensifying cough, the persistent fever, the running nose and the hostile spine were his only companions and he had grown accustomed to them. But if those drum-beaters had not come that night, he would never have found in himself the inspiration to do what he was then doing. Until that night, he had not even considered the possibility that he could be forgiven after all. In the last quarter of the cold night, when the dense fog stretched itself uninhibitedly in the darkness, these men invaded the desolate lanes with their beats. The dogs followed suit. He woke with a start.

'Rise, rise, rise now.'

Someone was commanding in the accompaniment of the beats. He didn't know why but the voice seemed non-human—almost angelic. The dogs persisted. The beats and the voice had slowly descended upon his doorstep. He was palpitating with a terror he didn't understand. The otherwise puny kerosene lamp lit up with a vengeance, bringing every object in the room to an unwarranted prominence. The voice moved away, still commanding, 'Rise, rise, rise now.' They were volunteers who had taken it upon themselves to wake people up for sehri. It was then that he realised that perhaps that was the beginning of the holy month of Ramzan and those men were fakirs who had assumed the responsibility of rescuing the believers from the apostasy of their dreams and usher them into the austere privilege of fasting. In return, they happily accepted whatever little alms they were offered at the end of the holy month. These selfless deeds helped them score both moral rewards as well as material remuneration. He had been hearing of their tales ever since he was a little boy and his life's experiences had taught him that in principle they held no religious significance whatsoever. When it echoed through the streets as part of a tradition, however, it became religious.

A religious word may be decreed but its mode of communication needn't be.

The beats which had jerked him out of sleep had sent ripples of pain across his back which he was now reeling under. It was these sudden movements that caused dislocations along his spine.

As he gazed at the fog slithering outside his window, he realised that the voice he was hearing was different—different from what he had heard as a child. He felt there was something between the drum-beaters and the dogs—a void that carried with it caravans of penitent pilgrims, none of whom knew what it is that they were pleading for and before whom. It was then that he realised that he was no different from them and that the only justice he sought was forgiveness. His soul had been for him a boon companion and a lifelong bolster to his body. After this incident, however, his soul had abandoned his body and followed the beats to the cold and bitter lanes outside. This was the first time in his life that his soul had betrayed him and abandoned its corporeal counterpart.

Apart from a few casual attempts as a child, he never remembered himself to have kept a fast. During the initial days of his married life, he did try to keep the alvida fast at his wife's insistence. It was during the summers and he was so ravaged by thirst that all the courtyard walls had been left with splattered white stains from his constant spitting. Escaping his wife's prying eye, he had gone ahead and taken a sip of water anyway. This was a secret that was still buried deep in his heart.

After the awakening, however, he started fasting with a surprising degree of diligence and secrecy. No one in the neighbourhood had any idea that he too was fasting this year. Because he still wasn't offering his prayers, perhaps these fasts were no different than the ones kids keep for their amusement. These were obviously faakas. Though they remained imperceptible to those around him, he was often noticed languishing outside the halwaayi's shop, staring into sweet nothingness. The halwaayi's pan would be brimming with a saccharine syrup in which he would then fry the jalebis. The saffron light of the mercury bulb outside the steamy shop coupled with the growing fog on the street outside pushed every other thing on the gloriously well-laden Ramzan street out of prominence. The role played by these jalebis in his affair with dysentery and the perpetual cramps is a story for another day. As far as his not offering namaz and taraabi during Ramzan is concerned, there is no witness who can testify to anything. Maybe the defiant spine and the lethargy therefrom are responsible for this. Or maybe it was his heart's covert desire to initiate the proceedings with the auspicious Eid namaz, for which he had already made all the preparations. Indeed, his enthusiasm was no different from a child's. He had excavated his sherwani from the trunk, which must have been made for his wedding and was in a pretty bad shape now, riddled with unceremonious stains incurred over the years. It had also lost most of its buttons. The motivation to wear it for the Eid namaz was so strong that he even bent down to lay it on the bed and run a cold iron over it. He also managed to dig his old shoes out of the ruins of his room. While they looked as old as he had wanted them to, they were now a little too small for his perpetually swollen feet.

In a corner of the room hung his father's cap since he didn't know when. The cap was a family heirloom of sorts, extending back to a few generations; age had taken its toll on it and it now bore several gaping holes left behind by gormandising insects. He could have easily bought a new one but somehow the idea of wearing his family cap seemed more proper to him on this momentous occasion. As soon as he wore it, the pungent odour of his forefathers' august heads was so overwhelming that it brought tears to his eyes and he hung his head—the hunch taking over the mantle.

But why did this pain him so? Maybe because he sought forgiveness on the grounds that he had himself forgiven everyone else he could have forgiven. That god would forgive him was a baseless presumption that he was acutely aware of.

The very possibility of forgiveness, however, is certainty enough.

But what was it really that he sought forgiveness for? He wasn't aware of his sins, but what difference does the knowledge of one's sins make anyway? The fact remains that you are a sinner because the very form of your eyes, your lips, your head, the structure of your bones are akin to that of a sinner. You also appear as alert as a sinner and that is just about enough reason. No, there is no point in defending yourself or procuring evidence to prove your innocence. It will certainly be in bad taste. The only way forward is that you are forgiven, forgiven for sins which you may not have committed but which are reflected in your body and your being.

Be that as it may, forgiveness can spare you the horror of public disgrace. 'But what difference does disgrace make anyway', he thought to himself. Only a few days ago he had been disgraced on the second floor of a tall building where he had gone to collect a few wretched pieces of paper. Those notes may have been his right, but he was condemned to collect them like a tramp.

And he had also been disgraced at that spiral staircase where the food he had worked so hard to procure on a hot and sultry day had been thrown in his face. What are disgrace and humiliation? One is born into them.

And there was no dearth of such humiliating incidents in his life.

Not many moons had passed after his wedding when, one night, after kissing his wife, he had moved his lips forward in the anticipation of being kissed back. His wife, however, had no such inclinations. Oh, and she wasn't being coy! He found the true reason for this dismissal a few days later when she remarked, 'No matter how hard you try, your face always looks dirty.' While he tried to cover it with an outward laugh, he was instantly reminded of the girl with the waddling gait. Maintaining the outward laugh, he clung to his wife's form with all his might but his heart was overwhelmed by the memory of the girl with the waddling gait. Despite all his efforts, when he couldn't bring about any progress in the bed, his wife threw him off like she would a creeping insect. 'Why do you come troubling me when you are incapable of this?' The sheer contempt and disgust in her tone had left him frightened. That wasn't even the worst part. It was the humiliation that scraped away at his very being like a termite. White ants don't have teeth, which is why it was only years later that he found out that his wife had been in love with someone else. She was in love with the same person whom he had hated his whole life.

'What is disgrace and humiliation?' he thought to himself. It is but the natural and predestined state of our existence. Perhaps every human being has been disgraced and humiliated at one time or another. When they beg for someone's mercy, when they borrow money, when they profess to love, when they slip and fall on the road, when they await their turn in the queue at a public feast. Is there even a single moment when the silent spasms of humiliation are not gnawing away at our bones? And this is because human beings reduce it all to a world unto themselves. One only feels humiliated when one confronts someone else's world, as a subject or as a spectacle. But this entire world is a spectacle before someone else's eyes, which is what has instilled shame in every single one of us. I, too, am a human being after all and have, therefore, had a long association with public humiliation. I can only worry about disgrace when I know I have been forgiven. Perhaps, he thought, he should have just made peace with the fact that his soul had abandoned him.

The mosque was still a long way off.

The spasms in his abdomen returned and his calves contorted with pain. The antique shoes were gnawing away at his feet. He had paid the fitra due unto him and one could hear the clattering of coins in his sherwani pocket. 'I will go to all my estranged relatives after the namaz and claim my long-due Eidi. Forgiveness is my right. The most merciful and the most beneficent god will finally have to settle an old score and forgive me.'

Indeed! This was an old score and if he had not been so vain as to keep track of all his unmanly moral achievements, perhaps he would not have derived this confidence to demand forgiveness from god. This petty habit turned out to be pretty profitable for him. And he was well aware of the fact that he may have been capitalising on his infirmity with this heightened awareness of his condition. As a consequence, he was also mindful of the fact that maybe he wasn't ready to be forgiven.

But what was this old score all about? With great pride, he had taken care to remember everyone he had ever forgiven along the way. During his teenage years, when the girl with the waddling gait and a flat nose had told him 'But your face is so dirty!', they had been standing at the top of a spiral staircase and he was holding a tiffin-box in his hand in which he had brought rice and yoghurt for her. While trying to cover it with a hollow laugh, he asserted his masculinity by planting a kiss on her flat nose. There were flickering kerosene flames along with the carved columns of the staircase. The girl pushed him away with such force that he lost his balance and the tiffin fell to the ground, betraying its contents to the floor beneath. A tear did manage to escape his eyes then but she never knew about it. As she lifted her heavy buttocks and walked away with her famously waddling gait, he wiped his tear and forgave her with all his heart.

He managed to scale even greater heights of humiliation in the days after. This is when the germs had taken over both his jaws and, whenever he ate anything, his surroundings resonated with the uncouth sound of his absent chewing. During his meals, he would sit with his right leg stretched forward and his left leg bent around the knee. Perhaps this posture was deemed discourteous. Therefore, he could feel a thousand contemptuous eyes staring angrily at him whenever he ate, at the realisation of which the bolus inside his mouth would start oozing out. As he would hastily wipe the sweat off his forehead, a pompous burp would escape his throat, announcing his victorious return from a battlefield.

And then, one day, he saw his clothes being bludgeoned against the water tap with such vengeance that he had trouble breathing. Breathing and having dirty clothes are the same thing. But this was the simmering month of June and, as he stood in a corner with a bottle of his blood-tinged urine, a pair of contemptuous eyes instilled fear in his heart that the blood in his urine could not.

The true purport of that look was conveyed to him when both his sons grew up. He often thought of himself as a punctured tyre from which air was ever so silently escaping through a tiny hole. While this air is generally cool, it had none of its coolness about it when it reached his tailbone. As cold and as nerve-wracking as the clutches of death, the sound of it escaping never really left him alone after that.

When his wife finally died of tuberculosis after a long-drawn-out battle, he stood up against her corpse in the courtyard and forgave her. He forgave her the contempt in her eyes when she fed him, the vengeance with which she beat his clothes, her feigned ignorance of the blood in his urine and her infidelity. He even forgave the person whom he had hated since his childhood and who had somehow managed to procure the much sought-after dried jujube branches for her funeral.

A slight slip in the mud while walking sent waves of pain across his back. He stopped for a while but then resumed as quickly as he could with as straight a back as he could manage. 'How much further is the mosque?'

His strength was waning.

A few years ago, when both his unemployed sons were leaving for Saudi Arabia in search of a job, he was dejected. He was reminded of the days when he would drop them off at school on his cycle, and, with panting breath, he would carry their colourful bags and bottles to their classrooms. While they were inside, he would either wait at the gates or languish away in the streets outside. The schoolbags did not come cheap. For fifteen years, he could not afford a change of clothes for himself. But his sons could not find jobs in the country.

'Have you made up your minds to leave?' he stuttered.

From their response, one can only imagine for how long they had held themselves back.

'Would you rather have us rot here like you? You somehow survived on your measly clerk job! We can't,' the first son replied.

'Where the hell do you see jobs here? You worked your whole life, what did you manage to achieve? Mother kept spitting blood on her way to heaven, without any proper medical supervision. Do you think you're honourable just because you didn't accept bribes? The truth is that your whole life you have done absolutely nothing for us.' It was the other son.

'He just has these silly ideas of virtue. I ask you today. Apart from these pointless words, what good deeds has he accumulated? The entire neighbourhood taunts us that our father has never offered a single namaz!'

In complete agreement with each other, they took turns to remind him of all his misdemeanours. Right at this moment, when he focused all his attention on the twins' forms, he saw in them a reflection of the man he had hated since his childhood. The only thing that surprised him was that he had taken so long to see this. Maybe it was because he had never looked at them carefully ever since they had grown up. Now he made no efforts to stop them. The twins did not even inform him on reaching their destination. He didn't care anymore. For their discourtesy and their ungratefulness, he had forgiven them.

He clearly remembered that he was in the eighth standard then. One day after school, an older and stronger boy offered to ride him home on his bike. When he took a detour and rode him towards the wilderness instead, he realised he was scared.

'Where are you taking me?'

The older boy stopped his cycle and led him to a desolate spot.

'I don't want to go with you,' he protested.

'Take off your shorts. I'll give you five bucks.'

He started wailing. 'Saale, come with me quietly or I'll put this knife in your stomach.' Overcome with fear, he closed his eyes to avoid his shadow in the dry bushes around him.

For a long time after that, he was overcome with fear and guilt and could never muster enough courage to look the older guy in the eye. It was only after his wife's death that he saw this man whom he had hated his whole life. However, when he got those jujube branches for the funeral, he forgave him his monstrosity. Maybe these instances in his life were events that just happened. But there was something else that convinced him that one's personal life could never be completely separated from the public one. In fact, there were uncanny similarities in the events that occurred in both respectively.

For instance, around 20 years ago, when he was travelling back from the tehsil, he entered a narrow lane which was inhabited by people from a different community. Those were tense times. It had grown dark and he noticed that quite a few people were huddled in a corner. Not one to poke his nose in others' businesses, he went ahead on his path. Coincidentally, he chanced to look above his head and saw a live electric wire coming for him. Frightened, he ducked the wire and slipped and fell into the drain at one end of the road. He looked back to watch the scorching wire land just where he had been standing.

When he finally managed to get out of the drain, his clothes were soaked in the muck and he was bleeding from his head and elbows. He had also sprained his left foot. When he tried to look at the people who had chosen to neither warn him about the wire nor help him out of the drain, with accusatory eyes, he couldn't even ascertain whether they were laughing or trying very hard not to. Since drops of sludge had gone into his eyes, he could not even look at them clearly to find out. Soaked in muck, he went ahead on his way.

There were numerous other episodes from his life that were equally trivial and keeping track of them was an occupation in itself. However, his overtly sadistic nature had made it a point to remember all the pardons that he had ever been a part of. He couldn't resist the idea of forgiving people. The interesting thing is that his accomplishment in forgiving was not just restricted to human beings. He had even forgiven the mad dog for biting him for no good reason. He had even forgiven the wasp that had pointlessly left a sting on his forehead. This list also included the monkey who would often steal his clothes and discard them on someone's terrace. That's not it. He had also forgiven the sun which made his 9-kilometre-walk home from the workplace painful and which had turned his complexion to ember. Even the rainfall was not any less guilty for seeping into that exact point in the ceiling under which he had placed his bed.

Indeed, he must be congratulated for relinquishing any fantasies of revenge, for throwing away his fair share of hatred. Our prophet will obtain forgiveness for all his followers but that is contingent on us forgiving each other first. We must forgive even the banalest of spirits, the sun, the rain, the wasp, the monkeys, the mad dogs and even the air. We must forgive them all.

Tragically, however, while these pardons were signs of a good heart, they not only ended up leaving a most gruesome reflection on his face but also kept smacking him like an incorrigible child. Exasperated by the constant mocking, he had lost his way in that aimless world. Having lost all hope, he then sought help from the dead—from those who were not in this world anymore—which is perhaps why they held a greater significance for him now. It is safe to say though that any attempt to seek help from the dead is a death in itself. A clueless and traceless death that embeds itself inside the person.

But what had been truly helpful was the beating drum piercing through a cold, dark night, carrying with it that command in an angelic voice—'Rise, rise, rise now.' He had lost his way in the void that held the drum-beaters and the dogs together. He found the caravan and lost himself in it.

'Is this the way to the Budhh mosque?' he sheepishly asked someone.

'Yes, but you must take the other route. There are knee-high swamps along this way.'

The spasms were now attacking his abdomen with a vengeance and his calves were becoming numb. Mustering all the strength he had in his body, he tried to hold his breath. Despite the bitter cold, drops of sweat were now trickling down his forehead. When he took a turn into the adjoining lane, he witnessed the familiar sight of the mosque's minaret.

He had made it.

Deriving as much happiness from the moment as one possibly could, he tried to walk with an even more erect gait. As soon as he reached the mosque, however, he realised that the people had already offered their namaz and were now raising their hands to the sky in prayer. He was crestfallen. The spine too started conveying its angst. When he saw a few men leaving the mosque, he hurried to them and asked, 'Is it over, brother?'

'Yes, only a couple of minutes ago. You're late. Anyway, if you turn right from here, you will reach the Green Mosque. They must be about to begin. Hurry!'

He quickly moved in the suggested direction. The muck slashes were now establishing themselves on his sherwani in the face of little to no resistance, and the coins in the pocket were confusedly clattering away. Because he had to move quickly, he couldn't maintain a straight back anymore and the hunch was more prominent than ever. According to his standards, he managed to reach the Green Mosque in record time but his best wasn't good enough. He realised to his horror that he was late again and the namaz had already been offered.

'Am I the one who is always late or do they begin before time?' He suddenly realised that, a little further ahead, there was another mosque where he would certainly be able to pray. Without wasting any more time, he dragged his aching back, sore feet and the hunched back to the mosque like a distracted camel.

He did not remember the number of puddles he stepped into and the number of mosques he shuttled between with his unbathed and impure body. With an agonising stomach and stinging back, he looked at all the mosques with empty eyes. He was but a dazed witness to other people's prayers. He was shaken back into wakefulness when he found himself standing outside a tiny mosque that lay in the compound of a graveyard located at the outskirts of the city and adjacent to the city asylum. There was another graveyard behind the asylum. In that graveyard of living people, all the prayers begin late. He remembered coming here as a child with his father on the eve of shab-e-barat—the festival of the dead, and the night of fortune and forgiveness, the day when all the graveyards light up. This mosque had also been decorated that day. Long streams of tiny lightbulbs would hang from the dome. Then there was a mass recital of the Qur'an, after which everyone was offered sweetmeat. He even remembered the gluey touch of the sticky syrup that was left on his fingers.

Perhaps this heavy door to the mosque was never opened, which explained the huge spiderwebs that now adorned its arches. 'Where is the main door?' he thought to himself. But it was all in vain now. His legs were shivering and the rest of his body was displaying mild contortions, reducing his spine to a painful blister. The swollen feet had been ravished by the shoes. The spasms now acted like sharp knives.

He gave up on the idea of finding the main door to the mosque and collapsed in front of the back door instead. 'Maybe there are a lot of people praying inside,' he fancied. He started banging on the door with such force that the webs came crumbling down on him. He kept knocking.

'What is it?' He found a man clad in white in the desolate graveyard.

'Eid … I have come to offer the Eid namaz,' he said in a broken voice.

'Eid namaz?' The man in white looked at him surprised. 'But it is dark now. Only a little while ago, I somehow managed to offer the *maghrib* prayers. What Eid, brother? These days even the farz namaz stands threatened, and you are reminded of Eid?' he asked.

He silently stood staring at him.

'Let's go, brother. What are you doing here? Don't you see the fog is thickening now? In a little while, the roads won't even be visible.'

Suddenly, the air became laden with azaans, the calls for prayer. No sooner had it ended than it began coming from somewhere else.

It didn't stop there. One after another, there were calls from every corner of the sky.

The man in white suddenly started looking dazed and distracted.

'You saw that, didn't you? The worst has come to pass. There is trouble in the city. These are people crying for help from their rooftops. These are not calls for prayers, these must be for the community's safety.' With huge distracted strides, the man in white vanished into the dense fog.

Allah-hu-Akbar!

Allah-hu-Akbar!

Despite his failure to comprehend the meaning of the lines, he felt a wave of chastity riding over his body as he sat listening to it. He felt as if these calls were the same as the ones that are made after a corpse has been placed inside its grave. Even before the incense stick has gone out, the people walk away from the site, leaving the dead man to face his grave alone.

And, finally, he thought, 'Everyone doesn't need to get a chance to offer the Eid namaz. God is indeed great. Greater than the azaans sung in his praise.'

The calls stopped after a while. Now it was just the silence of the graveyard and the descending fog. But, wait, there is another voice he could hear. The voice of the fakir that appeared to be coming to him from the sky. Perhaps it meant to carry with it this mass of muck and dirt to a place where he could finally seek forgiveness. He looked around him, and there was absolutely nothing left for him to forgive as he departed. It was now his turn. He looked around again, and there was nothing familiar in the world anymore. Dejected, he collapsed in front of the front door of the mosque.

When they tried to straighten his stiff body in the morning, his forefathers' cap fell to the ground, the hump was more prominent than ever and the coins in his sherwani filled the air with their clattering against the cold and silent graveyard.

WOH

(That Woman)

By Rashid Jahan

Introduction

By Editors

Rashid Jahan's short story, 'Woh', translated here as 'That Woman', does not pull any punches when depicting the humiliation that disabled bodies face, often every day, at the hands of the able-bodied. From the moment the story introduces the disfigured (suffering, perhaps, from syphilis) unnamed woman, she is shown to go through chastisements, ridicule, disrespect, disgrace and, by the end of the story, physical violence. Every 'upright' able-bodied character treats her as something that isn't even human and sentences both her physical and moral being as ugly, mutilated and hideous. From principals to doctors to teachers declaim her a loose woman, prostituting her body to whoever has the inclination and money. This assertion of her immorality, in fact, is never acknowledged as something extraneous to her physical appearance to the other characters of the story. There is, rather, an inimical link between her villainous physical presence and her equally unscrupulous moral being. Everyone seems to be assured of her disfigured face (with two holes for a nose and a missing eye) being a reflection of her immoral character. While her face is symptomatic of syphilis, nowhere does the narrative reveal the veracity of this diagnosis even as all characters treat her as syphilitic. Even if one assumes her to be afflicted, the presentation of the effects of the disease does not warrant a declamation of her immoral being. Yet, people continue to do so. By the end of the story, the able-bodied world is affected by her mere presence so much that Naseeban, the helper at the school where Safia, the narrator of the story, works, throws a slate at her face and begins hitting her.

Such forms of exclusion are, the story boldly says, the only fate awaiting the disfigured and the disabled body. The stigma that this community faces is widespread and normalised. Objectively, neither is Rashid Jahan mistaken in her presentation of this reality nor is she over exaggerating. Physical disability is, as Lerita Coleman Brown also argues, 'the most severely stigmatised difference', especially because they are 'physically salient and represent some deficiency or distortion in the bodily form … in most cases unalterable' (2013). But systems of stigmatisation are always specialised forms of marginalisation which necessitate a relationship between either side of the binary. Stigma allows one side to feel superior over the other to 'feel good about themselves' (ibid.); to ensure that their existence is somewhat better than others. In 'Woh', the classification of the unnamed woman's morality as corrupt based on her physical disfigurement is the acting out of this play of stigmatisations. It allows the 'normal' world to feel that not only are they better than her in terms of the retention of 'normal' physical features but they are better also because they choose to act in moral ways. In so choosing their own fates, to stick to the path set by god and goodness, they have actively averted turning into the hideousness that is her, thus, negating the play of chance in the acquisition of disablement. In other words, the 'normal' world is 'normal' simply because they have chosen to be moral. There is, then, nothing else to do but admonish the woman who has strayed, even if it means resorting to violence.

At the heart of this stigma lies disgust. Every character is disgusted with this woman and always acts in revulsion. It is, in other words, disgust that distances everyone in the story from the woman and allows the former to set in procedural stigmatisation against her. Safia, in fact, does not fail to mention or highlight how this disgust makes people avert their eyes from the woman's face each time she comes into view. Safia too, for that matter, has to force herself to look at the woman. Disgust, then, becomes the immediate and the sole emotion that the 'normal' world elicits at the sight of the disfigured woman. But this emotion of disgust in the face of disability is rather interesting in itself. It is, as Bill Hughes notes, 'a form of cowardice in the face of inevitability and a failure to recognise that mortality is not an enemy but simply the price one pays for life' (2012). As a response to the disabled body, disgust sets in when the disgusted is reminded of their 'visceral, animal, messy selves' (ibid.). Further, this reminder is also accompanied by a possibility of coming to embody the messiness of being human. The disabled subjects, therefore, 'invoke anxiety and revulsion because they are defined as literally embodying … loss of control, loss of autonomy, at its deepest level, finitude, confinement within the human condition, subjection to fate' (ibid.). Read from within, the characters of Jahan's story are disgusted by the unnamed woman precisely because the holes in place of her nose and eyes remind the characters of the holes that they have hidden inside the skins of their faces. This is a reminder that they cannot contend with. Neither can they come to terms with the fact that they do not have any control over their own fate and bodies to allow them to retain the skin that hides the truth of their 'hideousness'. The societal process of her invalidation is, thus, 'locked into the disavowal of [her] slimy self which is projected onto the other [characters], palpably displaying the signs of breakdown and defilement of what [they are] and will be but refuse to face' (ibid.). This inevitably leads them to stigmatise her as shown above and, in the process, regain, even if false, control over their lives.

The only exception to this rule is the narrator Safia. But even her exceptional treatment of the woman does not set her apart from society. For one, it feels as if her actions towards the woman is exceptional only because she has to drive the narrative of the story forward and she cannot do it if she rejects the woman at the first glance as others do. For another, even as she is interacting with the woman, Safia is still disgusted. She takes care to not even touch the chair that the woman sits on when she comes to meet her. The way Safia treats the woman, in that sense, is not all that different from the way the others do. She might not have, like Naseeban, hit the woman but her abhorrence at her presence has similar violence in it. The woman's parting words, '[n]ow you must know', then, has an over-arching reach to comment on the way how everyone in society, however ostensibly friendly, treats her. But more than being a hopeless representation of the state of the disabled human, in its showing of the injustices meted out to disability, Jahan's story does show a glimmer of hope. It shows the affectations that need to be squashed and stopped. What is, instead, required is something similar to the Jaina philosophy of nirvicikitsa which 'would enable one to feel no revulsion at the sight of disease, deformity or disfigurement of any kind in another human being' (Anand 2020). Shilpaa Anand, in fact, suggests a similar reaction arising out of 'Woh', where the rubric of the narrative necessitates a response to disability as a mixture of nirvicikitsa and a modern-day 'emphasis on compassion' (2012).

Works Cited

Anand, Shilpaa. 'Translating Rhetoricity and Everyday Experiences of Disablement: The Case of Rashid Jahan's "Woh"'. In *Disability in Translation: The Indian Experience*, edited by Someshwar Sati and G.J.V. Prasad, 231–242. London and New York: Routledge.

Brown, Lerita Coleman. 2013. 'Stigma: An Enigma Demystified'. In *The Disability Studies Reader*, edited by Lennard J. Davis, 147–160. New York and London: Routledge.

Hughes, Bill. 2012. 'Fear, Pity and Disgust: Emotions and the Non-Disabled Imaginary'. In *Routledge Handbook of Disability Studies*, edited by Nick Watson, Alan Roulstone and Carol Thomas, 67–77. London and New York: Routledge.

That Woman[1]

Translated from Urdu by Shilpaa Anand and Aneesa Mushtaq

I met that woman in the hospital. She was there to collect her medication and I was there for the same reason as well. On seeing her, the other women present there started turning away from her, averting their gazes. The doctor's disgust was apparent in the way she shut her eyes at the sight of that woman. I felt equally repulsed but somehow managed to look her in the eye and smile. The woman smiled back at me, at least she tried to smile. Her nose seemed to have disappeared. There were two gaping red holes where her nose would have been. She was also missing an eye and could not use the other eye without straining her neck.

I came face to face with her again, upstairs, a little later, where I had come to collect my medicines. Nasally, she asked, 'Where are you coming from?' I gave her my address. She collected her medicine and left; without my prompting, the compounder offered, 'This woman is a rogue. Slut! She's just a slut! She's rotting away to death and thinks she can get treated now! The doctor's also insane to be prescribing a remedy for her. She should be kicking this disgusting woman out of here.'

I was working at an all-girls school at the time. I had recently passed out of college. The world was at my feet. The future appeared to be a bed of flowers and every bloom a rose or jasmine. The world stood before me like a moonlit night in which the river flowed softly at moments and at other moments became a waterfall. I was happy and content. Distress and sadness were unknown to me. Teaching was an excuse, a way of killing time. All this self-indulgence seemed to be a way of waiting, waiting for something to happen.

The curtain lifted and that woman entered the office room in the school where I worked. I stood up astonished, and, without much thought, by force of habit said, 'Please take a seat.' At first, she hesitated but finally sat down. She had in her hand jasmine in full bloom. She placed it on the table, in front of me. I did feel repulsed as I reached to pick up the flower but I restrained my disgust and somehow placed the flower in my hair. The woman smiled, got up and left.

The woman's visit became an everyday affair. As the classes would end for the day, she would lift the curtain and come in. I would say 'Please take a seat.' She would sit. She would place one or another flower

---

1 The editors and authors have made all attempts to contact the copyright holders.

before me. My peers among the teaching staff had taken to teasing me about the woman. No one ever sat on the chair she had occupied. It was the woman's face that was so disgusting! Even I was careful not to touch that chair. After the woman left, old Naseeban would grumble saying, 'Nice new teacher you have there! One has to encounter this filthy woman now! Why should I wipe that chair? Why should it be cleaned'?

The principal would also express her disgust by saying, 'Why do you call that woman into the school? Parents will be upset by the fact that such obscene and characterless women come here.'

The next day would arrive and she would be there again. And I would once again say, 'Please take a seat.' We hardly ever made conversation. Did she believe that I didn't know the truth about her? She would just sit there and stare. Just stare with her misshapen eye from that nose-less disgusting face. Sometimes, I suspect that her eyes welled up with tears. What does that woman think about? Sometimes, I feel like just asking her outright, but where would I begin with the questions?

It would often turn out that she would come in and the other teachers in the staff room would get up to leave, teasing me in English, 'Safia's 'that one' has come. Come, let's go sit in the library. Just look at that wretched face!

Another teacher would say, 'Hai! Safia, after looking at that ill-fated woman I can't take even a bite of my food. I feel nauseated.'

'But how well that woman has chosen her object of interest! The best among all of us. She's so wretched that we need purdah to save ourselves from her,' such were the jealous comments of the stout teacher.

I would be doing my work and that woman would just sit there and watch. I would be restless. What is she looking at? What is she thinking? Had *this woman* also been like me sometime in her life? That thought would make my hair stand on edge.

Why does she come here? Doesn't *this woman* know that people hate her and are disgusted by her? Snot keeps streaming from those two red holes in her face and every day I would think of telling her to stop coming here. What the principal says is right. The girls have also been expressing their distaste in their own way. And the teachers are walking around being nauseous. But she would appear the next day and I would present her a chair, saying, 'Kindly, have a seat.'

Didn't that woman ever look in a mirror? Hadn't she realised that she was bearing the fruit of her sinful actions? Why doesn't someone just tell her! Does she even have someone she can call her own? Where does *this woman* live? From where does she come? Does she believe that I only think of her as a disease? I have become the butt of strange jokes in my school. And it doesn't just stop at ridicule, it has turned to a kind of contempt. But she would bring me some flower and I would put it in my hair and she would smile that frightening smile at me.

Why does this woman look at me like that? Who is *this woman*? Who was *this woman*? Where was she born and what brought her to this condition? What does she feel when she visits me this way? Does she feel pained or a kind of relief?

One day, as she was stepping out of the staff room, she sneezed and wiped the snot on a wall outside. Naseeban, who was scrubbing the little girls' slates with multani mitti while sitting down to catch her breath, sprang up with youthful sprightliness and hit the woman with the slate that was in her hand, scaring the woman.

Old Naseeban, with that one action, forgot all the decorum that she had acquired in the last 20 years of working in the school and would always remind the girls to imbibe. She returned to being that street-side Naseeban. 'Haramzadi, randi! Has come off here like some great lady who is fit to sit on these chairs! This has been on for days now! Only yesterday she was seen at the chowk. Now, the skin is literally falling off piece by piece from her body and she has shown up here to be some big madam....'

One kick, a second kick and a third punch...

I ran out and caught hold of Naseeban. 'Hai, hai, what are you doing!' The girls had all crowded around by then. It was as if Naseeban had forgotten who she was.

'You have given this woman such a high status! A stone from the gutter has been elevated to the top of a building. She's spoilt all the walls now! For 20 years I have been serving this place. And I have never heard of prostitutes coming to school! I refuse to continue working here. Get some other woman to replace me...' saying this, she charged at that woman again. People somehow managed to hold back the old woman. I bent down and helped the woman get up. She was crying uncontrollably. I held her and moved her towards the parapet. There was blood streaming down her neck. She probably didn't even know that. Hiding her face, still crying, the woman said nasally, 'Now you must know', and walked away.

KUSHTOROGIR BOU

(The Leprosy Patient's Wife)

By Manik Bandyopadhyay

Introduction

By Editors

Manik Bandyopadhyay's 'Kushtorogir Bou', translated here as 'The Leprosy Patient's Wife', presents a rather archetypal construction of a disabled character: a construction not only in terms of the creation of or a birthing anew of a character model but also as a producer of the typological affectation of disability. Seen objectively, then, there are, insofar as the disabled subject is concerned, two distinct phenomenological entities that Bandyopadhyay fashions—the man Jatin and his disease-induced disfigurement/disability—only to yoke them together by force in service of the story. This force effectively disallows Jatin to be a rounded character or, as shown later, even a human being. He, along with his disability, is simply a function; a transaction in the economy of the critique of patriarchal hierarchies. Jatin's entanglement with leprosy, therefore, is constructed to simply play a part. The story, after all, is not really about Jatin or the materiality of his disability, but his wife who happens to be wedded to a man who (after a period of a happy marital life) contracts leprosy. The title of the story makes this quite clear. The subject of the narrative is the wife while the kushtorogi is a mere adjective; someone (or something) that modifies the wife—Mahashweta's—existence. Naturally then, the story relates Mahashweta's struggles in being the wife of a diseased human being as leprosy rots Jatin's mind alongside his body. Mahashweta is berated, cursed, humiliated and made to feel less than human even as she does what a dutiful wife within a patriarchal setup is supposed to do. The story ends with her awakening and an answering back as she decides to stop attending to her (by now quite monstrous) husband and open up a care facility for leprosy patients in general.

That the story gravitates towards the problematisation of power hierarchies implicit with gendered realities is fair enough. After all, Mahashweta's suffering at the hands of her husband is quite prototypical and Bandyopadhyay's story does quite well in the presentation of the absurdity of such suffering. The problem, however, lies in the way this absurdity is related: a way that seems to necessitate a loss of Jatin's humanity and transfigure him into an altogether ugly thing—physically, mentally and literally. Mahashweta's problems, after all, begin only when Jatin is diagnosed with leprosy. He starts losing himself as he increasingly becomes hopeless, suspicious and, for the lack of a better word, emasculated. Notwithstanding the thing that he becomes, the story is quite clear in proposing that it is the onset of disability that is fundamentally responsible for the change that Jatin goes through and, subsequently, the humiliation that Mahashweta has to endure. Interestingly enough, nowhere in the story is Jatin belittled or berated because of his disease/disability. Not a single character comes up to him and makes him feel less. Neither is he ever segregated because of his condition. Everything that happens to Jatin, everything that he believes that the world is doing to him is, in fact, self-imposed. It is he who decides, for example, to lock himself in a room and not allow anyone near him. Within such a framework, two questions need to be asked. Firstly, what allows Bandyopadhyay (reportedly an able-bodied author) to use disability as a watershed event that converts a human being into a social, physical and mental wreck? Secondly, why is it *disability* that becomes responsible for Mahashweta's suffering?

The answer to both these questions lies in the ways that society engineers normalcy. Firstly, both Jatin and his author-creator have grown up in societies that venerate the resourcefulness of the able-bodied. To be able to do all that humans are meant to do is, after all, normal. In which case, any deviation of this ability to be human resources, relegated into the dark abyss of abnormalcy, is always conjured up as monstrous—to be segregated from the rest of the people and, if not subsequently fixed, then locked up. The disabled body, then, is nothing but sub-human; to be included within the ambit of society only upon proof of function. Further, considering that society as a whole believes this, the naturality of such a dichotomous existence is incontestable. It is the objective truth in a sense, never to be doubted because how can someone, who is perceptibly not whole, become a part of society. Obviously then such socio-topographical layouts not only govern the abled world but the disabled one as well; making the latter keep themselves in check. This is a society that Jatin has grown up in. There is no real need for another character to come and tell Jatin that he is a lesser human being. He already knows that. But, more than Jatin's knowledge about his 'inhumanity', as it were, what is important here is the naturalness of this inhumanity. Neither Jatin nor Bandyopadhyay questions the veracity of such a claim and accepts the lesser being of the disabled subject. Jatin's metamorphosis into a monster-like figure who keeps on berating and abusing his wife (who, as a good human being, is always ready to help him) and finds her responsible for his predicament is then but natural. It's as if the author is trying to show that acquisition of impairment/s necessitates the loss of humanity. This, in itself, becomes a strong critique of the processes of naturalisation that society contrives towards the formation of the abled natural and the disabled deviant. Jatin, hence, doesn't stand a chance. Not only is he fated to become the villain, but also find his disabled self in a constant battle with normalcy. There is no question of talking about the material or existential nature of his disability. It is, the story proclaims, a phenomenon that turns good people bad and nothing else. The question that readers need to ask, especially in light of the presentation of this normal of the monstrous disabled, is if it is right to present the absurdity of the marginalisation of one kind of identity at the cost of another. Is there no other way to exacerbate Jatin's patriarchal moorings besides and/or through disability?

Among other things, what is majorly responsible for turning Jatin 'bad' is the pity that he feels his wife has for him. Crafted rather naturally within the vicissitudes of ability, Jatin's increasing admonishment of his wife's pity for him comes equally naturally. While the narrator of the story does not colour (quite comfortably) Mahashweta's devotion to her husband as either pity or charity, Jatin sees in his wife's eyes nothing but pity. One can argue here that it is Jatin who sees pity where there is none. This, however, does not redeem the society which has drilled into Jatin (and, subsequently, the author) the idea that the disabled body is always to be pitied. If nothing else, Jatin's surety, that his wife takes care of him out of pity and not genuine love, reinforces the vaudevillian nature of the disabled subject: living life as per a tight script written by society. In other words, insofar as Jatin is concerned, the world will always pity the disabled body. There is absolutely no other way that the abled interact with them. What makes it worse is that it doesn't matter for Jatin if Mahashweta feels pity for him or not. As long as he thinks that it is pity which is driving his wife, the veracity of the claim is baseless for he feels what a 'genuinely' pitied human feels like. Bill Hughes, in his seminal essay, 'Fear, Pity and Disgust: Emotions and the Disabled', notes what being pitied feels like. For him, it hierarchises the two parties concerned as the superior (the one who feels pity) and the inferior (the target) and demarcates 'populations into moral categories of the normal and the pathological' where the latter is 'socially invalidated'. The pitied disabled, then, are cast as '"less fortunate" [and] the subaltern, neither fully fledged citizens nor fully fledged persons' (Hughes 2012). In feeling pitied, Jatin becomes the site of all the negativity that Hughes talks about. It is, finally, this feeling of otherness, of inferiority, that propels him into the monstrous state that claws and gnaws at his own wife despite her devotion. The reason for this change is as immaterial as the legitimacy of Mahashweta's pity. Perhaps his feelings of inferiority emasculate him or perhaps it forces him to draw upon the patriarchal power, even more, to compensate for the power that has been taken away from him. The result, in either, is the same: his monstrosity.

Works Cited

Hughes, Bill. 2012. 'Fear, Pity and Disgust: Emotions and the Non-Disabled Imaginary'. In *Routledge Handbook of Disability Studies*, edited by Nick Watson, Alan Roulstone and Carol Thomas, 67–77. London and New York: Routledge.

The Leprosy Patient's Wife[1]

Translated from Bengali by Brati Biswas

Occasionally, people's words come true in the most amazing manner. If there is some heavenly reason behind this, god alone knows. God does not spend sleepless nights to give credence to the collective wishes of humans. A curse is nothing but an expression of human suffering and ineffectiveness. But, at times, curses reach poisonous and horrible fruition.

Who does not know that to earn is to get others' money home? When it is done on a large scale, one becomes rich. Like women, all the money in the world, except that which slips out of the pocket and gets lost among the roadside rubbish heap, has a master. The ways of earning less and more money are almost always decided by either the sweat of the brow or a cunning evil mind. If you do not want to harm anyone and wish to live like a harmless common person, you will shed five hundred drops of sweat to earn a rupee; everyone will thump your back and bless you. But if you want to be rich, you will have to cheat people and destroy them. Before you are born, all the money in the world has already been divided and grabbed by everyone. When you cheat, use muscle power and expertise to empty everyone else's coffers and fill your bank account, people will fall at your feet crying and curse you. There is no other way to be rich.

Therefore, it must be said that Jatin's father used various means to destroy many people and earn some money. Had there been a means to earn money by doing good, he would have done that. This is the reason why he cannot be blamed entirely for the curses and envy he accrued in the nooks and crannies of his life. Maybe, to prove the adage that, in this world, virtue always wins and sin loses, before he could savour the hoarded wealth of his father, at the young age of 28, Jatin, the son, was afflicted with leprosy.

One day, Mahashweta asked her husband, 'What has happened to your finger?'

'Don't know, there is a small boil.'

Mahashweta touched the finger and observed.

'It is red all over. It cannot be a boil.'

'The finger seems insensitive to touch, Shweta.'

1 Translated with permission.

'Should I put some tincture iodine? Otherwise, let me kiss it. The kiss will heal it.'

Mahashweta kissed the finger and smiled. 'This is not a human's finger. You seem to have borrowed it from the celestial Urvashi and Menaka. God has never seen a human finger so bright. Blood seems to be at bursting point.'

Mahashweta draped his hand around her neck and repeated what she had spoken many times before in her life.

'You are being very unfair, you know? You are so handsome, I am confused. Do I love you or do I love your face? I don't know. Is it only this? I worry and worry day and night. If you had to face this, you would know. Envy consumes me.'

After that, for some more time, things remained unclear. Even when circular coin-like copper-like blotches appeared at two or three places beside his fingers, things did not become clear. Mahashweta felt that Jatin was not well; the colour of his skin was becoming dull due to bad blood. He needed to take a tonic.

'Please take a tonic.'

'What will happen by taking a tonic?'

'Oh ho, take it. Your health might improve.'

Jatin drank the tonic. But a tonic cannot heal this disease.

Gradually, the rings appeared on his other fingers as well. His skin became rough and looked dead. The ones around the well of his eyes and lips broke and took on an unhealthy lifeless look. His sense of touch gradually decreased. He stopped feeling pain after being pinched. Day and night, a dull unhealthy feeling made him depressed and irritable. Then, the finger which had been affected first, which Mahashweta had kissed and lovingly put tincture iodine on, began to rot.

The 16-rupees-a-visit doctor said, 'I'm feeling hesitant to tell you, you have leprosy.'

The 32-rupees-a-visit doctor said, 'Bad type. It will take time to heal completely.'

'Will it heal doctor?'

'Why not? Why are you scared? It can be certainly cured.'

The doctor's reassurance was spoken in such a plain and forceful manner that it was clear to everyone that Jatin's dreaded disease would never be cured.

The 100-rupees-a-visit doctor said, 'There is no option but to try and localise the disease's spread as much as possible. It is impossible to do more than this. You know that this is contagious, be careful. It is needless to tell you that children … you understand?'

Didn't they? Jatin understood. Mahashweta understood. If only this understanding could have happened six months ago.

Mahashweta was like someone struck dead; like someone who just had had an unjust, inappropriate, unnatural and painful death. In an extreme panic, like a senseless perplexed person, she exclaimed, 'You have got leprosy? Oh god, leprosy?'

Jatin was not dead yet. But he was dying. He gave up the normal tenor of speech and said, 'What sin led me to this, Mahashweta?'

'Why should it be your sin dear? What about my fate?'

In his own house, amidst relatives, Jatin became untouchable. Had he a desire to roam about the house freely, no one would be able to stop him. But he chose seclusion. He exiled and incarcerated himself in a separated portion of the house. As per his orders, no one else was allowed to go in there except Mahashweta. Friends who came to visit had to return from outside the house. Relatives who tried to express their sympathies face to face, failed. Jatin refused to bring his rotting body in front of other people's eyes. He installed a radio in his room, collected a heap of books and got a phone set up to link himself in an unclear subdued voice to not only the other part of the house but with the outside world as well. There was a sudden change in his life and there was no end, no boundary set for the misfortune.

Though he had shunned all the people in this world, he could not leave Mahashweta. It is difficult to say where he got his will to live. After all, he had rejected even the sight of his closest relatives. But, with Mahashweta, he remained weak-willed; like a baby clinging to its mother. He stuck to his mental resolve to contain his contagious disease within his body till death and turn it to ashes in the funeral pyre. But, it appeared as though he had not included Mahashweta within the ambit of this resolve. In his attempt to be careful towards relatives and others, he completely forgot about the danger to Mahashweta. Till that time, they had shared everything in their lives and if today Mahashweta had to accept and share his body's ugly disease, he had nothing to say about it.

He continuously called his wife and wanted her near him. He wanted her to sit with him and either talk or read to him. A beautiful song being played on the radio was enjoyed only when the two of them were together. If he wanted to talk on the phone, she had to search out the number and dial it and give the receiver to him. If nothing else, she would just sit near him and he would watch her.

Mahashweta did everything. Something like a cyborg, she surrendered herself to all the new whims and fancies of Jatin. Whatever Jatin said, she followed with an unmoved heart. She never tried to change or improve on his wishes. If one watched her following her husband's uninterrupted wishes, it did not appear as though she needed to bathe and eat, be in the company of healthy people or simply needed to spend time with herself. If Jatin remembered to give her leave, she ate. She would take a stroll in the garden in the evening only if Jatin reminded her of it. Otherwise, she completely forgot about herself and tirelessly endeavoured to fulfil Jatin's ever-changing wishes indefatigably.

She kept an eye on all things required for Jatin's convenience and well-being and ensured that all the guidelines were followed. To increase Jatin's sense of ease and to give him something above happiness, she could not devise or discover any means in 24 hours of a day.

Slowly, their relationship changed. Moving together on life's path, their life had a pace and followed certain norms. That pace of their life had, with Jatin's illness, stopped. All the rituals had changed as well. Old love, old affection, old curiosity had been put into a new mould. After four years of marriage, there was a need to establish a new relationship. The earlier understanding and equation had to be changed completely. So that they could overcome the situation they were faced with, small but many transformations happened on their own—they did not even get the time to notice those. Corresponding with the elaborate preparations for the patient's treatment, the bed of the patient and the healthy became separate. While speaking, the need to laugh got completely lost. Nine out of ten components of conjugal bliss disappeared and faced a silent death in the chasm of the two separated beds.

With the illness in the equation, throughout the day and night, not a single kiss existed in their whole world. They forgot the language of the eyes as well, through which they used to communicate earlier. Not all of it, though. Now, through their eyes, they gave expression to a moving fearful question. Their eyes expressed an unbelievable, unexpressed pain, questioning what happened?

Day and night, Mahashweta probably thought about this. Her lips were always pursed tightly, taking short breaths. When she felt the need to take in more oxygen, she took a deeper breath. It sounded like a deep sigh like a curse to an unseen fate.

Jatin reprimanded her and said, 'Why do you behave like this day in and out?'

Mahashweta replied, 'What do I do? I don't do anything.'

Jatin suddenly became teary-eyed and said, 'As it is, I am already dead. If you too give me pain...'

Jatin forgot and took hold of Mahashweta's hand tightly. In the beginning, his sores would be bandaged; nowadays, to give them light and air, they were kept open. The doctor had asked him to wash his fingers five times a day and dry them in the sun. The bandage was only for the night.

Mahashweta kept staring at his three de-skinned fingers. The fingers were touching her hand but she did not flinch for a moment. It appeared that, had Jatin pleaded, she would have kissed his fingers and sore hands. Jatin removed his hand and angrily said, 'You hate me Shweta?'

Mahashweta spoke angrily, 'When did I hate you?'

'Then why do you look at me like that?'

'How do I look'?

Can a person, in such a state, tolerate this type of counter-questioning? Jatin got up, walked to the verandah and plopped down into the easy chair kept under the strong noon sun. The hot sun of Baisakh could not be tolerated by an ordinary person. But Jatin's senses had died. For hours on end, he spread himself out in the hot sun. As the sun moved, he moved the easy chair. He had heard from the doctor about the beneficial effects of the ultraviolet rays of the sun. Jatin tried to use the sunlight wholeheartedly. He could not waste it.

After a while, he called out, 'Come here Shweta.'

When Mahashweta came, he said, 'Sit here.'

Mahashweta sat near Jatin in the shade. The heat from the sun burnt her sweating body but she did not get up. She sat by her husband like a bright glorious husband-worshipping wife and drooped.

Jatin said, 'I am thirsty.'

Mahashweta brought him water.

Jatin said, 'I need another pillow.'

Mahashweta brought him another pillow.

Jatin asked, 'Is just bringing enough? Put it behind my head.'

Mahashweta put the pillow under his head.

Jatin looked at her dryly and said, 'Tell me what you are thinking.'

Mahashweta said, 'What shall I think?'

The Baisakh afternoon became more and more sultry. At night, Mahashweta woke up to find Jatin in her bed. She closed her eyes. The whole night, she kept her eyes shut.

Everything in this world is fragile. So, the fragility of humanity cannot come as a surprise. As humans change, so do their nature—building and breaking. A king today can become a beggar tomorrow. All one can make out is that he was not a beggar always, nothing more.

Spending his days and nights imprisoned within a narrow confine and with a poisoned mind, Jatin, day by day, began to turn more and more inhuman. His horrible disease kept on growing and his handsome good-looking face turned ugly. Soon enough, his ugly exterior left its mark on his inside too.

It became almost impossible for Mahashweta to spend even a few hours together with him. Jatin's mental state had completely gone awry. The blood rushing into his brain caused what turmoil, no one knows. But his bloodshot eyes reflected his state of mind. His voice became hoarse and unclear, and the hair on his head thinned considerably. His nose begun to take on a copper-ish hue. The flush on his face and body appeared old, rotting and fermenting. Like a cornered, ferocious animal, his rough scary behaviour began to terrorise Mahashweta. Jatin understood that he did not, anymore, have a place amongst humans. In this lifetime, he had lost all hope of ever receiving human respect, honour and love. Since he did not allow anyone to come near him, no one inquired about his health. He was not ready to accept this self-beguiling truth. In fact, he began to identify Mahashweta's voiceless and unaffected self-surrender as an abnormal manifestation of uncommon hatred. Jatin had nothing to give to another human being. That is why he was angry towards humans and became selfish. Since he was suffering, he was not hesitant to hurt another.

But, Mahashweta was the only one he could reach. She, alone, had to carry the burden of his diseased body and mind! Gradually, she became very quiet. Her detached cold manner too abated a little. It appeared as if her dormant instinct for self-preservation was no longer somnambulant. She decided to live a little and not willingly choose to die with Jatin.

She asked Jatin, 'Will you go somewhere?'

Jatin replied, 'No.'

'It might lessen with seawater.'

Jatin looked with cunning doubting eyes and said, 'Lessen? Your head! The doctor did not say so.'

Mahashweta said angrily, 'All is being done as per the doctor's advice.'

After a while, she said again, 'We can try and visit the holy place. Maybe you might get some divine revelation.' To this, Jatin stared at Mahashweta's healthy strong body with bloodshot eyes, 'After devouring your son, why this sudden devotion to god? Divine revelation! No god will ever give any sign to the husband of a sinful woman like you!'

This incident was a month old. Jatin had been given a brief recount of the incident. But, he did not believe it to be an accident. He was suspicious of Mahashweta. Toying with this suspicion in his mind, he had begun to soon believe it. Due to this, he spent whole days in violent maddening agitation.

Mahashweta did not reveal anything. When interrogated, she gave replies that Jatin refused to believe. Insofar as he is concerned, she attempted to cover up the whole thing but was caught. Besides this,

Mahashweta behaved in such a manner as if the events were related to only her life and self. But, the truth is, even if this was the case, that it was she who is responsible for the event and not god, Jatin did not have the right to say so. He was unnecessarily becoming agitated and raising the issue of her relation-less, irrelevant life. It was her fate to suffer. She was predestined to be denied all joys. That was why she was suffering: because of being denied. What was it to Jatin? Why should he get agitated?

Just because he was her husband, Jatin would not get any sign from god. Mahashweta could not tolerate this belief that Jatin clung to—that he would be told the 'truth'. Finally, she said, 'You are dying for a son. Has there been any prediction for a son?'

Jatin's eyes had a revelatory look.

'Not a boy? But they said it was a boy.'

'They do not know more than I do!'

Jatin did not say anything else but remained silently immersed in thoughts. The next day, in the afternoon, dark clouds stole away Jatin's sunshine and beckoned Mahashweta.

Outside, the rain poured without restraint and Jatin spoke in a complaining petulant tone as if remembering their few days' old conversation, 'As if girls do not have any value.'

Mahashweta, surprised, answered, 'You are still thinking about that thing?'

Jatin said, 'What did you do? You could not have killed by strangulating? Or were you able to?'

Mahashweta said, 'What reply should I give to such nonsense? You keep on jabbering about things you do not understand. Had it lived, it would have suffered so much pain. Thinking this, I have reconciled myself. Can you not do the same? What a downpour! Let me see.'

Mahashweta got up to stand by the window. The water kept on pouring tirelessly and Jatin continuously swore at her. Mahashweta's eyes watched the rain and ears listened to her husband's words.

A long time ago, they had this conversation.

'What sin led me to this, Mahashweta?'

'Why should it be your sin dear? What about my fate?'

That time was long gone. Now, the manner of their conversation had completely reversed. Jatin shouted at the top of his voice and said, 'Because of your sin, I'm in this condition; you son-devouring monster. Why did you not die? Oh no, your desires are not yet fulfilled? Do you have someone who loves you even now?'

His suspicion had become Jatin's prime weapon of attack. If one looked at Mahashweta's face, it would not appear as if she was happy.

But Jatin's manner of seeing was different. That dark pallor of her face appeared to him as if exuding beauty and the empty look of her eyes, a mark left by tiredness, appeared to him as contentment. Her attempt to remain neat and clean Jatin interpreted as making up to look good. All this Jatin construed as a highly suspicious attempt to increase the ambit of her life behind his back. Why else would she go out in the afternoon and leave him alone? Did she rest in another room? He did not believe it. If she required another room to rest, what was the fault with the room next to his?

'I'm not such a fool. Do you understand?'

Her habit to counter-question had not left Mahashweta completely, 'Who is calling you a fool?'

Jatin adamantly retorted, 'All this will not do. You cannot stay at my house and do all this. I'm warning you. I'm not dead yet.'

'What are you saying?'

'I'm saying bullshit. Oh dear, I have been destroyed from all corners.'

Jatin started to cry loudly. Mahashweta stood still like a picture and watched his distorted face. As Jatin's crying intensified, she became calmer. Slowly, her eyelids dropped and the hazy pictures hanging on the walls of the room seemed to slowly revolve around her. The sounds from the outside gradually began to filter into her ears and she began to realise these sounds bit by bit. She felt that someone somewhere was crying.

A kind of madness had overcome Mahashweta as well. It was inevitable.

Madness is what people do not do in their normal state. Mad things will only be done by a person whose life has gone beyond the boundaries of their typical lives. Such insanity births certain curious new habits of the mind. Some perceive a friend as an enemy while others think of a loved one as hated. Life, for them, seems a trick by a magician. Faced with sorrow, some cry their heart out. Some just look sad and think that their headache is because they have not had the evening tea. Or, they look at the strange birds that just fly in the sky.

Mahashweta stopped staying in the room at night. She began making her bed in the adjacent room.

Jatin asked, 'Why?'

She did not say anything but entered her room and bolted the door. The whole night she framed a clear reply. Jatin stood outside the closed door and said, 'I have loaded the bullets into the revolver. Tomorrow morning, the moment you come out of the room, I will shoot you.'

He said, 'I cannot tolerate this insult Shweta. Do you hate me so much?'

In his room, Jatin stayed awake. Alone and rejected. In the other room, Mahashweta, on her empty bed, searched breathlessly for some meaning—something to hold her life together. She wanted to think about so many things but was unable to. She wanted to understand so many things but could not. Everything got mixed up. Memories of her maidenhood, like an unimaginable, unthinkable feeling, kept circling her head. When she started to think about the four years of marriage when Jatin was healthy and handsome, her power to think became ineffective. She moved from that primitive, sinless celebration and arrived at a life centred around Jatin's rotten body and distorted, fermented life—where a newborn baby, a complete marvel, died as soon as it was born. Where it is repeatedly born only to die. All the light that was within Jatin's mind had been put off. And, in this deep darkness of his mind, countless laughable superstitions had taken birth. After thinking for a few days, he had developed an unshakable belief in god's sign. God was once for him a mere hazy imagination and religion a compensation for old age. Knowledge was rationality. Now he had begun to hope that if god had mercy on him, then he might reveal the path to be healthy again.

But which God? Tarakeshwar, Baidyanath, Kamakhya? From where would his sign come?

Jatin was not able to decide on his own! He called Mahashweta to discuss it with her.

'Where would it be good to go? To wait for god's sign, Shweta?'

Mahashweta tried to think of a holy place that was far off and said, 'Go to Kamakhya.'

'I will go?' Jatin was surprised, 'How can I go in this condition?'

Mahashweta asked, 'Who will go then?'

'Why? You will go. When a husband is ill, the wife goes and prays to get god's sign.'

'Me? If I go, I will not get any sign. I have no belief in god.'

'Do you have no faith?' Jatin found this viewpoint unbelievable.

'Not a single drop. When I think of waiting for god's sign, I feel like laughing.'

Jatin got angry.

'Oh, you feel like laughing? You are immersed in laughter. Your husband is dying here, and you are indulging in laughter with someone else? You think I do not understand anything.'

Mahashweta asked, 'With whom have I been laughing?'

'If I knew that, do you think you would still be in this house?' Jatin breathed in loudly through his rotting nose and held up his festering fingers in front of her eyes. Crying out loudly, he spoke on, 'Do not think a lot. You too will get it as well. It will be more severe than mine. So much sin needs recompense.'

Under the influence of his fierce anger, he rubbed his sore fingers hard into Mahashweta's hands. Like lighting a fire with fire, he seemed to have transferred his contagious disease into her body and took extreme pleasure in this fact and said, 'Caught you. Now it will catch you. You will get punished for hating me. It is not far.'

After this curse, Mahashweta discarded Jatin. She not only did not serve him anymore but stopped coming close to him as well. She would come only once in the morning and check up on Jatin. The rest of the day, she would keep her distance. At night, before going to bed, she would just peep in, just for a second, like a joke.

It is impossible to say if Jatin would have thrown her out of the house in anger had he not gone to Kamakhya to get a sign from god. Mahashweta agreed to go with him as well. But only because his insistence oscillated between angry order and pitiable begging. But, on the day they had to leave for the pilgrimage, Mahashweta was nowhere to be found. Finally, the paternal aunt of Jatin told him, 'Mahashweta has gone to Kalighat. She has taken your servant and car and left for Kalighat a few moments ago.'

At Kalighat, something new began. Mahashweta had told Jatin that she didn't believe in god but that was not the truth. Had it been true, she would not have spent so much money on the puja the day Jatin had to leave for Kamakhya. Neither would she have distributed an entire basket full of change among beggars. All this, Mahashweta did of her own volition. On both sides of the path, leading to the entry of the temple, beggars sat in rows. She made the servant and the driver hold the basket and distributed fistfuls of money among them. It was like a big congregation. Not just beggars but people gathered to watch the distribution of alms.

Among the beggars, there were lepers as well. Some had a piece of jute covering their hands and legs. Someone else's nose had rotted and become like an indention on their face. Yet another's swollen face was full of big blotches and his hands had wasted away from the wrist. While giving the money to these people, Mahashweta felt a handful was not enough. One basket of money was not enough for them.

She returned home and opened a leper's ashram that evening.

The servant caught and brought home five beggars from the street. Despite the promise of thousands of kinds of luxury, two among them did not agree to stay in the house. The remaining three settled into an easy life. They ate, slept and gave repeated blessings of wealth and sons to Mahashweta. They had no other work. Within the next seven days, Mahashweta's retreat had 21 residents.

Having shifted all relatives to a different house, she began to live alone in a house full of leprosy patients and a few servants she hired. She had also arranged for a doctor to come in the morning and evening to check on the patients. An advertisement had been given for two experienced nurses. The doctor said:

'No one will allow you to open a leper's village here.'

'Why?'

'This is the heart of the city. Who will give you permission for a shelter like this?'

Mahashweta said in surprise, 'They roamed about the streets of the city. I have reduced the risk by containing them in the house.'

The doctor smiled and said, 'Even so they will not permit. But, you know this is very good work. No one wants to obstruct such work. The colony people will complain; that complaint will be analysed, then you will be given notice. You can remain silent for two months. Then, when another notice comes, you can slowly arrange to remove them.'

In reply to the doctor's words, Mahashweta said, 'Leprosy is a dangerous disease, doctor.'

The doctor with his immense experience smiled, 'There are so many similar diseases in this world! They destroy a human being completely. They move with the family bloodline and are hereditary.'

Family lineage! Hereditary! Who knows how much the doctor could divine?

Jatin had become ferocious based on mere suspicion. He had thought that Mahashweta had insulted him. The doctor knew and yet was unmoved. Maybe, the doctor supported her in his mind. There is bound to be a difference between the knowledgeable and the layman.

Jatin returned before the nurse could be appointed. He had not received a clear signal. The only thing he had had was a dream. So, he took a white flower from a 'kund', converted it into a talisman and wore it. Upon returning, he was shocked to see what had happened to his house. 'What all have you done Shweta?' Mahashweta's mind was calmer and, therefore, her head clearer. She said, 'I'm doing it for your good. I met a sanyasi at Kalighat. I have not seen such a bright tejasvi sanyasi in my life. His eyes were bright like fire. He said, "Set up a leper village, your husband will become well".'

The effect of bearing the talisman was still on Jatin's mind and he said, 'Really?'

'Do you think that I am lying to you? You have not seen that sanyasi. Had you seen him, there would be goosebumps all over your body! He spoke to me and disappeared.'

Jatin regretfully said, 'You could have asked for some medicine from him, Shweta?'

Jatin took refuge in his portion of the house. Depending on the talisman and the sanyasi, he had become considerably calm and quiet. But Mahashweta still did not go near him. She kept her distance as she used to before his visit to Kamakhya. But now, she was completely preoccupied with the leper's village. When the number of occupants of the village increased to 25, her joy knew no bounds. Day and night she served these disfigured and rotting people she had collected from the streets. Her love and service were like that of a mother. It appeared as if her chest was made up of these 25 rotten bones of the rib cage: they received all the warmth of her heart. One day, Jatin weepily said, 'You only serve those people, Shweta. You do not even look at me.'

Mahashweta remained standing with a bowed head. She could not say anything.

Once, she used to love her healthy husband and hate the lepers on the streets.

Now she hated her husband and loved the lepers from the streets. There is no complex psychology involved here. Only a simple mind's spontaneous response.

Mahashweta was not a goddess. She was just a leprosy patient's wife.

THAKARA

By P. Padmarajan

Introduction

By Editors

One of the first problems encountered when thinking of disability as an identity category is its porous nature. For one, it is quite difficult to narrow down the genus of disability, especially in definitive terms, to singularities that would then, in turn, include afflicted selves. For another, as Lennard Davis reasons out in his essay, titled 'Crips Strike Back', not only can 'anyone...become disabled' but, in time, 'most people [do] develop impairments [as they] age' (1999). This porosity is a problem because it hinders specific modes of demarcations that allow the categorisation of individuals as either this or that. In other words, it is very difficult to say who is, in definite terms, disabled not only because of its fluctuating definitive boundaries but also because the non-disabled of today can become the disabled of tomorrow. Davis, in line with this argument, calls the able-bodied as TAB: 'Temporarily Able-Bodied' (ibid.). Interestingly, however, this difficulty becomes far more disconcerting for those who don't wish to be classified as disabled rather than for those who are. In fact, the very idea of disability 'disturbs people who think of themselves as nondisabled' (ibid.). This disturbance, as it were, is due to the aforementioned permeability of disability. The fact that the non-disabled can always, and, rather, quite easily, become disabled, scares the former. Having witnessed the process of disability in others, either in real life or representations, the able-bodied world is always fundamentally worried about the retention of their ability. Therefore, they prefer to live in a state of denial when it comes to the question of recognising the frugality of their able-bodied identity. The figure of the disabled character, particularly if they develop impairment later on in life, is, in such a scheme of things, a dreadful reminder of the 'shaky footing on which normalcy rests' (ibid.) and a shocking presentation of the amorphous nature of their normative identity. It is, finally, this that evokes a paralysing sense of dread and fear in the non-disabled human. In this sense, disability, as Davis puts it, becomes a 'spectre haunting normalcy' (ibid.).

It is this denial followed by a fear of disability that is, to an extent, responsible for the stigma that the non-disabled world associates with the phenomenon. The disabled subjects, in other words, are always seen as incomplete, because the superiority that the abled feel counteracts their fear of the former. It is in thinking themselves to be better that they negate the horror of their impending impairment. Quite strangely, this inferior position that they delegate to the disabled human is a double-edged sword. A large part of the fear that the non-disabled feel when confronted with either the disabled body or disability is *because* of the inferior position that they have allotted the latter. In a strange twist of fate, the constructs of the able-bodied meant to make them feel superior come back to bite them, hence, destabilising not only the construct but their abled normative identities as well. P. Padmarajan's short story 'Thakara' exemplifies this strange double-edged process of stigmatisation. At the beginning of the narrative, the subjectivity of the cognitively impaired Thakara is defined by the non-disabled gaze of the narrator and his friend Chellappanasari. For the two of them, Thakara is nothing more than an object of amusement. They ceaselessly taunt him for not being a 'man', thus, constantly questioning and mocking his masculinity. They then try to arouse him by narrating erotic stories of their often feigned sexual encounters and even suggest that he should befriend Subhashini, the village heartthrob, who simply refuses to be seduced by men. This challenge that the narrator and his friend levy become quite important in the scheme of representation of the disabled subjects in the story because, in the non-disabled imaginary, disabled people are often thought of as de-sexed entities. But, as the plot unfolds, Thakara resists assimilation into the non-disabled world's subjective system of meaning and can have somewhat of a semi-successful relationship with Subhashini. Unexpectedly, Subhashini develops a soft corner for her disabled lover and their cross-ability romance becomes a reality. In trying to show the 'inferior' Thakara his rightful place, the narrator and Chellappanasari inevitably slip and come face to face with their inferiority. Had, in other words, the two of them constructed a world where Thakara could have a successful romantic relationship, they wouldn't have had to face a situation where they would end up feeling inferior to him. It is, ultimately, because of this uneasiness of feeling small at the hands of someone who should have stayed below him that Chellappanasari tells Subhashini's father Mathumooppan about her affair with Thakara; a complaint that ends with Thakara being beaten to a near-death state by Mathumooppan.

Thakara's success at winning Subhashini's heart is, in a way, quite liberating. Sexuality, after all, is a culturally feared aspect of corporeally different bodies with serious implications for people like Thakara whose body (and mind) falls outside the narrow and rigid normative conceptions of corporeality. The threat posed by Thakara to the non-disabled world is, therefore, considerable. Not only does he, by asserting his sexuality, disturb normative expectations of the corporeally different other but, by establishing a romantic relationship with a non-disabled woman, he also destabilises the hierarchy of power between the non-disabled and disabled world and renders fluid the line of demarcation between the two. But, such fluctuations, always being unwelcome, prompt rather violent responses from the 'normal' world. Bill Hughes argues this rather succinctly:

> In the context of such an encounter non-disabled persons are most likely to attempt to resolve the element of fear manifest in the challenge of difference by erasure, by putting clear emotional, physical and social distance between themselves and the source of this kind of visceral identity shock. This can be achieved by an act of 'reclassification' that dehumanises and objectifies the aberrant body. (2012)

Though Hughes speaks of processes of erasure in terms of a mere distancing, the 'normal' world, to preserve its normalcy, not only can but also often applies far more insidious ways of erasure. Chellappanasari's complaint to Mathumooppan is a prime example of this. He isn't simply jealous of Thakara but is quite afraid of the defiance that Thakara dares to show to the preconceived notions that Chellappanasari harbours about people like him. The only way out is, then, a systematic erasure of not only the victory that Thakara achieves through his affair with Subhashini but Thakara himself as well.

Thakara, however, does not allow society's violence against him to succeed. He rises like Davis's eponymous spectre haunting normalcy and strikes back at not only Chellappanasari but Mathumooppan as well. Challenging his lover's father, he manages to stab Mathumooppan. Though the latter survives, Thakara is able to reclaim the societal position that had been taken away from him by force. His act establishes him as someone who refuses to sit down and take society's machinations to either keep him as the incomplete half-man or, failing that, seek his erasure. In fact, as he plans his comeback (not only a metaphorical but also a quite literal one—from the eastern shore of the river back to the western shore), the narrator doesn't seem to recognise Thakara as Thakara anymore. He is perplexed because his non-disabled subjectivity could never imagine that Thakara could become someone who can assert himself. He begins to almost fear and dread him in literal terms. While the author's feverish fantasy borders on a revenge scenario, Thakara's act of retribution, in a sense then, presents a perfect example of the imagined dread that non-disabled people have of their corporeally different other. The disabled subject, who has been infantilised throughout the story, is, at once, transformed into a fearful monstrous figure. But, Thakara's monstrosity can be read as a good thing. Such encounters with the monstrous 'are emotionally powerful because they challenge the stable view of embodied self that is characteristic of non-disabled identity. Such encounters push at the walls of the architecture of ableism' (Hughes 2012). In being a 'monster', Thakara can break apart the normative modes of comprehension that define the abled body against the disabled one.

Works Cited

Davis, Lennard J. 1999. 'Crips Strike Back: The Rise of Disability Studies'. *American Literary History*, 11(3): 500–512.

Hughes, Bill. 'Fear, Pity and Disgust: Emotions and the Non-Disabled Imaginary'. In *Routledge Handbook of Disability Studies*, edited by Nick Watson, Alan Roulstone and Carol Thomas, 67–77. London and New York: Routledge.

Thakara[1]

Translated from Malayalam by Sanju Thomas

Thakara was a close friend of mine during my adolescent years. He figures in the list of my friends who committed suicide.

It says nothing about him if I just say that he was a friend of mine who committed suicide. Time has, without much delay, wiped from my mind the faces of all those who committed suicide. Still, Thakara remains. With the resilience of the common weed that sprouts with every first rain.

We were all sad when he died. To us, schoolchildren, it was like a dreadful bolt from the blue. Since death itself was a rare experience for most of us, it became a mental trauma for quite a few days. We remembered him on our way to school and our way back. During school intervals, there was no enthusiasm amongst us when we gathered around the peanut seller at the gate. The next day, many of us would have stories to secretly exchange about not being able to sleep or seeing Thakara in our dream. Our minds just would not stay still. Then, one by one, all forgot Thakara. The unexpected attack of death retreated as it had arrived.

But I wasn't too surprised that Thakara hanged himself. I had a feeling that he might do that. I even knew that to die by hanging was his most cherished wish. Only Chellappanasari knew that wish other than me. He had said it to only the two of us. He would repeatedly say that to us on days when he would be too happy or too sad. Every time he said it, he would warn us, 'Look here! It's just the two of you! Thakara hasn't mentioned it to a third person. Don't say it to anyone—if you do, Thakara will hang himself.' Chellappanasari and I would laugh at this refrain.

Chellappanasari used to wear a pair of blue ear studs. That was why we admired him—Thakara and I. The second desire of Thakara was to wear those studs and stroll around in the market. But Chellappanasari didn't give it to him. He only kept on reassuring Thakara till the very end that he would—but then what's the point in blaming him? How could one trust Thakara? It's not as if he would steal them. Thakara didn't know how to steal. But if someone whom he might meet on the way very pleasantly asked him for them, Thakara might very well hand them over to him. If one asked him later whom he gave them to, he

1 Translated with permission. All rights reserved with the copyright owners.

wouldn't even remember. If one persisted, he could only stand there and smile, like an idiot. If one got angry, he might even burst into tears.

Thakara had sprouted in the market even before Chellappanasari and I were born. Our first memories include Thakara running errands for all and sundry. By then, he had already passed his days of abuse in the market and many traumatic nights. I was scared of him then. I used to have nightmares about his big form in loose khaki knickers asking after everyone and drooling from the mouth. Once we started going to school, that fear disappeared. Thakara became close to us. We started loving that mentally retarded man as we would a large doll. He too wanted only that.

Chellappanasari was two or three classes senior to me. He deserves a prime position amongst those who taught me waywardness. He was an expert in imparting sex education through the medium of day-to-day routine talks. As we would walk back four miles from school along the lonely village path, he would speak about sex in a very natural style. He also had an experience of all that by then. He made up ten times more stories than he had experienced. I displayed enthusiasm even when I knew that he was bluffing. Those stories and the events in them that anyone could make out to be imaginative, excited me in those days. Sometimes we would sit by the broken bridge at the river and speak for hours. The stories that he would narrate, while smelling the stench of his sweat after the football game as if it were a matter of great pride, would always add something to my knowledge. Many times the stories would run into some similarities. In all the stories, Chellappanasari would figure. And also, a woman. What attracted me most was the variety of women in those stories. I could relate to them more when they were about his secret liaisons with women I was familiar with. Thakara just intruded into our intimate evenings, and what he wanted were those stone ear studs.

Chellappanasari promised to give the ear studs.

'When will you give them?'

'Immediately after I finish telling this story,' replied Chellappanasari and got back to his story-telling.

It was a great story. I got lost in it. I forgot about Thakara. It was only later when the story ended that we realised that Thakara too was lost in the story.

He was drooling. The spit spilt along his mouth and made holes in the sand as they fell. We could faintly recognise an unusual gleam in his short breaths. Chellappanasari and I looked at each other. We burst into laughter. Thakara didn't understand why we were laughing, but, after watching us for a while, he too joined in our mirth.

'What were we talking about?' Chellappanasari asked.

'I know,' Thakara was bashful.

'What do you know?' asked Chellappanasari. I saw in his face the delight of finding a new victim.

Thakara didn't answer. But we understood that he had some ideas about the man–woman relationship. Is it that he knew, or that he wanted to know … something in between, maybe.

We spoke to each other in whatever English we knew. Let's ask him if he has slept with a woman. We asked. He hadn't slept with a woman. He confessed. He didn't have any interest in doing it either. Thakara hung around with us till evening. By the time we left for home that day, Chellappanasari had included him in the list of his disciples.

Initially, I didn't like it that Chellappanasari made Thakara his disciple. It's nothing much … I just felt that there was some devious thinking behind this move. I might also have been a bit jealous. Jealousy mingled with fear about an intruder into my private world. But it just happened. Gradually, it became a habit with Thakara to talk with us by the bridge or by the bamboo thicket near the ruined temple courtyard. Chellappanasari happily took up the responsibility of expanding the horizon of his knowledge along with mine. I felt hatred and disgust. I felt pity when I saw that stupid large being getting enchanted so easily by the new world. I also feared that this would lead to some mishap or the other. I hinted towards this to Chellappanasari once. He only smiled mysteriously. A deceitful smile! Then he said: 'You are even worse! A bigger idiot than him!' He said that Thakara wouldn't do anything. 'What will he do anyway? He will only roam around with his mouth open. Can't you see, those tufts of black hair in his armpits are like stalk. His muscles are of no use. They are as dead as logs.'

'Then what's your plan?' I asked him angrily.

'I have no plan. What shall I do if he comes running after me every day? Should I just give him a thrashing and send him away? I can't do that.'

'Just tell him that you will not give him your stone ear studs.'

'It's not the studs he is after now,' Chellappanasari said. 'You are such a fool! It is now that he has started an interest in vulgar things. That's how it is with some people. They just grow big like trees till 30–35. Some just remain sterile. Some turn poisonous a little later.'

'What do you gain by making Thakara poisonous?'

'I do not want anything. But isn't it fun?'

But I understood later that it was not just for fun that Chellappanasari had recruited Thakara. He had a special affection for Thakara once he understood that Thakara could become a good guinea pig for his experiments.

Once, as we sat watching Chellappanasari playing football, Thakara softly asked me, 'Have you ever slept with a woman, kunje?'

He was very shy to ask it. I noticed a faint red spreading across his stubbly cheek.

'Oh yes! Whenever I feel like, I go sleep with a woman.'

Thakara's eyes widened with surprise. I started telling him a story in the style of Chellappanasari as I watched his tongue rotating in his mouth and wrinkles appearing on his forehead. The heroine of my story was Radha, my househelp.

Thakara had seen Radha. In fact, Thakara knew all the women who went to the market to buy fish.

Thakara showed great interest in how my liaison with Radha happened. I told him that story in a very simple narrative.

'One day I felt like sleeping with her. So, when everyone in the house fell asleep, I went and lay next to her on her mat.'

'Didn't she scream?'

'No,' I declared with a triumphant smile. 'No woman screams.'

'Why is it so?'

'That's how it is.'

That day, when the gathering by the bridge disbursed, I told Chellappanasari about it. He congratulated me. He of course didn't forget to ask if what I said to Thakara was true. When I told him that was just a desire, he didn't forget to tease me.

'Anyway, Thakara is growing well,' Chellappanasari assessed. 'We should get him to do some things. Shouldn't leave him like this.'

It was easier said than done. In fact, it proved to be a strenuous effort. We read out to him from sleazy magazines. We gave him books with pictures of naked women and sexual intercourse. In the soft coolness of the temple pond, Chellappanasari demonstrated to him how to masturbate. Though Thakara ran away embarrassed, we gradually understood that he did try it out the next day. According to Chellappanasari, it was his big victory.

'I have identified a girl for Thakara,' Chellappanasari said one day.

'Who is it? Who is it?' I asked anxiously.

'There is someone.' He revealed the name after a lot of cajoling.

'Subhashini.'

That was the moment when I felt the utmost regard for Chellappanasari. At the given point, there could not have been a more intelligent choice in our village.

Subhashini was the talking point among young men of the generation immediately older than us. Her name could provoke many fights amongst them. In due course of time, her father Mathumooppan, a ruffian sans any conscience, would thrash up or stomp on many a young man. The story goes that one had even been stabbed.

Those days, our village had only one stud bull. Mathu was famous as the owner of that celebrated fornicator. Mathu was a terrifying figure who would let the bull rest after noon and would turn towards the tapioca trade. He would be drinking arrack all the time.

Mathu's father too had a stud bull. After getting drunk, Mathumooppan would come to the junction and speak about this proud lineage. If anyone disagreed, he would be beaten up. Mathu obtained many stud bulls one after another. His bulls had a free run fornicating as much as they wanted with the cows that grazed all along with the village. The woman who had come to live with Mathu ran away in fear. He got a daughter in that deal. He didn't send her with the mother; forced her to stay back. Subhashini!

Subhashini was a good girl. Everybody in the village liked her. The villagers were thrilled by her seductive youthfulness that blossomed in the backdrop of the mysterious world of stud bulls. Subhashini used to talk and laugh with boys, but if anyone made any wrong advances, she would warn him. If she could not handle them by herself, she would complain to her father. She generally liked people fighting over her once in a while.

Another reason to choose her was also that there was ample scope for Thakara to be close to her. Mathumooppan used to take Thakara along during afternoons to carry the tapioca which he would uproot from everywhere in the village. If it were a small bundle, Mathu would carry it. If it were big, either Thakara or someone else like him would carry it. If it were Thakara, he would not argue over wages. In the market, during evenings, Thakara would hang around with Mathumooppan while he sold his tapioca. On days when Mathu was too drunk, his daughter would join in to weigh out the tapioca and bargain with the buyers. Thakara had the freedom to be close to her even in the presence of her father.

I admired Chellappanasari's intellect, still, I was also scared. I somehow didn't like the idea of Chellappanasari's arena getting bigger with Thakara, Subhashini and Mathumooppan.

'Chellappanasari! This is going to end in disaster!' I said.

He said nothing would happen.

'Thakara is a fool. He is retarded. He will do something crazy. She will complain to her father.'

'Nothing will happen, Pillai,' Chellappanasari consoled me. 'Even if Thakara does something, she will not take it seriously. After all, it's Thakara!'

'Can Thakara do anything?'

'Oh yes! That's his privilege'.

I understood that no one took seriously anything that Thakara did when I watched the tapioca business for two days. I watched them enviously as they talked and argued and pinched each other in Mathumooppan's presence.

I told this to Chellappanasari. He smiled that devious smile. I felt hatred towards those blue ear studs.

Thakara's chief advantage was that he was unaware of the consequences. Therefore, we understood that he had his eyes fixed on Subhashini. Chellappanasari sniffed out any mild move of his and advised him remedies whenever he required them.

One day, Chellappanasari told me at the courtyard, 'Today you must leave as soon as Thakara comes.'

'Why?' I felt as if I had been slapped.

'There is something. I need to tell him a secret.'

'What secret?'

'Didn't I say a secret'? He stared at me. 'Then I will leave right away. Why would I give you company till he comes?'

I couldn't sleep that day. What could be Chellappanasari's secret advice to Thakara? I was sure that it could be a very risky move that he was doing all by himself.

During lunch interval the next day, he came to me. Though we had met in the morning, I pretended as if I had not seen him. If he was such an important person, I would just leave him to himself!

'Why are you so solemn?' Chellappanasari approached me while I was washing my lunch box at the lake.

I felt angry. I thought there was sarcasm in his voice. 'Poda…' I forcefully spat out the water in my mouth and climbed back the steps, but Chellappanasari came after me. I went to the yard of the lonely old couple to collect ilanji fruits and he followed me there. I understood from his face that he had something very important to tell me. He looked very nervous.

I raised the bar. I pretended as if I had not heard him and started walking away. He stopped me.

'Please stop Pillai!' he requested. 'We need to brainstorm too.'

'That's what you feel now?'

'Yes,' he shrivelled before me.

'What did you advise Thakara privately?'

Chellappanasari didn't reply.

'What is it Chellappanasari?' I got annoyed when he hesitated. 'Would some mishap have happened?'

'Most probably,' he said.

He said that something would have happened that morning. Mathumooppan would have left early in the morning with his bull. Thakara would have entered the house where Subhashini was all alone. He would try to have sex with her. Chellappanasari had advised him to use whatever force that was necessary.

My heart beat faster while I sat in class after lunch. There was a buzzing sound in my ears. That afternoon whatever was written on the blackboard turned into white zeroes.

As soon as the bell rang, we ran and checked at the village junction. Thakara wasn't there. He ought to have been there at this time. Our face fell. Chellappanasari didn't stay for his football game. We didn't talk at all on the way. We were worried about what could have happened to Thakara.

But nothing had happened to him.

He was waiting for us at the thicket by the dried-up river. He was in a hurry to tell us what had happened. We ran up to him. He was almost sobbing with joy. 'I feel like hanging myself,' he told us with such delight. Subhashini had made him promise that he wouldn't say it to anyone. Still, I have to tell both of you.

Our mouths fell open. What Thakara told us was that Subhashini yielded to him happily. Though, initially, she kept on saying she was scared, at the end she almost bit his shoulder off! We didn't want to believe him. He must be lying. We consoled ourselves that Thakara had made up a story just like Chellappanasari and I did. But Thakara beat his chest and promised it was true. 'It's true. Thakara is saying the truth. If you doubt, do come and see for yourself tomorrow.'

The next day, both of us didn't go to school. We dodged everyone and reached Subhashini's house and peeped in. Thakara was there. What Thakara told us was the truth.

That year, there was a drought in our sesame fields. Here and there, one or two shrunken plants still stood. Many didn't even venture out to sow the seeds since there was no rain. But, weeds grew wild in all the fields. They carried different kinds of flowers and undulated everywhere. Chellappanasari told me dejectedly that even nature seemed to be in favour of Thakara.

'How else can this craziness happen?' He asked. 'Look at stupid Thakara's fortune!'

Both of us felt disdainful anger at ourselves.

Though Thakara didn't try deliberately to move away from us, we felt that he was moving away. The pull towards the first woman whom he won over in life was kind of quite quick. He lost interest in anything other than Subhashini. And that girl was an expert in carrying things along without evoking any suspicion in anybody. Thakara too started keeping secrets from us. We got envious. The secret of the wondrous liaison of Thakara and Subhashini was an exclusive and difficult thought to deal with. We also had another doubt: Was Thakara turning out not to be Thakara, bit by bit? Chellappanasari substantiated with evidence that Thakara's dullness had reduced with his knowledge of sex.

Thakara had indeed put on a little weight. We felt that his broad muscles hid in them a machismo that not many in the village could boast of and that was where a thorny flower-like Subhashini floundered. Jealousy ruined our peace. The evenings under the bridge got another hue. The stories of Chellappanasari stopped all of a sudden. With twilight, the silence of sombreness and accusation came to wrap around us.

'Didn't I tell you not to get Thakara into this useless game?' I scolded Chellappanasari every day. His blue ear studs had long lost their sheen for me.

One day, when I met Subhashini on the way, I murmured, 'Hmm ... I know!'

She turned back sharply, 'Mmm? What do you know?'

She didn't let me slip away. She forced me to stay and tell her more about it.

'Why are you stopping girls on their way to exchange pleasantries?' She hissed.

I turned into a mature adult and said to her, 'Look Subhashini! People have started talking here and there. Thakara is retarded. He can say anything to anyone.'

I expected her to be devastated but nothing happened.

Instead, she blasted me, 'Phaaa!! Don't you dare cook up filthy stories! I don't mind who you are and what you are! I will shower you with expletives....' She started mouthing whatever came to her mind. 'Fine, you told me this. But if I happen to hear anything from anywhere, I will catch hold of you and that carpenter boy who roams around with you. Both of you will end up at my father's knifepoint.'

She walked away thrusting her chest. I stood there and trembled.

Chellappanasari scolded me when I told him about that encounter. I also felt that it was a bit risky to have approached Subhashini in such a crooked way without even consulting him.

'Now I can't undo what I did. I will bear the consequences if anybody creates trouble.' I promised and he was pacified.

But we got to know many things from Subhashni's plucky attitude. Most of that knowledge only made us more troubled. To our astonishment, we understood that Subhashini trusted Thakara completely. It was clear to us that she wouldn't let go of him even if she got to know about some mild rumours from here and there.

That awareness weakened us. Our enthusiasm and general interest in day-to-day things waned. Chellappanasari got suddenly bored of football. At times, we went to the evening market and watched in sly Thakara and Subhashini. If ever they happened to notice us, they behaved very cautiously. Mathumooppan will go to the arrack shop in between his tapioca trade. We noticed that during those intervals Thakara would behave like an efficient adult and try to handle the business seriously. He was a new slave for Mathu. He struggled to display the responsibility of an heir. Subhashini laughed out at his nervousness.

That must have been the triggering point for Chellappanasari. In the evening, he ground his teeth callously and said to me: 'I think I am going to put an end to this.'

'How?' Even I wanted to see it end.

'I will tell Mathu.'

'He will stab you, and Thakara,' I told him fearfully. 'Don't go for all this mess, Chellappanasari!'

Though I told him this, in my mind I thought let him do it if he wanted.

The next day, Chellappanasari didn't come to school. I sniffed danger. That evening, as I was coming back from school, I saw a gathering at the market. I ran up there and saw that Mathumooppan was thrashing Thakara. A big crowd stood around not able to do anything, overwhelmed by the brutality of the blows.

Thakara had fallen. Blood streamed from his face and shoulder. Mathu abused him and hit him on the back of his head with a weighing balance and with each hit blood spurted out. Thakara cried out and made some gestures in his unconscious state. I didn't wait till he passed out. I ran away before that. Mathumooppan's ferocious face didn't let me sleep all night. No one saw Thakara from the next day.

The previous day, he was seen lying in a pool of blood. Mathumooppan sat on guard at a distance with his blood-stained weighing balance to stop anyone from giving water to Thakara.

Various stories did the rounds in the village as to what must have happened to Thakara. The most convincing one was that he was dead. Someone said that he was admitted to the hospital. Anyway, no one cared to investigate after him. Everyone was scared of Mathu. The villagers also knew that nothing much would come of complaining to the police on Thakara's behalf.

The enquiries and curiosity lasted only for a few days. Mathu appeared in the market again with his blood-stained weighing balance. He didn't bring Subhashini along.

It was said that Mathu had beaten up Subhashini too that night. All of us, school children, were shocked when Satheeshan who stayed across the paddy fields said that he could hear Mathu's yelling and her screams at his house.

All believed Thakara to be dead since no one saw him for a week. It made a wound in my heart. I tried to convince myself that Thakara wouldn't die just like that. I felt that if at all he had to die, he would hang himself. I stopped talking to Chellappanasari. I was even scared of his blue ear studs.

One day, I met Subhashini. The old playfulness and flirtatiousness in her had disappeared completely. Her face got all the more sullen when she saw me at a distance. I was emboldened that nothing would go wrong if I got into an argument with her then. 'That day when I tried to warn you, you were ready to kill me,' I said. 'See what has happened now.'

She didn't say anything. I felt bad.

'I felt right then that something like this would happen.' I turned an approver, but she didn't like my pretence.

'Hey, boy!' she said sternly. 'Don't you try your games on me!'

I got angry.

'But now your game has turned grim, hasn't it?'

'What?'

'Hasn't Thakara been battered to death?'

'By whom?'

'Your father?'

'Huh! I don't know.' She just stood there as if she knew nothing. 'My father would beat and kill many like him. Why? Are you smart enough to question him?'

'Weren't you beaten up too?'

'What for?'

'Look here, don't lie staring into my face.'

'It must be someone in your home that's lying.' She got furious. She toned down her voice when she saw my panic. 'My father hasn't as much as thrown a speck of sand on my body so far.' I didn't remain there since I knew that she could lie through her teeth.

But one thing I understood. She hadn't taken Thakara seriously. In fact, she would not have much problem in letting him go either.

One day, we got to know from the fishermen from the west that Thakara was at the beach. Everyone was relieved to know that Thakara wasn't dead, especially we schoolchildren. We heard the news as if it were one of great joy.

Thakara isn't dead. He has sprouted on the beach two–three days back. He was tired because of the beatings. Still, he was mostly alright. He found means to live by collecting small fish and helping fishermen pull the net. We thought of going to the western shore like an excursion. We should devote one Sunday to that. We should go there and garland Thakara. We took these decisions, laughed and dispersed. Nothing happened. No one went in search of Thakara. It was as if he would come by himself.

But, when next Sunday came, I couldn't help but go to the west shore. I told a lie at home that I needed to go to a friend's place to borrow a book. As I stood waiting for the ferry, I wondered to myself: What is it between Thakara and me?

It was not just because of guilt that I went to meet Thakara that day. That was when I understood that there was something more than just a curiosity that I had towards him. When it was time for the ferry, one more person joined the passengers, Chellappanasari.

He looked awkward when he saw me. We didn't utter a word in the boat. We sat at a distance and kept silent as if we were on a vow. It was very hot. The water in the lake was blue. Chellappanasari and I sat looking at our reflections on the wavering water. As we sat looking, my feeling of anger towards him deteriorated. I somehow felt pity for him. (He told me later that he had felt the same.)

We didn't speak to each other even when we reached the bank. Both of us knew where the other was headed towards. Then what was there to ask?

When I started walking fast, he slowed down.

Thakara was at the beach. He lay in the shadow of a boat staring at the sea. Thakara didn't look too weak as people said. In one or two places on his head where hair was cut too short, dry pieces of cotton stood in the wind.

Seeing Chellappanasari and me one after another delighted him. He ran to us with a wide smile and started talking to us holding our hands. We were surprised because we had thought that he would be angry with us. Thakara himself didn't know how he had reached the western shore. He only knew what people said.

Boatman Viswambharan, drunk, and on his way back from ferrying a dead body across the river, had dragged Thakara to the western shore. He got him admitted to a charitable hospital and left. Thakara regained consciousness only after two or three days. The days after he regained consciousness were the most intolerable. As he had lain there without anyone to speak to and quashing the flies that covered his open wounds, he took a decision. He revealed it to us.

He would come back to the market. Then he would stab Mathu. Chellappanasari and I trembled within but we laughed.

'Don't, Thakare', we said. 'What will you do after stabbing Mathu to death?'

Thakara said that he would marry Subhashini. And they would live happily ever after. With no nuisance whatsoever. We laughed.

That entire day we spent at the beach. We didn't feel like leaving Thakara. Whenever we started to, he would stop us. We tried our best to get him to rethink his decisions, but we didn't succeed. He had taken his decisions.

'What if Subhashini is not willing to marry you?' I asked.

'Oh, she will,' he replied with conviction.

'She doesn't love you much,' I said. 'We talked. She changed her mind fearing Mathu's beatings.' But Thakara wasn't affected. He somehow was convinced that both of them would marry and have a blissful life together.

'You are just saying this to pull my leg.' Thakara washed away my seriousness with his joy. 'Nothing will happen. She will say "yes".'

Thakara got us huge tender coconuts from the coconut trees on the beach. We experienced his friendship in the clear wind of the beach and the slightly salty taste of the tender coconut water.

Thakara had started belonging in that deserted beach. People had begun to call him Thakara. He took us to a desolate spot and showed us the sunset. All of us turned red.

As the red faded, Chellappanasari said to Thakara, 'It is because of me that you got thrashed up.' Thakara didn't say anything. 'It was I who had told Mathu.'

I understood that he had come to the western shore just to confess this. But Thakara didn't give it any thought. It was as if someday or the other Mathu had to know about it. But he felt bad that Mathu tried to kill him when he got to know about it. That would mean that he would not get Subhashini as long as Mathu lived.

'Thakara will kill him,' Thakara growled again and again.

He came to the ferry to see us off. Just before the boat arrived, he told us one more thing. He would come to the eastern shore only after he bought a knife. He was saving up for a knife. He would come as soon as he bought one. Then he would meet us. Chellappanasari and I remained silent on our way back. We had nothing against each other at that time.

We didn't tell anyone that Thakara was saving up money to buy a knife. Still, all came to know about it. Thakara had been saying this to many. The fishermen who came from the western shore joked with Mathu about it. 'Of course, let him come with his knife.' Mathumooppan announced in the market, 'I am waiting to have a go at him. Tell him I will give him the knife. He just needs to come this far.'

The villagers arranged with the fisherwomen to tell him not to come to the western shore. Whether they told him or not, Thakara didn't come.

The schoolchildren were sure that he would not come. Thakara would not come. He would just stay put on the western shore. He would have forgotten us and that girl by now. After all, it's Thakara!

But Chellappanasari and I knew that Thakara would come.

On our way back from school, we would sit by the bridge and analyse what would happen if Thakara had an encounter with Mathu. All those analyses were distressing.

One day after school, we got to know that Thakara had arrived in the market. We held our breath and ran to the market:

Thakara was in the market. A crowd had already gathered there. No one dared to approach him. With a long knife in his hand, Thakara was standing in waiting under the tree where Mathumooppan usually sat selling his tapioca. As we schoolchildren joined in, the crowd grew bigger. Thakara wasn't noticing anyone. His gaze was fixed at the end of the road.

People said that he had arrived in the afternoon on the ferry. It was not the Thakara that they were familiar with. He had a knife in his hand. People gave way when they realised that he had come to kill. A crowd followed him right from the river bank noticing his movements.

Someone said that Mathumooppan also had come to know about Thakara's arrival. He was getting tapioca collected from some field. He sent word that he would come to Thakara immediately after he had finished with it. He would start his tapioca sale that day only after he settled the matter with Thakara.

All of us waited with bated breath. Our stare was transfixed at the end of the road. Many children ran home scared when they got to know about the gravity of the matter. Chellappanasari and I could not run away. We hid from people and waited. As I stood there, I had a premonition as to what Thakara would do. It played out exactly that way.

Mathumooppan appeared with his weighing balance and his new slave who lifted the tapioca. The boy ran away when he saw Thakara's pose.

Mathumooppan approached Thakara with his weighing balance. Without saying a word, Thakara stabbed Mathumooppan. Just one jab.

No one could believe that Mathumooppan would fall if Thakara stabbed him. People looked on astonished as he lay on the ground convulsing.

In that state of shock, Thakara ran away. The village had gone numb that evening. Some people took Mathu to the hospital. Two policemen came in the evening. They threatened some asking for Thakara. No one knew where Thakara went.

A rumour spread in the evening that Mathu was dead. Later, it was proven wrong. He just had one wound. And that was not life-threatening. He would be out of the hospital in a few days. Then he would go after Thakara. There would be more trouble in the village if Thakara was not handed over to the police, villagers evaluated. Thakara had gone completely mad.

But Chellappanasari and I thought otherwise. We realised that Thakara had stopped being Thakara.

I asked Chellappanasari where Thakara would have hid. He didn't know. Would he have gone to Subhashini? We were sure that he would try to meet her.

I couldn't sleep at night. Thakara would have met Subhashini. She would have rejected him. Would he stab her too? I was scared that something of that sort was hinted at in the conversation that happened on the beach that day.

The next day, I went by Subhashini's house. She was there. She was tensed. She didn't try to hide her tearful eyes and frightened gaze. An old woman from the neighbourhood who kept her company told me that a policeman had come to interrogate her the previous day. When the old woman moved somewhere else, I asked her, 'Did Thakara come?'

She nodded fearfully.

'Did you send him here?' She asked.

I didn't say 'yes' or 'no'. I understood that she was scared of me and Chellappanasari. I thought that was good.

'What did he say?' I ignored her question.

She didn't reply.

'Did he propose marriage?'

She looked at me, stunned. Then she nodded her head, almost benumbed.

'What did you say?'

'I got scared. I told him never to meet me again.'

She should not have told him that, I felt.

'Where did he go then?'

'He just ran away,' she said.

During the school interval, we got to hear that Thakara had hung himself. Many schoolchildren ran to see him hanging from the ruined bridge across the dried-up stream. Chellappanasari and I didn't go. That day, there weren't many students in class after lunch. Even the teachers had lost interest in classes hearing about Thakara's death. By the time we came back from school, the police had untied his dead body and taken it away.

We could hear our heartbeats as we approached the bridge. We didn't stay there. We could only glance at the many footprints on the sand below and walk away terrified.

BEETHOVEN

By Saurabh Kumar Chaliha

Introduction

By Editors

In an essay titled 'Superpowers for the Blind and Deaf' published in a journal called the *Scientific American*, Mary Bates notes how the human brain, upon the loss of one sense, compensates with another. This compensation, Bates notes, is not a simple re-education that the brain goes through but is in the form of a fundamental adaptation that gives the brain a complete makeover: 'If one sense is lost, the areas of the brain normally devoted to handling that sensory information do not go unused—they get rewired and put to work processing other senses' (2012). Giving the example of a study published in the *Journal of Neuroscience*, Bates shows how, in people who are born deaf, the area of the brain, typically meant to process sound, instead, processes touch and vision. This augmentation of the brain to compensate for senses that are not functioning, Bates shows, is called cross-modal neuroplasty. The study of this condition has far-reaching implications; a prime one being, in Bates's own words, the creation and propagation of modalities for the rehabilitation of disabled people. Quite like Bates, the *Science Daily* reports a 2017 research conducted by the Massachusetts Eye and Ear Infirmary, proving cross-modal neuroplasty in people who lose their sight early in their lives. The report, rather distinctively, notes: 'The brains of those who are born blind make new connections in the absence of visual information, resulting in enhanced, compensatory abilities such as a heightened sense of hearing, smell and touch, as well as cognitive functions (such as memory and language).' The inclusion of the words 'enhanced' and 'heightened' in the report unmistakably make the visually impaired into compensated superheroes who have received a superpower by going through a *small* sacrifice. In yet another science journal called *Live Science,* Sara Miller confirms that '[p]eople who are blind do have enhanced abilities in their other senses…' (Miller 2017). Once again, the use of the word 'enhanced' projects the sensory compensation as a boon that besets a human who has undergone sensory deprivation.

That these scientific journals are busy granting such superhuman qualifications to the disabled body isn't surprising. For science, after all, the disabled subject is an individually problematic being who needs some kind of cure for their return to normalcy. In the absence of such a cure (or at least till one is figured out), cross-modal neuroplasty becomes a rather good condition. It not only allows the impaired to do what they otherwise could not, but also, at the same time, grant them something grand; the likes of which even the abled don't have. Notwithstanding medicine's fascination with such compensations, it is important to see such positions as inherently problematic. Firstly, they, ultimately, absolve society from their responsibility of being the disabling entities. Such discourses proclaim that since other senses come to the rescue of the absent one, impaired bodies overcome their 'lack' on their own and society, as and for an infrastructural construct, does not need to bother itself with the disabled body. Secondly, this discourse overlooks the lived reality of disability as well. In having one sense working in a heightened fashion for another, the original loss and the life being lived with that loss is completely ignored. What matters more is the compensation rather than the reason for it. These two points are not, obviously, working individually of each other. There is, rather, an intimate connection between the two as a part of the reason of society's absolution of itself from taking any responsibility of disability lies in its disavowal of the experiential reality of the impaired; a disavowal that stems from society's insistence on sensory compensation. A note of caution needs to be struck here. The question that is being raised here is not against the studies or the phenomenon itself. Cross-modal neuroplasty may (as science shows) be true. What is problematic, however, is seeing such a rewiring as compensation or, as is the case of *Science Daily* and Miller, enhanced and heightened superpowers. It is the discourse of the phenomenon that creates the problem rather than the phenomenon itself. One sense working for another does not mean a replacement. Each time such neural activity is seen as compensation, it creates nothing but problems.

Disability scholars have noted this situation rather succinctly; especially as it contributes towards the creation of the supercrip. Understandably, if impaired develops 'enhanced' and 'heightened' sensory negotiations, they are almost halfway into their creation as the superhuman. Strus, for example, notes how the 'familiar idea of "compensatory faculties"' grants people with disabilities with 'gifts' that 'compensate for and may result from their deficiencies', thus, justifying their 'savant' existence (2013). Schalk similarly writes how supercrip narratives 'emphasize (over) compensation for the perceived "lack" created by disability … [setting] … unreal expectations for people with disabilities to "overcome" the effects of their disabilities through sheer force of will' (2016). In the presentation of the facticity of sensory compensations in the disabled body, often as enhanced and heightened, therefore, the subjects in question get converted to beings in whom nature has, ostensibly, given the power to rise above their impairment by themselves. Such narratives are not only 'complicit in the ableism that constructs such low expectations for people with disabilities that all achievements are considered extraordinary' (ibid.) but also posit individuals as being responsible for themselves. Amidst such narratives, the misery that the abled world wrecks on them is conveniently made to disappear and then forgotten. While such narratives always include journalistic and factual discursive pieces, rift with stories of disabled athletes and mountaineers, it is the representational and literary realm that uses the scientific concept of the cross-modal neuroplasty to create veritable superheroes. Marvel comics' Daredevil, a blind lawyer by day and a crime-fighting vigilante (as all his other senses work to give him heightened knowledge of the world) by night, is a case in point. Between these two kinds of narratives—the journalistic and the fictional—however, there is another layer: that of the creation of narratives of historically disabled people who have ended up being masters of their crafts.

Take Saurabh Kumar Chaliha's Assamese short story, 'Beethoven', for example. The story presents a frame narrative where two friends are discussing Beethoven's musical genius and his subsequent deafness. The narrative, semi-historical in nature, goes on to construct how Beethoven's music is one of a kind and has touched infinite hearts in sorrow and pathos across the world. This inclusion of pathos that sets his music apart, the friends seem to suggest, comes, in fact, from and because of his deafness. In other words, his disability grants him a superhuman and extraordinary sixth sense (as an accumulation of all other functioning senses) of understanding music in a manner that he can bring the entire world to tears; thus, moving them and their souls. This correlation as well as causation is further proved by the friends when, towards the end of the narrative, they speculate what would have happened had medicine been evolved enough to operate on Beethoven's ears and make him be able to listen again. The obvious conclusion to such speculation shows Beethoven's eventual failure to produce the same kind of music that he made when he was deaf. Being able to hear, thus, the friends note, would have robbed him of his genial spirits, rendering him just another musician among many. So, Chaliha's story ends with what is, perhaps, the most problematic sentence of the entire narrative: 'Maybe we are grateful for that—because, our hearts weep for him, but could we lose this music?' The friends, in other words, are thankful that Beethoven remained deaf throughout his life because that gave the world his music. This sense of gratitude, expertly hiding below a misplaced sense of self-righteousness (in the friends and the author), however, does not pay any attention to the distress and misery that Beethoven has to go through because of his deafness. As a matter of fact, the story does include a letter that Beethoven writes, explaining his general misanthropic demeanour and squarely blaming his disability for his misery. But, in light of the display of his super power, this lived reality of his despair (as haunting as it is) is completely ignored. The only thing the friends could feel is empty remorse. For them, comfortable in their abled world, only the music matters and never the man.

Works Cited

Bates, Mary. 2012. 'Super Powers for the Blind and Deaf'. Available at: https://www.scientificamerican.com/article/superpowers-for-the-blind-and-deaf/ (accessed on 15 November 2020).

Miller, Sara G. 2017. 'Why Other Senses May Be Heightened in Blind People'. Available at: https://www.livescience.com/58373-blindness-heightened-senses.html (accessed on 15 November 2020).

Schalk, Sami. 2016. 'Reevaluating the Supercrip'. *Journal of Literary and Cultural Disability Studies,* 10(1): 71–86.

Science Daily. 2017. 'Brain "rewires" itself to enhance other senses in blind people'. Available at: https://www.sciencedaily.com/releases/2017/03/170322143236.htm (accessed on 16 November 2020).

Straus, Joseph N. 2013. 'Autism as Culture'. In *The Disability Studies Reader*, edited by Lennard J Davis, 460–485. UK and New York: Routledge.

Beethoven[1]

Translated from Assamese by Rajashree Bargohain

Gentle rise and fall of three notes in harmony. Primarily, there is sorrow; this music seems to be saying. But, in this joyous spring of four tunes that keep surging up at intervals, there is an anxious pursuit of happiness as well. There is the blind injustice of the one who is unseen and unknown, but a struggle towards liberty readily exists too; an unflinching ascent of the ladder of sounds, the unequivocal trumpet sounds of victory at the end of an endeavour or perhaps victory and jubilance are not that certain. The ladder of sounds still resolute and undaunted but descending, subdued, because destiny, the unseen is merciless, irrational—

The final modulation of the instrument faded away, and the musician friend said, 'Speak.'

'Primarily there is sorrow,' I said, quoting a line I had heard somewhere, 'but there's a hint of joy too that pierces through that sorrow—'

'Quest for happiness—?'

'Music critics say it is the universal circumstance of life, this is its musical expression. He manifested in music yours and my heartburn and yours and my laughter. There's unfairness, there's injustice, undue misfortune, unwarranted hardships, but then, yes, there's life, there's youth, there's an unwavering persistent struggle, one has to rise, one has to rise, one must strip the unseen destiny naked and rise to achieve the glory of heroism—'

'Mainly, life force?'

'Correct. Lifeforce. Imagine then, a young musician on Viennese street, 22 years of age, a fancy glittering tidy dress of the eighteenth century, lace-work shirt, well-groomed hair, graceful strong body, sensuous eager face, brilliant confident eyes. He has arrived from birthplace Bonn city, has already visited Vienna once before, has already met Mozart, has received the good fortune of learning music from him, has learnt music from Haydn and Salieri. He is already an accomplished pianist, his first symphony has already been publicised and has fetched him praise and renown—but Bonn is a small city, an insignificant city. The centre of the music world—Vienna has to be conquered, the universe must be conquered. Ardent lofty ambitions in his heart, merry, fun-loving and a little conceit and hubris. The feel

1 Translated with permission.

of tremendous strength in his body and mind. Wants acclaim, fame, honour, wealth, title, glory, mixing with kings–queens–dukes–counts, and attractive women, love, happy domesticity. New musical notes, ground-breaking tempos, original harmonies—they are all boons of God. Among crores and crores of people on earth, God has chosen him alone for this timeless creative genius. Such musical vibrations that will quicken your blood flow that you will hear the language of eternity; and you will find joy—signs of the natural universe. You will lose yourself inside you. Vienna mine, the world mine, whatever I desire is mine, whoever I desire is mine! Mine! Mine!

'But what's this? What's this? You tell me, shepherds are singing in the distance? Someone plays the flute out there? But why am I not hearing it? Why are my ears not capturing those vibrations? What's wrong with me? What is happening to me?

'Yes, he is gradually turning deaf. Him, whom God had picked out from among crores and crores of people and bestowed with the boon of matchless moving music-creation, his auditory senses—his senses of all—are beginning to turn dysfunctional, someone whose need of the ears is hundred and thousandfold more than you or I. What kind of mockery is this from God? What cruel humour is this by the unseen powers?—Imagine, then, a young musician on a Viennese street has not yet completed a score and half of years in age (but already famous in every direction), untidy dishevelled dress, unkempt grubby face, parched hair, stiff heavy footsteps, lustreless eyes full of crude suspicion, as if someone is out to deceive him, as if someone is demeaning him. What if someone is laughing at him? Uncontrollable anger, he is hurling abuses at people at the slightest provocation, throwing his plate full of food at people over trivial matters—the doctor says, move to a quiet place, hiding in his room in Heiligenstadt village on the outskirts of Vienna, he is putting his agony into words—'My dear mates, when you think I have no geniality, and describe me as bad-tempered or even anti-social, what injustice you do to me. Because you do not know, for what untold reasons you end up feeling that way. Although my nature used to be passionate and ebullient, even entertainments of society used to be dear to me, very soon I was compelled to detach myself, to lead a life of solitude . . . it's impossible for me to ask people, "Speak loudly, I am deaf." The sense which should have been more terrific in me than in anyone else, the sense which was most supremely developed in me, how can I accept the flaw in that very sense. What shame, when one standing beside me can hear a flute playing in the distance, and I hear nothing. Incidents of this kind have brought me to the edge of sheer despondence—had anything more of this kind occurred, I would have ended my life itself'—in the secluded solitude of Heiligenstadt village the lonesome self-exiled ailing irate musician sat and wrote these things, the desired milieu of patrician students and admiring devotees and lauding scholars is now too far away, there is no hope left of finding in life those things that are for him supremely (perhaps absolutely) coveted— friendship, affection, love, marriage, domesticity—his body is broken and untidy, reeking stench in his room and vermin in his bed, he doesn't allow anyone to take care of him, he doesn't trust anyone, people avoid him, little kids are scared on seeing him, already (at the age of 25) his marriage proposal has been turned down (he was not completely deaf yet), and today all that is even beyond his imagination, women flee from his company . . . detached from the bountiful sounds of the universe the heartbroken musician with dishevelled hair is wandering in the woods all by himself. Flowers are in blossom, birds sing, a murmur runs through plants–trees–woods–park, merry streams flow by making babbling noises, in the evening, music sparkling with exuberance plays in some distant tavern in the country, throngs of young men and women are moving in that direction—but his ears do not hear any of this, perhaps his soul hears them, his entire body and mind, entire being feels crushed. This irrational joylessness of life and this marvellous joyous hubbub of the world becomes vocal through the tip of his pen, through the movements of his fingers sometimes dancing, at other times sighing or at times crying out in intolerable pain, in protest, in defiance.

'This loneliness of his, this penury in his heart, this non-fulfilment of his being—what was its purpose? Its purpose was that we might find in music the pathos and sorrow of life, the joys and yearnings of life so that we find in music a protest against the injustices and imperfections of human life—its result is all his many piano-sonatas, this many violin sonatas, this many quartets, and so on, and the invaluable wealth of our achievements—these nine symphonies, its result is your tearful eyes even after these 200 years, this transfixed body, the reverberating but stilled astounded air in your room, you have merged into yourself—critics say, the high pedestal on which Haydn and Mozart had installed music, he brought the music down from it, he broke the smoothness and softness to pieces and built it up in the mould of the rough arid hardness of life, he immersed music in the whirlpool of life—

'Our hearts cry out for him, but we cannot lose this music—'

'Irrational unhappiness?' I said, 'Pointless? Perhaps, it may not be entirely irrational, entirely pointless. We have heard that he probably turned deaf due to some malfunction in his blood circulation, or, maybe, he lost his hearing powers due to some disease like syphilis—not impossible, because he is a careless, rash artist type of a person. His spirit is fierce, physical urges vigorous, fervent youth licentious. It's not unnatural for him to contract a venereal disease—and perhaps there were hardly any preventives in the eighteenth century. Let us again imagine, then, a young musician on Viennese street, 30 years of age not completed yet, he has understood that his ears are becoming incapable of capturing the high notes, but he is in Vienna now, the city which is also a vital centre of medical science (of both the physical and psychiatric kinds). We imagine, then, the deaf musician in a physician's room, bright rays of light from a lantern through the famous physician's magnifying glass over his naughty ears. We know, the ears have been divided into three parts by physicians—the external ear, which lies outside the head, collects sounds and sends them to the tympanic membrane or eardrum inside and sound waves create vibrations on the membrane; middle ear, a hollow or cavity containing one round and one oval 'window', three bones within which, with hammer-like motions, transmit these vibrations to the oval 'window' lying towards the interior; behind this window, lies the inner ear or 'labyrinth' or the interior part of the ear, a cavity surrounded by a wall of bones, through the liquid substances of which the vibration moves forward, and creates vibrations on the liquid substance of a tube with conch-like spiral structures—the name of these spirals is 'cochlea'—and from there goes to the brain in the form of electric signals through auditory nerves, those transmissions take the form of sounds in our senses there. Some tiny strings stir to create an electric field inside the ear—as a result, electricity is produced—ah, this inner ear that is visible, there are a few tiny excess bones starting to grow here, which are called cochlear osteosclerosis, which result in the obstruction in the process of conversion of sound-waves falling on the eardrums into neural transmissions, as a result of which those transmissions do not reach the brain—do not worry (the physician says), do not worry, Herr Kapellmeister (or Herr Hofforganist, or something of that kind), once these bones are removed, everything will be fine, after a small surgery, the nervous transmission will again function as before, it is no big deal—well, did you ever have typhoid?—and, thus, as a result of a small simple surgery, the musician's auditory powers revived, he heard as if someone was blowing a long deep note on a flute, his heart fluttered, he opened his eyes with fear—and, oh, what relief! Putting his mouth to the flute in the distance ... the world is so vibrant, the natural universe so delightful, human beings so beautiful—

We are relieved too, then, because he is just 27 years old, at such young age, a blood-flow-related ailment is not that destructive, damage of this scale to hearing cannot be caused by 'syphilis'—it is very likely that he had typhoid, just like the experienced Viennese doctor had guessed, which takes only a minor surgery to remove the bones it produces—or if not that, examine thoroughly using X-rays, if a string is broken, attach a prosthetic string, if the eardrum is ruptured, replace it, sew it up, using waves of ultrasound, insert a battery-run hearing device in the ear, the articulate world will reveal itself to the senses again, how simple—

The young musician is not lonely anymore, his dress is luxurious and tidy, the brilliance of eagerness in his eyes, renown, fame, wealth, loyalty, friendship, beautiful woman, love, marriage, domesticity, luxury, entertainment come to him at a sign of his fingers, sparkling bliss in every beat of his life, his life complete, there's no sorrow anymore in every layer of his being—

And this completeness, this absolute bliss—what is its result? Its result is all these sonatas of his; all these many symphonies—good, melodious like the symphonies of tens of others, quite good, quite skilful, there's a hint of sorrow and pathos and struggle too, but it's as if a few tunes are missing, as if some notes are in excess, and our eyes do not moisten that spontaneously anymore, my being is not transfixed that way anymore—'

Musician friend said, 'I never heard it happened this way, have never heard that he recovered his hearing.'

'No', I said, 'because medical science did not know of this surgery at that point of time, the battery-operated hearing-device had not been invented yet, x-rays had not been discovered—and maybe we are grateful for that—because, our hearts weep for him, but could we lose this music?'

KHITIN BABU

By Sachidanand Hiranandan Vatsyayan 'Ajnyeya'

Introduction

By Editors

In his book *Disability Studies: An Interdisciplinary Introduction*, Dan Goodley recalls a BBC interview with Richard Reiser, the then director of Disability Equality in Education, the United Kingdom. In the interview, Reiser tells BBC how as a young disabled child, he was sent to special schools to become a 'collection of super-crip' (2011) and made to undergo procedures that would systematically root out his identification of himself as an impaired body. So, one day, as he walks by a shop window and catches a glimpse of himself, he gets the shock of his life: 'I did not recognise myself in the reflection. I can remember thinking: who is that child with the lop-sided gait' (ibid.). His failure to recognise himself, especially when his corporeality is re-presented to him in completeness, reveals the enforced symbolic realities that disabled subjects are regularly endowed with. Within such realities, the impairments of the disabled body are not impairments at all but challenges that they need to individually overcome. Thus, disabled humans are 'honoured' with the position of the super cripple. Reiser's training to be so, to disregard his disabled self, is a stark example of such symbolic attestations. Further, it is not just in the west that such realities are created and presented to the disabled subject. The Indian government's insistence on calling the disabled divyang—a piece of divinity—does the same thing. But, such conversions of the disabled body into, to use Goodley's terminology, 'super-crips' does not negate their impairment, but merely hide it. The symbolism of the 'super' does not offset, in that sense, the reality of the 'crip', thus, converting the subject into an entity that is governed by something chimerical. This object that thus emerges is exoticised and fetishised—often made an example of. While the immediate effect of this conversion is the effacement of the lived reality of the impaired, it also, simultaneously, disallows any possibility of cohesion between people who find themselves sharing this reality. In other words, if the super-crips can achieve whatever they have achieved, despite their impairment, then society is redeemed of its disabling tendencies. It is the individual, then, who is declared unable because another individual, the super-crip, has successfully done what the first could not. If society were responsible, such a construction says, why could one impaired body do it? Disability, for the abled world then, becomes something that needs to be overcome on an individual level. This individuation, further, dissolves any possibility of a political community that could come and demand societal changes to remove disability.

The reasons for such bodily extrapolations become rather plain then. The abled world does not want to be disturbed. So, the best way to rest in their complacency is to create the disabled individual as the singular site of deviancy and disfigurement. To do so, the best way is to create heroes who, despite the odds, overcome. The abled world, in such a scenario, is, at least ostensibly, not afraid of their corporeal others anymore but simply awed. Their awe serves to concretise the individual disabled identity and, in turn, redeem the naturally normalising world of its disabling tendencies. Obviously, it is important to see this awe as a function of the fear that Hughes talks about; as something that is constructed on the basis of a fundamental rejection of the normalcy of impairment. Goodley, hence, writes (with emphasis) that '*To demand disabled people to meet the symbolic* [of the super] *is clearly an act of cultural violence*' (2011: 20). One manner by which the abled world propagates this violence is through their narratives of the disabled. For, such symbolic additions are, in literal terms, re-presentations of the disabled being, thus, making it quite easy for narrative representational spaces to become agents of such symbolising tendencies. Ajnyeya's short story 'Khitin Babu' is a rather good example of this tendency. On the face of it, 'Khitin Babu' is a story that is all over the place. It neither has a lot of activity in its content nor any apparent cohesion to its structure. The entire tale is a piecemeal recollection of the multiple meetings that the narrator has had with the titular character. At times, this recall is interspaced with musings about the most random of subjects: from human faces to food to the soul. At other times, the narrator just cuts short of what he is saying and moves on. Then there is a parable about a food tester and a bed tester lodged uncomfortably almost halfway into the story. The fable does not make any sense vis-à-vis its location. It's an aberration that is visibly disassociated from its surroundings. Taken individually then, all these multiple elements present a story that is chaotic in conception and doesn't have any internal stability to it.

But, this structural instability is not a mistake. It seems deliberate, as a fine synthesising thread of logic holds the otherwise unstable chunks of the narration together: a logic that is revealed only in hindsight, once the disintegrated parts of the story are allowed to settle in the mind of the reader as a whole. In other words, Ajnyeya's story is not a sum of all its parts, but all its parts are just sections of the whole. This deliberate, somewhat broken formation of the story, is extremely important when concerned with the titular protagonist and the subject matter of the story. Khitin Babu, from the moment he is introduced, is fragmented. With the different parts of the story coming together, Khitin Babu keeps on losing one body part after another till he cannot lose anymore and dies. But, the narrative presses, his loss is not a loss of the 'whole' of his self. The narrator shows this clearly towards the end when he says that one does not require the material of the body to be. Each limb is just a part that while presents the 'soul' with an appearance, is not the soul itself. The essence of the whole remains unchanged and undivided. This is the reason that, the narrator can see Khitin babu after the latter's death. The body itself becomes a part—a vestibule for the essence. Just like Khitin Babu's body, the many broken parts of the story are parts of its essence and its meaning. The moment the whole is seen, the individual elements make sense. This parallel between the formal construction of the narrative and Khitin Babu's adventitious disability is important because it shows how 'wholeness' lies outside the body. If, in other words, the narrative is understood quite well from a position outside and despite its broken self, then the 'soul' of the human body should also be true. The reality of the disability of the body in such a scheme does not matter because being is marked not by the physical but the metaphysical. What happens to the reality of the human living body then? Interestingly, aside from its philosophical profundity, the narrator never really shows the 'real' life of Khitin Babu. It is, as if, he is afraid that if he witnesses the disabled body in its disability, this construction of the wonderful supercrip that he has created will fall apart.

For, Khitin Babu is a supercrip. Or, at least a prime example of one. The narrator's reaction to Khitin Babu's increasing order of impairment is always in terms of awe and, dare one say, reverence. It is this veneration that allows the narrator to talk in terms of Khitin Babu's soul. This reaction, further, literally conjures up Khitin Babu as someone more than human, ultimately negating or overlooking the real material nature of his humanity and, subsequently, disability. This conjuration presents two further problems when concerned with the disabled body. Firstly, the norm of the human that the narrator sets up is not of the conventional able-bodied human, but the impaired superhuman. In other words, it is against Khitin Babu's 'superhuman' self that the narrator re-defines his own 'human' self. His theory about the soul, more importantly, his own soul, for example, is verified only when he is able to think about Khitin Babu's condition and the statement: 'Now I know that it is possible to live without this as well'. This shows, in quite clear and succinct terms, how Khitin Babu's superhuman nature is evaluated as such only so that it defines a normal, abled self. Secondly, insofar as the narrator validates his theory of the soul from Khitin Babu's aforementioned statement, completeness becomes contingent on the loss of extraneous weight. Khitin Babu is more complete than the narrator, in a sense, because he has shed the dead weight that god has burdened everyone with.

Ironically then, the more limbs the protagonist loses, the denser his soul becomes and the more complete he gets. This effectively removes all traces of the reality of Khitin Babu's disability. It becomes something that is, in fact, welcome. The story, in other words, says that it is, in quite definite terms, Khitin Babu's disability that makes him so much more. If that's the case, then every disabled self has the possibility of achieving such heights because, like the divyang discourse, disability is liberating.

The story is as problematic as it can get. But, quoting Michalko, Goodley gives a way to combat such representations as well:

> This strategy involves finding 'cracks' in the symbolic nature of culture, developing alternative signifiers around, for example, disability politics and arts, which allow other routes for interpolation for disabled people.... Increasingly, in this ocean of signifiers that threatens to engulf, we can make choices about those to use, mindful of the fact that even the big signifiers ... may be omnipotent but offer us very little. (2011)

Khitin Babu's mythical soul, something that stands to redefine all other souls, is this big signifier that, although seemingly 'omnipotent', offers very little.

Works Cited

Goodley, Dan. 2011. *Disability Studies: An Interdisciplinary Introduction.* London: Sage Publications.

Khitin Babu [1]

Translated from Hindi by Ritwick Bhattacharjee

These faces—these innumerable, infinite faces—they haunt me; rush at me; overwhelm me. It's never been a question of which faces. Or, for that matter, whose face. Every single one that I have seen, that I have come across, each as well-defined as the other, all of them conspire to fill my being with their ephemeral presence. All of them. Never just one. For someone who has spent his entire life storing the mental imprint, the essence of all these faces, it becomes impossible to pick just one and say 'this … this is the one that I will never forget'. No. Never just one. When someone sees a face, really sees it, they can never forget it. No matter if it is a human's face or an animal's. Yes, people look. Europeans look at Indian faces and find them all the same. Indians look at European faces and find them the same. Yes, people look. But they never see. To see a face in its wholeness is to simultaneously know that each being is an individual—someone who cannot be divided or replicated—and each face is memorable in its own right. The only question is if we have the eye to find that individuality, that uniqueness.

So, that's what I am left with. These innumerable, infinite faces. Never just one. Even if I try to focus on one, all the others burst into my consciousness, screaming 'Why? Are we not here? Do we not exist? Have you forgotten us?' Every single one. There are men, women and kids. There are horses, dogs and parrots. There is a squirrel that I had once kept as a pet and used to carry around in my pocket. There is one monal who howling from being struck by my bullet had run for miles. There is a dog that used to sit and cry near my head when I was sick. There is a crow whom I had befriended at the Multan jail. I had named it Parkata on account of its cut wing and half a beak. I remember the way its face used to glow when it half hopped and half flew upon my command. How many more do I list? Is it even possible to capture the sublimity that these faces present? Thank heavens that trees don't have faces or they too would have stood up in attendance and come swirling to my vision. No. I don't think I can even empathise with the trees to the extent that Kalidas, for example, does when he writes about the saddened flora shedding tears after Shakuntala's departure from the forest.

What I have, then, is a museum. Of faces and for faces. Each is inimitable and yet memorable as the one before that and the one before that and the one before that. And, in that labyrinth, if I do manage

---

1 Translated with permission. All rights reserved with the copyright owners.

to duck the others and focus on a face, it's never for its unusualness or deviancy. I pick the most common of faces of the most common of people because—and this is what I have been trying to say—remembrance does not depend on rarity. Every house has a superstar. All that is left is for you to make the effort to come back and see.

These faces. And within them, that one face. Khitin Babu's face was neither beautiful nor exceptional. It was the face of a common clerk with some rudimentary common education. The first time I met him, he didn't have a lot that was worth seeing. The only thing that he had was, well, some pieces missing from the jigsaw of the body. The first was an absent eye in a face marked by smallpox and the other, the hollow arm of his coat conspicuously pinned to his body. Upon enquiring from our mutual friend, I was informed that Khitin Babu had lost his eye to smallpox and his arm had to be cut off after he fell from a tree. Whatever these absences are, however, there was always a strange romantic openness and innocence in Khitin Babu's laughter. Everyone praised him for it. For his laughter, his smiling face and his friendly demeanour.

It was at this mutual friend's home that I had met Khitin Babu for the first time. I was to go abroad for an official tour and was visiting all my friends to bid them farewell. It must have taken me two, or maybe three, months to finish my work and come back. Truth be told, I had expected to meet Khitin babu once again when I was back. But, it was only six months later that I finally saw him again. This time, there was another piece missing—one of his legs. It was, in fact, this new loss because of which I hadn't seen him for so long. His leg had been cut off in a railway accident and he had been in the hospital for so long. It is only after he had learnt how to use crutches that he was allowed to be discharged.

While his accident was old news for Khitin Babu, it was quite new and arguably shocking for me. I wanted to tell him how sorry I was. But, then I realised that maybe my pity wasn't what he needed. Sometimes pointing out someone's disability puts them in a strange dilemma. Before I could make up my mind what to say and what not to say, however, Khitin Babu extended his remaining hand to me and exclaimed: 'Come in. Come in. I have to tell you about my new invention.' And, just like that, all of my hesitations were gone. Reaching out and shaking his hand made me realise how the loss of one limb grants extraordinary strength to the others. I don't think I had had my hands shaken with that much strength more than two or three times in my life. I was about to sit when Khitin Babu started talking again: 'Do you see how much dead weight a human being has to carry throughout their life? I had my tonsils cut out and haven't missed it to date; the only thing that was lost after my appendix was removed was the pain. God just gives uncontrollably. Immeasurably. Most things are useless—two arms, two ears, two eyes. What's the need? Have you ever felt that something is missing while tasting food because we have only one tongue? No. What is the use of having everything doubled over again?' Saying so, he started laughing.

Listening to all this, I just stared at him astounded. But his laughter was pure: emanating from somewhere deep inside of him. There was a joy that sparkled through his remaining eye. I don't believe that he was ever sad about his incompleteness. After all, one doesn't need all the pieces of a jigsaw to know what the picture hidden in the puzzle is. Once, I don't remember when, Khitin Babu had explained this one strange theory that he had about his body. Or maybe he had told it to me in bits and pieces over three or four meetings. I don't remember. What I do remember is that theory. Well, the truth is, it was not just a theory. Khitin Babu had been the living proof of that idea.

By our third meeting, Khitin Babu had lost his second arm as well. I was told by the same mutual friend that, while de-boarding a rickshaw, Khitin Babu had fallen and injured his arm. The injury had soon turned septic, forcing his doctors to hack the arm off from below the elbow. Although this third meeting was at our friend's house, it was from inside the kitchen that I had heard Khitin Babu's voice. He was sitting on a stool and giving instructions to our friend's wife on what to cook and how to cook it. While Khitin Babu was just about fond of eating, he was downright passionate about feeding. The fact that he was a master chef accentuated his passion. Our friend was simply organising the feast. It was Khitin Babu who was preparing it. The reason for this, what one can easily call a banquet, hadn't been told to us. But, we had figured out that it was on account of Khitin Babu's safe return from the hospital. This time his visit to the emergency ward had been very serious and the shadow of death had almost taken him. It was because Khitinda too had realised this that he had given the disclaimer to our friend: 'Yes, the feast will happen and it will happen at your house. But, I will be the one who will give the feast. I shall cook everything as well.' The final decision was taken that, while our friend's wife would do the cooking, Khitin Babu would sit beside her and give her all the necessary instructions. Khitinda's excitement, not only at this decision but also in general, was both contagious and a source of strength for the rest of us.

I pulled up a stool and sat down next to him. Looking at the friend's wife, I asked: 'So, what are you cooking for lunch today?' To which she replied: 'I am not cooking anything. Khitinda is.' Hearing her, Khitin babu chimed in: 'Yes. I hope you'll eat the food that I have touched.' Saying so, he roared into laughter and asked me: 'And you sir, will you eat everything that he has touched? Touched by a person who doesn't have hands.' Still guffawing, Khitin babu asked me further: 'Have you heard the story of the food tester and the bed tester?'

I hadn't heard the story, so he started reciting. Once upon a time, two men walk into a king's court looking for work. When asked what sort of work they do, the first replies, 'I test if the food served to the king is luxurious or not.' What does that mean? It means that when the king sits down for a meal, this person will taste it first and tell if the food is worthy for a king or not. Promptly, he is given that day's meal as a test. The food plate doesn't even reach anywhere near him when this guy pinches down his nose and shouts: 'Take it away! Take it away! The food smells of the dead.' After a lot of research, the king's men finally find out that a dead bird was hanging from a tree beside the field in which the rice that was given to the king was grown. The food tester gets hired. The bed tester then says that he will similarly test the king's bed. Towards that end, he is taken to the king's bedroom. This second guy doesn't even properly take his place on the king's soft silk bed before leaping up and crying: 'My back! My back! I have broken my back. Who calls this a bed?' Once again, all the king's men start looking through the perfectly made bed. No one finds anything out of the ordinary that might have hurt the guy's back. Finally, when the last mattress is removed, the men find a single strand of hair. And, just like this, the bed tester gets hired as well.

Having finished his story, Khitin Babu retorted: 'Those were good times. Good times indeed.'

Listening to him, our friend's wife replied, 'Imagine if you were born in those times. It would have been brilliant.'

Khitinda answered back, 'Of course. If I had been there, the king would not need two different testers.'

The friend's wife turned to me and added, 'Did you know that Khitinda is an excellent singer as well?'

Khitin Babu laughed and said to her, 'Yes, why not. I could have taken the job of the song tester as well.'

The cooking ended at around 4 in the afternoon. Eight to ten of us ate. While the taste of the food was not at the top of the list of things I remember, the lunch that day was so delicious that I haven't been able to forget it.

After the feast, I kept on meeting Khitin Babu for the next two to three days. Then there was another long hiatus. The next time I met him, he had lost his second leg.

Both arms, both legs and an eye. All gone. Tonsils and appendix, as he had said, were useless anyway. He was sitting atop a cushioned stool on an immovable lounge. He had been brought to the friend's house in a special wheelchair. He didn't want to bring that chair inside the house because it is a chair meant for disabled humans. So he had been carried in and placed on the lounge where he was sitting like a lord. He seemed like an idol sculpted by a world-famous sculptor who had only made the torso and left the rest of the body untouched.

I found a corner for myself, sat down and started listening to what he was saying. Looking at Khitinda, I got reminded of the long deliberations concerning the human soul that I used to have in my youth. If the soul exists, does it permeate through the entire body? Or does it reside in just one part? If it is the former, then what happens to it when one part of that whole is cut off? Maybe, the part of the soul which existed inside the cut limb redistributes itself into the rest of the body. I don't know how valid this idea is. Scientists all over the world have been trying to find an answer to the question of the human soul for ages. But looking at Khitinda made me believe that somehow, somewhere, I was right. It seemed as if the only truth about Khitin Babu's soul was its indestructibility. I believe that every time Khitinda lost one appendage or a part, his soul used to become denser by its reduplication through its re-inscription. The soul from each part would enter into that of the remaining body. One could see it—see this ethereal density radiating not from just the body, but also that one cyclopean eye. It was as if there was this big zero inside him that was being slowly filled by the ghosts of forgotten parts and rendering him as an unshakable island hung from the middle of the sky....

Suddenly, seeing that I had already come, Khitin Babu stopped mid-speech, looked at me and said, 'I told you. One does not need a lot to live.' Then he laughed.

I never saw Khitin Babu after this. As an end of this story, I should have. But, I am not narrating a story. I am showing the truth. Telling the truth. Hence, I didn't see him after that. But truth and reality are outside our being. Completely objective and completely unattainable at its purest. Stories do not end with the absence of their listeners and life's theatre doesn't end with the absence of an audience. I also learnt by hearing that Khitin Babu's story ended only after it had reached its zenith. One day, when he had been taken out for a stroll, his wheelchair had collided with a motor rickshaw. Khitin Babu was thrown out of his chair and onto the road. The motor rickshaw had, then, driven over his shoulders, shattering the remainder of his arm. He was taken to the hospital where his arm was further cut down and his shoulders bandaged. Waking up after the operation, Khitinda had asked if his shoulders were intact or not and had said, 'Now I know that it is possible to live without this as well.' This time, however, the possibility of life wasn't very long. He never left the hospital. The wound had poisoned his entire body and he had died.

Khitin Babu: a common clerk: a common accident: a common death. But is it so? I can still see him. At times, I think that the person I see is not simply one who is missing limbs. It is as if he is a body-less spirit. An entity unto itself. What is this singular body? What are its parts? 'Now I know that it is possible to live without this as well.' Maybe, one can live on without the material of the body. The only thing that is needed is pure will. Our will to be. Our will to power. We all shout for food, clothes and shelter. Yes, they are important insofar as human life needs to be lived to a standard. But the true requirement, the true need is just our will.

SEH DA TAKKLA

(The Mute Fury)

By Gurdial Singh

Introduction

By Editors

The rapidly industrialising world of the past 300 odd years has necessitated a simultaneously rapid dissipation of a discourse of the industrious. After all, it is only through this industrious human that profitability becomes possible; thus, upholding the true values of capitalistic conglomerates and societies alike. For such a society, work, in quite physical terms, gets translated into capital and feeds into the existential realities of all humans who find themselves (inevitably) attached to such economic systems. What this insistence on work, often converted and coveted into and as the sacred, results in, is the systematic valorisation of the physical and mental ability to *do* certain things; to move about and use bodily functions and make alterations in the machines of the world. These humans are the norm and the normal: defined such by their literal ability to produce something and, hence, becoming a member of the social corporation. In other words, as long as a human can integrate themselves within structures of production and be 'productive', they are welcome to join the society. On the other hand, put against these productive beings of the world are the wastrels and the deviants. While some get defined so because of their refusal to fit into the schema presented to them by this drive to make a profit, others get clumped up here because of a physical lack. These latter are the ones who, for one reason or another, are not able to use their bodily function as efficiently as their abled others and are, thus, considered dis-abled. Obviously, the disabled subjects are not a creation of the industrialised world. Neither is their marginalisation as the extras of society something that comes up with the rise of industries. In fact, the industrial revolution (not just in England, but the world over) ends up further marginalising a community that was anyway marginalised by history, society, culture, tradition and religion. The point to note, however, in this interaction between the profit-making machines and their disregard of the disabled body is the introduction of the discourse of the apparent failure to be 'productive'. Since the disabled subject, in other words, fails to produce as per the wishes of the governors of capitalist tendencies, they have to be necessarily set aside as second-class citizens.

This insistence on production and its failure thereof becomes quite important because, at times, to the astonishment and surprise of the abled world, some disabled persons seem to overcome their bodily impairments and produce as per the wishes of the abled. The idea of production here is not necessarily restricted to just the manufacture of goods in factories. Capitalism has understood that it cannot ask people to always work and has, therefore, given them other 'productive' activities to do. But whatever the act be, there have been times when the disabled—the ones who are unable to act physically—have managed to and have, thus, become supercrips. But they are not beings who should be celebrated. Firstly, they are, ultimately, discursive (and often physical) creations of the abled world. Such creations are enforced not only through their rampant valorisation by the abled world, but also their necessitated normalisation through cultural representations. David Mitchell and Sharon Snyder pick up the example of the X-Men comic books and films to show the same. These narratives permeate the world with forms of 'positive and affirming' kinds of disability (Mitchell and Snyder 2012), thus, encouraging the supercrip at both the ontological and epistemological levels. The X Men, for example, lead glorified existences despite their 'significant—even severe—incapacities' by simultaneously harbouring 'extra-human compensatory abilities. Compensation or, rather, schemes of superpower overcompensation … enshrine those bodies different yet enabled enough to ask nothing of their crumbling, obstruction-ridden infrastructure, continually naturalised as environments made for most but (unfortunately) not all bodies' (ibid.).

What this implies is that the X Men find existential validation by the abled world only because their extraordinary selves allow them to move closer to the normal. This creation of the supercrip, therefore, is problematic because the abled world is ready to grant the stature of the normal human to only those 'disabled' who are endowed with superhuman qualities, ready to become 'more' abled than their counterparts. Secondly, these supercrips, in thus becoming normal(ish) grant a kind of legitimacy to the systems of marginalisation that the abled world wrecks on the disabled one. The supercrips, in a sense, undercut all challenges put to this industrialist discourse of the productive versus the unproductive where the impaired, obviously slotted in the latter category, are kept out of society because of their inability to work as per the wishes of governments. The abled world looks at the supercrip and seems to say that their system works because it motivates those who cannot work to be superhuman and put in the kind of productive labour that all humans need to put. Mitchell and Snyder sum this argument up rather succinctly, when they write that 'Enhanced supercrips are celebrated by capitalist commodity cultures and social democratic governments alike as symbols of the success of systems that further marginalise their "less able" disabled kin in the shadow of committed researchers conjoined to "creaming" practices for the *non-impaired impaired*' (2012).

It's not just the western cultural representative industry that is busy in the creation of the supercrips. Indian discursive practices across the nation and multiple languages have given rise to these super-powered beings as well. In fact, unlike the X Men, who are fundamentally fantastical entities, Indian discourses of the supercrip tend to situate themselves in more realistic situations, thus, giving more credence to their being. The Indian prime minister's insistence on calling the disabled bodies 'divyang' instead of 'viklang' since 2015 is a striking example of this. The word divyang, finding its roots in Hindu divinity, allots the disabled body a position next to the gods/esses, thus, ensuring their movement away from being human. Such a nomenclature seems to call them out to be the semi-divine creatures that they are 'meant' to be rather than be humans who live similar lives as the abled world. Further, the Indian government's renaming of the entire disabled community is not an odd moment out in the creation of the supercrip. Narratives from across the nation and time have done similar things. As shown below, such discourses have transcended their capitalist beginnings and borders and seeped into economies that, while might rely on the market, are not necessarily so. Gurdial Singh's Punjabi short story (translated here as) 'The Mute Fury' is a case in point. The story, set in a village in Punjab, is about the deaf and dumb Bhoonda, who, after coming to know about Jallo's molestation at the hands of the local goon, decides to step in and seek justice. The goon has had the entire village running scared of him and retaliates swiftly if someone wishes to stand up to him. So, no one dares to, except Bhoonda. By the end of the narrative, the mute, with his near-superhuman strength, breaks his farming tool into two and stabs the goon dead with it. The last line of the story tells how the villagers, as Bhoonda is being taken away by the police, praise him for ridding the village of evil. That it is the disabled Bhoonda who ultimately takes action while the rest of the abled world sits silently and endures the goon's shenanigans, becomes the perfect example of the supercrip. In fact, at multiple points, the story shows how, though mute, Bhoonda is inhumanly strong and can achieve feats that no others can. It is of little wonder then that, in the end, the abled world venerates him. Truth be told, his muteness is completely incidental to the story. Had he not been disabled but had done the same thing he anyway does, he would have had received the same kind of praise. But, in making him disabled, the author ensures the creation of the supercrip. Singh shows how the disabled body has the potential to rise above, as it were, their disability and do deeds that even the abled world is unable to do. It is only after achieving such feats that the disabled subjects can be known because, till then, they are confined to the shadows of the margins. The problem, in a sense then, is centrally a discursive one where the idea of the productive, irrespective of the mode of economic production, ends up defining the super-productive as well; simply because not a lot was expected out of the disabled body anyway. Their endeavour to go over and beyond, thus, sets them apart as the uniquely super.

The most apparent effect of such constructions is, as Smith and Sparkes write, the fostering of 'unrealistic expectations about what disabled people can achieve, or what they should achieve, if only they tried hard enough' (2012). This, in turn, suggests that those who cannot achieve or meet this expectation, for whichever reason, are expectedly and justifiably lower than everyone is. Thus, these discourses 'perpetuate heroic and hegemonic notions of masculinity and "reinforce social systems of domination, equating individuals' self-worth with coming out on top in the competitive struggle for achievement"' (ibid.).

Works Cited

Mitchell, David and Sharon Snyder. 2012. 'Minority Model: From Liberal to Neo Liberal Futures of Disability'. In *Routledge Handbook of Disability Studies*, edited by Nick Watson, Alan Roulstone and Carol Thomas, 42–51. London and New York: Routledge.

Smith, Brett and Andrew C. Sparkes. 2012. 'Disability, Sport, and Physical Activity: A Critical Review'. In *Routledge Handbook of Disability Studies*, edited by Nick Watson, Alan Roulstone and Carol Thomas, 336–348. London and New York: Routledge.

The Mute Fury[1]

Translated from Punjabi by Jasdeep Singh

On this round as well, Bhoonda the Mute could not stop himself from pulling the lever of the cultivator near the pathway, and the bulls stopped. Squinting his eyes, he took a sweeping look at the long pathway. He saw a woman carrying lunch on her head just at the turn of the path. He watched more carefully, it was Jallo, Naamha the Mazhabi's daughter.

'Ooo- hoo- hoo- hoo,' the Mute laughed and stood laughing like this for a while, squinting and widening his eyes time and again.

Jallo was at an acre's distance. The Mute shrieked at the bulls, signalling them to stay where they were; and started walking towards the pathway. Cleaning the dirt-ridden cotton head-cloth with the strokes of both hands, he took long strides and came to stand in the middle of the pathway. With hands placed on his haunches, legs stretched and a stiff neck, he seemed like a bull waiting to charge at Jallo. Jallo had seen him too; intimidated by him, she started walking by the side of the pathway. But her slow gait did not show any signs of fear.

When she was 10 steps away, the Mute uttered 'Ooo-baa' in a shriek, and his eyes seemed to swell with surprise. Jallo was drying her teary eyes with her chunni as she came. The Mute ran towards her, held her arm without any inhibition, and saying 'Ooo-baa, Ooo-baa,' pointing towards the vann tree in his farm field, started pulling her towards that side. Jallo stuck her feet initially, but then started walking behind him uninhibitedly. Her demeanor was still not affected in any way.

Under the vann tree, the Mute took the lunch packed in a cloth and the pitcher of buttermilk from her head, placed these on the ground and pulled her arm to make her sit. But Jallo looked first towards the pathway and then all around the fields in fear, with her red moist eyes. The Mute recognised her fear. He looked all around and brought his mouth close to her, swinging his hands like a tabor, to say 'Ooo-baa, Ooo-baa' in a low voice to explain to her that nobody was around.

The Mute held Jallo's gentle arm gripped in his sturdy hand. When he jerked her arm again to make her sit, the welled-up tears in Jallo's eyes shook and fell over his hairy hand. Jallo sat half-heartedly, and, cleaning her eyes with the side of her chunni, covered her whole face.

---

1 Translated with permission.

'Ooo-baa-aaa!' The Mute raised his hands in front of Jallo's face, and made the gesture as if asking, 'What happened, Jallo, why are you spoiling such beautiful eyes with this salty water?'

But Jallo started to cry more loudly. Her petite body was shaking with her wails. The Mute's grip on Jallo's arm loosened and, at last, he let it free. His strong fingers, which were like the claws of a pincer, became softer than cotton wool. Jallo's wails were sucking all the living force from his giant body. For a moment, he looked at Jallo from head to toe and then, saying 'Ooo-baa-baa-aaa' with a broken voice, pulled her chunni a little and joined his hands together. In his expressionless eyes was an unbearable plea that could melt even the coldest heart. Such expressions arose on his harsh plain face that his big face seemed like a beehive from which honey was dripping.

Jallo had not moved the chunni away from her eyes but she could feel all the expressions that were on his face, in his voice. Whenever he uttered 'Ooo-baa-aaa' in a prolonged and uneven tone, softly touching her arm, knee or forehead, Jallo could feel his mute heart's plea stirring her body. This pleading seemed to overcome the experience of the incident that happened near the harvesting pit, and she felt as if her unsettled self was regaining balance. And when Jallo dried her teary eyes and looked towards the Mute, she saw such softness on his tough and harsh features that she was not able to recognise if it was his face or someone else's.

'Ooo-baa-aaa-aaa,' stretching his voice, he joined his hands together and, bowing down to Jallo, he seemed to say, 'Would you please tell me now, what is the matter?'

And when the Mute lifted his head again to look straight into Jallo's eyes, she could not bear his gaze. (One wonders if Majnu ever looked towards his Laila, Ranjha looked towards his Heer, or Mirza looked towards his Sahiban like this ... whether their tongues could utter such enigmatic words or not, that the bereft eyes of the Mute were saying today). Jallo could feel a peculiar sensation in her body but still, she was unable to break away her moist eyes locked into his, and, when she did, it was as if she was gauging her eyes out. She felt an unfathomable pain in her eyes as she looked away, and the eyes became moist again.

'*Hoon-oon-oon-aan*,' the Mute said this softly and lowered his eyes. A reddish glow came over his face—the glow of a mute shyness.

But when he looked up again, his face looked as tough and harsh as before. He grabbed Jallo's arm in his strong fingers again, and started shaking her, uttering, '*Ooo-baa, ooo-baa*.' He was asking her sternly, 'Tell me quickly, what has happened?'

Jallo pointed hesitatingly towards the harvesting pits and, gesturing to her arm held in his hand, explained to him that somebody grabbed her arm like that near the harvesting pit.

Saying '*Ooo-baa-baa-ooo*', the Mute opened his eyes with such strength as if he wanted to gobble the man with them who had dared to hold her arm.

Bhoonda kept asking Jallo about that man, swiftly shaking her arm but Jallo had lowered her gaze. Her eyes welled up. For a moment, he sat quietly thinking about something, and then he touched Jallo's chin lightly to make her look towards him, and then murmuring '*Ooo-ooo*', he started making faces to her. He puffed his cheeks, swirled his moustaches and enlarged his eyes as if asking, 'Was it the same person who keeps twirling his moustaches all day long, who has puffy eyes and swollen cheeks?' When Jallo nodded her head in a 'yes' with her tearful eyes, he got up to clear any further confusion. He stood exactly the way Kaaka of the zaildaars stands folding his chadra in front of the porch of his baithak. And he swirled his moustaches again, and, looking around, tried to bring the same expressions in his eyes as Kaaka's inebriated eyes did while looking at the women in the street. After this, he quickly sat down again in front of Jallo and shaking his head in 'Ooo-baa-aaa' asked, 'Was it him, Kaaka of the zaildaars, who held your arm?'

Jallo was convinced that the Mute understood everything. But when she nodded her head to say 'yes', she again felt Kaaka's inebriated eyes and the defiant grip on her arm. When she had leapt to rescue her arm from his grasp, she heard his harsh words in her ears again, 'Such tantrums! If I had to, I can grab you any evening. Beware! Don't play with the wolves.' For a moment, Jallo's eyes expressed blood-red anger. But when she realised the next words uttered by Kaaka, 'Okay then, let's show it to you this evening only!' her entire body shivered with fear and her eyes welled up again.

'*Ooo-ooo-eee*!' the Mute let a horrific shriek out and got up abruptly.

Jallo was startled with fear. Drying her eyes, when she looked towards the Mute, her heart started pounding with anxiety. She had not seen such a terrifying face even in her imagination. The features of the Mute which dripped honey a moment ago appeared to be made of stone now. His eyeballs swelled out as if they had been gouged out. He was standing as still as the banyan tree by the pond and was looking at the village as if he wanted to set fire to all its brick and clay houses.

Jallo could not look at him anymore. She hastily took the pitcher of buttermilk and the lunch case with her shivering hands, placed them on her head and got up. Before leaving, she brought her hand close to the Mute's face, and, gesturing with the finger, she said in a shaken voice,

'Don't get into any trouble for me. If I had better luck, God would have given me a brother who would have saved me from such goons.'

And without realising that the Mute could neither hear her words nor pay attention to her gesture, Jallo walked away drying her teary eyes. The Mute, swirling the thick hair of his moustache, stood there like a pillar stiffening his neck like a bull, and kept staring towards the village. (Now he could see nothing else than the glittering paint on the mansion of the zaildaars, among the small mud houses of the village).

'*Ooo-baa-aaa-aaa*!' The Mute yelled another shriek and bit the palm of his left hand so vehemently that deep marks of his teeth appeared there.

Crossing over the pathway to the trail, Jallo heard the shriek of the Mute, and her already racing heart started beating faster out of fear. For a moment, she turned to look back and started walking anxiously again.

The Mute was still standing there like a log of hardwood under the vann tree. The image of the Kaaka of zaildaars kept appearing and disappearing in front of his eyes. The Mute knew about all his misdeeds and, even in the past, he had felt a rage against him (but never like today!). In an instant, the Mute recalled many of his misdeeds.

For the last two years, this elder son of the zaildaar (though he was 30 years old, everyone still called him 'Kaaka', a child) had been a nuisance in the village. All day long, drunk with booze, he kept playing cards with his gang of goons, bawling '*ha-ha-hee-hee*' in his baithak. Whenever he felt like it, he would go stand on the platform outside and leer at the women of the village passing by in the street. If he was too drunk, he would utter nonsense as well. (Afraid of his powerful status, nobody meddled with him. The year before, two other rowdies of the village had tried to confront him but he showed them their place. He got illegal arms planted in their houses and got them arrested. They were still in jail. Another reason for his arrogance was the fact that the politician he had helped in the last elections was holding a high position in the government. Kaaka was on his high horse because of that politician. (All the lower or middle-ranking officials of the region knew this and feared him.)

He had been after Jallo since the year before. Wherever he found her, he would stand in her way. Jallo, dreadful of facing him, would pass by ignoring him or would just turn back. He would loudly laugh at this as a hunter laughs at the bird trying to free itself from the net (whose neck he can break whenever he wants). He would go to Jallo's house as well, at odd moments. Swirling his moustaches, he would call from outside addressing her father, 'Are you inside, Sardar Bahadur'? and then he would just go away with a sly smile. At such moments, hidden inside the house in fear, Jallo's anger would leap out of bounds: the snide tone in which he uttered 'Sardar Bahadur' was intolerable. She wanted to take the cleaver and hack his neck with it. But when she thought of his 'status', she would console her heart crying bitterly.

A year ago, when Jallo's father was employed with the family of the Mute, she wanted to tell all about this to the Mute. But then she would think, 'Who is the Mute to me?'; she was still unclear about who the Mute was to her.

During employment with the Mute's family, she would go to their home as help for their chores or to bring fodder from their fields for the cattle. The Mute would look at her and smile. In the beginning, she felt fear on seeing the Mute smiling like this. But when he met her alone several times, he did not say anything to her other than laughing heartily, and so her fear vanished. And when many times the Mute helped her with throwing cattle-dung to the heap, fodder cutting, helped her carry it on her head, and took the food to the fields instead of her, Jallo started liking him. At times, he would look directly into Jallo's eyes, and she would lower her gaze. The Mute would laugh, hold her arm and then leave it in a blink and go away. His expressionless eyes were unable to look at Jallo for many days afterwards, and Jallo could see the red shade of shyness on his tough features. At such moments, Jallo felt like holding his hairy arm and turning him towards her ... but she could not do it.

Slowly, the Mute became Jallo's ally. The young daughter of a blind mother and a humble father, she started to feel secure in the presence of the Mute. (Once, she confronted some well-known rowdies, and seeing her mysterious courage, they left. But she was helpless in front of Kaaka. Neither could she speak up to him nor could she tell the Mute about it. She was unaware that the Mute had seen Kaaka trying to harass Jallo a few times.)

Jallo looked back once again; the Mute was still standing there. Then she lowered her eyes and with sad eyes, kept on walking, gazing at the dust of the trail. She could not see that at that very moment, the Mute yelled, bit his hand again and ran back towards the plough.

Seeing the Mute running like this, the bullocks were startled but in just two strides, he held them from the horns and in a blink, he removed the harrow from their necks. Then he slapped their backs and made them run towards the vann tree. After this, he put his foot on the beam of the plough lying there and pushed its ploughshare with a jerk; the beam split like a muskmelon. He placed the ploughshare on his shoulder and stood with his legs stretched as he did under the vann tree before.

He squinted his eyes and looked towards the mansion of the zaildaars, his eyes swelled up like burning embers.

'Ooo-baa-baa-aaa-aaa...!' He bit his palm once again and planted his right foot forward with such strength that a big mud chunk flattened under his heel.

And then he ran headlong towards the village. His zealous eyes seemed as if wanting to burn the earth...? He ran like that up to the harvest pits but stopped as he reached there. '*Khoonh*!' he stood and snorted, and shrieked such a loud 'Ooo-baa-aaa' that his body started shaking.

Then stretching his legs, swelling his broad chest and with a stiff neck, he slowly walked forward as if a wrestler was walking to the wrestling pit. And he went on up to the village with the same proud gait. (His gaze was still fixed on the mansion of the zaildaars.) As he reached the outer street, he looked straight ahead and stood in the middle of the street again.

Kaaka was standing on the platform outside his baithak wearing his tilla-embroidered jutti. He was wearing a long linen shirt and a chaadra. His right hand was on his hip, and with the left, he was twirling his moustache. Four or five of his goons were playing cards inside and making quite a noise.

'*Ooo-baa-baa-baa-eee-ooo*,' upon seeing the edge of Kaaka's shirt, the Mute yelled again and grabbed the left part of his moustache and jerked it so hard that many of its hair got plucked.

And from there, he ran frantically towards Kaaka. Seeing him running like this, the children playing in the street moved to the sides of the walls. But Kaaka laughed animatedly and turned back to call the goons playing inside—'Come outside; let me show you an amusing scene….'

However, by the time he turned his head to see the Mute again; the Mute was already over him….

'*Ooo-baa…eee..*!' Another shriek and the ploughshare dug deep inside the left side of befuddled Kaaka. His heavy body fell on the platform and then on the ground like rolled bedding.

'Ooo-baa..!' the Mute shrieked angrily and thumped his chest and swelled it as if he was challenging. 'Is there anyone else who wants to fight me? Come forward!'

But who would have dared come forward, all around, there was silence like a graveyard.

'*Ooo-baa-thooh*,' the Mute spat on Kaaka lying upside down in a pool of blood, and like a raging bull, looking all around, started twirling his moustache.

In the evening, when the police were taking the Mute to the police station in the motor vehicle, the people, gathered outside the village, heard a grey-bearded, feeble-looking man saying encouragingly—'Bravo, lionheart! You have earned glory by taking this porcupine's spike out of the village's flesh.'

SHWAAS

(Breath)

By Madhavi Gharpure

Introduction

By Editors

Written from the perspective of an oncologist whose 'feet are still firmly on the ground' despite his self-declared quasi-god-like stature, Madhavi Gharpure's short story 'Shwaas' (translated here as 'Breath') is about a child's 'brave' acceptance of his blindness. Given somewhat of Sophie's choice between dying and losing his eyesight, the 10-year-old Vidyadhar is forced to come face to face with the facticity of the temporariness of the human sense. Though sad at first, the young boy comes to uneasy terms with this knowledge; especially in the way it affects him. Taking some inspiration from Hellen Keller's life, Vidyadhar realises that he can still become someone if he joins special schools for blind children and work hard. His grandfather, however, has a completely different reaction. The narrator's diagnosis of Vidyadhar's adventitious blindness as a cancer of the eye breaks the old man down. In the narrator's words, Ajoba (the grandfather) ages almost 20 years in the 20 seconds that the news of his grandson's (impending) blindness takes to set in. His first and immediate reaction is a rejection of the inevitability of his grandson's blindness and perhaps, though unsaid, a consideration of the economy of life against this 'perpetual darkness'. After all, as he says towards the end of the narrative, '[this] darkness too is like death'.

The adult and experienced Ajoba's disdain against blindness in such a way is not surprising at all. In having seen the world, both literally and metaphorically, Ajoba has naturalised the primacy of the visual. For him, sight is the yardstick by which existence is both experienced and judged. Compared to it, other modes of sensing are always somewhat incomplete. That his son's loss of a hand in an accident does not perturb him as much as his grandson's blindness stands testimony to Ajoba's ascription of sight's primacy. He is not the only one. He is simply an archetype of a society that, historically, has always seen the world. The narrator too, despite being a doctor, acknowledges the immense gravity of the loss of the young boy's sight. Both of them, standing in for the world, claim that Vidya is, after all, just a kid and the world has so many things that necessarily need to be seen to be experienced and appreciated. Blindness, on the other hand, will either lead to pity or need charity. So, getting, rather miraculously, an extra day before Vidyadhar's operation, Ajoba sneaks him out to see the sights of the world for one last time. It is like fulfilling the last wish of a prisoner on death row: feeding the mind as much as possible before eternal darkness takes over. In

Ajoba, one can find an exemplification of what Rosemarie Garland-Thomson calls the normate: a 'constructed identity … [that] … by way of the bodily configurations and cultural capital … assume … a position of authority and wield the power it grants them' (1997). This sociocultural power allows Ajoba to stigmatise his grandson's impending blindness as something ontologically bad, thus, enforcing its negation by making Vidyadhar see as much of the world as possible before his operation. Interestingly, this position of power that Ajoba occupies comes out of a 'cognitive dissonance' (Bolt 2012) that disallows Ajoba to comprehend the state of his grandson's blindness. The only reaction he can thus have is to reinforce the primacy of the visual because, being the normate, he cannot think of any other state of being. Vidyadhar's darkness, in that sense, is comprehended in terms of death because that is the only way Ajoba understands disability. Society, by extension, becomes rift with similar normate beings itching to pigeonhole the 'deviant' disabled in accordance to their incomplete (imaginative and empathetic) conceptions.

Ajoba and the narrator's situation of blindness as something akin to death is the first pitfall that 'Shwaas' stumbles over. After all, it blatantly disregards even the possibility of a decent life after blindness. The only two people who seemingly accept the loss of sight as simply a different mode of life are children who, unlike the adults, have not 'seen' the world enough and, therefore, don't know what they are missing out on. The need for Vidyadhar to see is urgent enough to warrant Ajoba's sacrifice of his sight. This martyrdom, for the narrator, exemplifies selfless love. For why would it not? The elder man, at almost the end of his life, realising the necessity of sight, is ready to gift it to the younger generation. Vidyadhar's need is, in that respect, greater than his. After all, within Ajoba's worldview, disability necessarily needs correction. He follows a fundamentally medical understanding of disability in which, as Talcon Parsons notes, health is normal and disability physically and socially deviant. As a result, the latter essentially requires medical intervention for regulation, control and correction (Barnes 2012). Added to this necessity, Vidyadhar's age makes corrective intercessions all the more important. In all these interactions, the story, quite unwittingly, shows what is wrong in the way the world treats blindness. It reflects the automatic requirement of normally undesired pity and charity that the disabled develop. In doing so, the story becomes a party to the societal marginalisation that creates the disabled. But, as said above, this is just the first stumble that the story takes. The second one is far more profound and telling.

In trying to tell the story of a child about to lose his eyes, 'Shwaas' forces an emotional response from its readers often at the cost of its narrative integrity. On a formal level, the story is rift with unnatural coincidences—a child happens to undergo a similar problem as the protagonist of the story; Vidyadhar and his grandfather suddenly get an unplanned extra day before the surgery to do the things they were thinking of doing if they got an extra day; the two of them happen to come across the very schools Vidyadhar would later need to survive; and, finally, the story of Helen Keller's life, being played out in theatres, seemingly allows the young boy to accept his blindness. The story's insistence on concerning itself with eliciting an emotional response from its readers rather than tying up its formal inconsistencies reveals the author's comprehension of a child's blindness as nothing but emotional. It's as if Gharpure is saying that disability can never lead to anything but sadness. This misery, further, is not only a part of the life of the afflicted but also those who come into contact with the disabled. So, it is always better to find ways back into the land of the abled; even if it, perhaps, means death. That the story makes the two blind children—Vidyadhar and the unnamed boy who loses his sight in an accident—superheroes furthers this mission of emotion. The story points out two children, not having the wisdom or the intellect of adults, accepting a fate that the grown-ups shudder and bawl at. The narrator's description of the way Vidyadhar takes the news of his blindness is nothing short of reverential. The story does not even fail to ascribe a sage-like calmness to Vidyadhar that allows him to be more than human. This is where 'Shwaas' fails to stand either on its own or as a narrative that does not think of the disabled existence as a curse. For Gharpure, the disabled are either sub-human or supra-human, provoking nothing but pathos. This, in turn, augments a strange form of admiration that arises from a disabled person acting the way 'normal' humans do. Never, the story says, can the disabled be a human. They will always be deviant.

Works Cited

Barnes, Colin. 2012. 'Understanding the Social Model of Disability: Past, Present and Future'. In *Routledge Handbook of Disability Studies*, edited by Nick Watson, Alan Roulstone and Carol Thomas, 12–29. London and New York: Routledge.

Bolt, David. 2012. 'Social Encounters, Cultural Representation and Critical Avoidance'. In *Routledge Handbook of Disability Studies*, edited by Nick

Watson, Alan Roulstone and Carol Thomas, 287–297. London and New York: Routledge

Garland-Thomson, Rosmarie. 1997. *Extraordinary Bodies: Figuring Physical Disability in American Culture and Literature*. New York: Columbia University Press.

Breath[1]

Translated from Marathi by Rohini Mukashi Punekar

I am defeated at this moment. Comprehensively defeated. I, a surgeon, who has beaten many diseases into submission. But this common simple person has silenced me. I stand in the general ward beside bed number 8 on the ground floor. I stand, feet planted firmly on the ground. I am struck dumb with astonishment. Confounded; by the question put to me.

I am a well-known cancer specialist. Anyone would be proud of the way my name has spread far and wide. Some of my theories have gained acceptance in seminars organised by international forums. I hold a magic wand in my hand. Patients fondly (though perhaps wrongly) believe that the minute I touch an illness, it vanishes. Some think I am not a believer. That is not completely misplaced. I am never present at any prayer, or puja or ritual. My patients are my god. I serve them with the utmost sincerity. My real worship consists in smoothing the lines of worry from the faces of patients and their relatives. Therefore, I have many relations. I am someone's son, somebody else's brother; an uncle to yet someone else and a friend to another. I am surrounded by closely knit, loving ties of kith and kin. I am comforted, gladdened. In all this, the most important thing is my feet are still firmly on the ground; I have not been carried away by the feeling that I am someone of great significance, since this feeling has never taken hold in my mind. I relate to my patients like an ordinary person. As a result, they share all their joys and sorrows most naturally with me.

In one such similar incident, Vidyadhar's grandfather unwound a silken thread of emotion which threw me off guard and shook me.

I remember that evening in my clinic, some three or four months ago, when I first met Vidyadhar and his grandfather. Not having given too many appointments, I thought I'd go home early.

I had come straight to Pune after returning from England that morning. I was very tired. And, of course, there was jetlag. But appointments taken a month ago waited. It was not possible to disappoint people.

I examined the last patient and said to my assistant, Dr Shirish, 'That's all for today. Come on now. Let's have some coffee.'

---

1 Translated with permission.

The receptionist poured the coffee. Hardly had we taken a couple of sips when conversation taking place with the receptionist just outside my chamber fell on our ears.

'The doctor is still there, isn't he?'

'Yes, he is.'

'Come, Vidya, let's go. Thank God he is in.'

'Where are you going, Ajoba? Time is up.'

'We've come from a great distance you know. We haven't taken an appointment, but please don't say no. We would have come in time, but a goods train derailed on the way, and our train got late. Otherwise, we were on time.'

'Sorry. You can come tomorrow. Doctor is very tired. He returned from England and came to the clinic straight from Mumbai Airport.'

'Baap re! Where will we spend the night? We have no one here. Once we meet the Doctor, there is a train that will take us back. We will be greatly obliged if the Doctor can see us!' The old man was beseeching. One could sense the helplessness in his voice. I was listening to the entire conversation from inside. I said to Dr Shirish,'Bring that patient inside, will you!'

'Sir, you are always doing this!' saying this, Shirish brought the patient in. There were two of them. One a grandfather of around 70 years of age and, with him, there was a boy of about 9 to 10 years. Must be his grandson.

They felt the cold of the AC as soon as they stepped in. But more than that, the relief that the Doctor had called them in to examine the patient was paramount.

'Please sit,' I said.

Shyly, they sat down in the chairs in front of me, trying to compress themselves into as little space as possible. Chairs with seats of double foam. As they sat down, they seemed to lose their composure but soon collected themselves. The well-appointed interiors of my clinic, the clean glass on the table in front that showed reflections as clear as a mirror, the faint lingering perfume wafted in by the cooled air and the muted sound of Ghulam Ali's music falling on the ears. One could see they felt the difference in the ambience of this space keenly.

It was apparent from their expression and movements that they were not acquainted with many of the things here.

'So, please tell, for whom have you come in this hurry?' I asked.

'For my grandson. This boy, Vidyadhar. We have come from a village near Nagpur especially to meet you.'

'What is the complaint'?

'Vidya is not able to see clearly.'

'He must have been examined before, na?'

'I showed him to many people in Nagpur.'

'Well, then?'

'In the end, Dr Sharan gave a referral letter addressed to you, and said, "You go to this doctor and he will completely cure Vidyadhar".'

Sharan, my favourite student. He had been an assistant with me for five years. I have never had any need to change his diagnosis earlier. It is a matter of great pride and challenge to have gained a student such as Sharan.

'Let me see what Dr Sharan has to say.' I opened the letter while saying this and read it. The last two words shook me—'Suspected cancer'. I looked at Vidyadhar. The grandfather was looking at me. But doctors are always anchored by two stones under their feet. The first is equanimity and the second, an indomitable hope.

I said, 'Come Vidyadhar. Sit here.'

He sat down. 'Now tell me what exactly is the problem please.'

'Doctor kaka, two months back I could not see what Sir was writing on the blackboard. I could only see a blur. Then the eye specialist gave me glasses. I could see well then; but after 15–20 days again, it was like before!'

'What did you do then?'

The grandfather recounted what took place afterwards, 'We changed the doctor. One more pair of spectacles, some more medicines, more examinations. It's been the same thing for the past six months. Now his eyes constantly water.'

'Doctor kaka, I have missed many days of school,'

'Chhod do yaar! Your name is Vidyadhar. Don't worry. You can make it up easily.'

'I will be able to see clearly, won't I? Since my eyes have started watering, I am seeing everything in double. I cannot see even the big figures on the calendar clearly.'

'Vidya, you didn't tell me this?' This had given the grandfather another shock.

Vidyadhar turned to see his grandfather and rubbed his eyes with his closed fist. Which was the water from the affliction? Which the water from sorrow? There was no way to find the difference.

There was silence for a minute. I said to him, 'Don't cry, Vidyadhar. Your grandfather has brought you here so that you can get well. We will get all tests done. There is a remedy for everything.' My two sentences seemed to comfort him. Hope sprang a tender shoot.

I made Vidyadhar sit in front of me. Even before I could examine his eyes, I realised that his eyelids looked larger. Even his eyes seemed to bulge out a little. Fundoscopy had been done. Sharan's conjecture seemed correct. Now only an X-ray orbit had to be taken and sent for B scanning. I asked them to visit me in K.E.M. Hospital in Raasta Peth for the scanning.

The grandfather appeared to fall into confusion.

'Is there any problem?' I asked.

'Nothing special, but there is a problem. We haven't brought any clothes. We also don't have money and where will we make arrangements for our stay? We said we'd be back by the night train. My son and daughter-in-law will be worried.'

'Ajoba, you travelled this long distance at your age to bring Vidya here?'

The old man only glanced at Vidya; the boy immediately got up from his chair.

'Ajoba, I'll look at the pictures outside. I'll see if I can manage to read something.' Vidya went out.

Ajoba started speaking, 'When misfortune starts to follow you, it keeps to your heels constantly, never letting you go. My son Vasant worked in a factory.'

'"Worked", what do you mean by that?'

'My son lives, but two years ago his right hand was trapped in a machine and was severed at the wrist. The company gave him a little compensation and took him off his job. For a skilled worker, can money ever compensate the loss of a hand?'

'Since then, Vasant stays at home. We don't have any education. I used to work as an overseer on construction sites.'

'What does Vasant Rao do at present?'

'We have taken up the work of making cardboard boxes at home, which are used by sweet shops to pack their mithai. My daughter-in-law helps a great deal. Vasant goes out and gets orders, and delivers them.'

'Now, to add to our problems, this boy's ailment has started. Where do I get so much money from? I have very little of the strength or confidence that I used to have before. We have to set limits on what we can do for the boy. We had to come without reservation; I had to get the boy here because this city is new.'

I felt the sting of countless scorpions. It came over me suddenly that no one understands the twists and turns of destiny. What is man? Here today, gone tomorrow. He is caught up in the time between being and nothingness.

'Ajoba, what you are saying is right. You can do it this way. You return with Vidya today. Try to make arrangements for some money in about four days. You will have to stay here, please keep this in mind. It may also be necessary to have an operation, this is a possibility that cannot be put away.'

'Doctor...'

'Ajoba, don't be afraid. I only told you about a possibility. Rest assured about your stay here. A few rooms in my outhouse are vacant. My bungalow is quite close to K.E.M. Hospital. Even if some need for more money crops up, please don't worry.'

Ajoba held my feet. I raised him. It was the truth that unknown to myself, I was tied to these two human beings.

*

In four days, Ajoba came back with Vidya. I made arrangements for them in the outhouse. All tests were completed in two days. Signed and stamped pathology reports confirmed the root of the cause. Retinoblastoma—in short, cancer of the eyes.

In the afternoon, when Vidyadhar was sleeping, I asked Ajoba to come over to my house. He stood before me very frightened.

'Ajoba...'

'Speak, Doctor, speak.'

'It's a difficult situation.'

'Tell me anything, spell it out clearly. Even if this tree is wasted, it is still a banyan tree. It still can absorb anything. I can hold fate by its throat. I will not allow the untoward to happen.'

'Ajoba, please steel yourself. Vidyadhar has cancer of the eyes. Why did it happen? How did it happen? Please don't ask. There is no answer. Now, for this, there is only one remedy. Both his eyes have to be removed. His life can be prolonged only by this; otherwise nothing.' I told this in one breath. How many patients, how many decisions have I explained with poise, equanimity as a professional; but, in this case, I was myself entangled.

'Doctorrrr...,' he tried to say and a lowing wail broke out from him.

He held my wrists tightly with his trembling hands. The strength seemed to have gone from his legs. It seemed wiser not to stem the force of his sorrow; it had to find a flow outward. In about five minutes, the intensity subsided a little. His grip loosened. But the marks on my wrists were testimony to the depth of his desolation.

Hope whispered in his heart. 'Would it be possible to transplant another pair of eyes, Doctor? Even if one eye could be fixed it would still be all right. I can give one of my eyes. There would be no need to buy it from someone else. Even the colour of our eyes is the same.'

What is selfless love? What do they call a mother's love? Vidya's grandfather standing before me was a living embodiment of it.

Not wanting to keep him in the dark, I told him frankly. 'In this case, nothing can be done. It is impossible. On the contrary, this operation has to be performed at the earliest. Or else, the cancer will spread quickly throughout his body. Then we will not be able to save him.'

'I said I would hold destiny by its throat! That I would conquer fate. How can I?' Saying something like this, Ajoba tried to stand up, holding on to the teapot for support. His eyes dripping grief, quivering lips, powerless legs and helpless hands, 70-year-old Ajoba seemed to have suddenly become 90 years of age.

*

Ajoba had to compose himself. After he had somewhat collected himself, he said, 'Till my son lost his hand, I always tried to deal with many different events with a smile. Tried to find happiness in what was there. Wasn't it better to have my son alive, even with the loss of a hand? At least he has a second, I kept consoling myself. I didn't give grief too much due, told myself that there was never a lack of joy; but today I am defeated.'

Ajoba climbed down the steps. How would a lifeless puppet walk? He seemed like one!

Two days passed. On the third day, I sent for ice cream and called Vidya over to have some. After these days of cohabitation, he had opened up and had become very free and forthcoming with me. When he was busy with his ice cream, I asked him casually, 'Vidyadhar, tell me what is your hobby?'

'Playing cricket,' was the eager reply. 'So who do you want to be? Sunil or Sachin?'

'I want to be only Vidyadhar.'

His reply struck me. I had not expected this or this kind of an answer.

'Doctor kaka, can I tell you the absolute truth?'

'What son? Tell, na.'

'I want to be a doctor.'

His answer stumped me. Vidya spoke as I sat dumb, 'Doctor kaka, why are you so quiet? You will make my eyes all right again, na? Then what's so difficult?'

'Vidya, why do you want to be a doctor?'

'Kaka, firstly, I love science, and, on top of it, our teacher always tells me, Vidyadhar you are clever. You have won a scholarship. The children from our village who became doctors have all gone to Nagpur and become a part of the crowd there. Not one lives here. What is the point of digging a well where there is already enough water? Where there is no water, and people are thirsty, there a well should be dug. So you become a doctor and live here. But Doctor kaka, I haven't understood all his talk about wells.'

I couldn't think of a reply, but Vidya had narrated to me his science teacher's words just as they had been spoken, full of ardour and passion. I was struck by them. Every word had been weighed and measured, and it was uttered with clarity and confidence. But how would he know what was hidden in the folds of time? Time and tide have little respect for anybody or thing as they say! My wordless conversation was going on in my mind when Vidyadhar continued with the greatest enthusiasm,

'Doctor kaka, you won't laugh, will you? Now, after seeing you, I am very certain about becoming a doctor. When you do the rounds of the wards to check the patients in the morning and the evening, there are so many nurses and doctors running behind you saying, "Sir, Sir!", I love watching that. When I grow up and become a doctor, there will be so many people trailing me saying "Sir, Sir!", na? Like a retinue trailing the king. Tell me na, Doctor kaka.'

'What can I tell you, Vidyadhar?'

'What can you tell? Then tell me some stories of your clinic, the hospital! There must be new patients every day, na? Doctor kaka, are there any patients as old as me?'

It was Vidyadhar who helped me edge close to the crucial point. I said, 'Arrey, Vidyadhar, yesterday there were some patients involved in an accident. It was a crash between a car and a truck. There was no loss of life, but there is a boy as old as you, his eyes are badly injured. Perhaps it may be possible that he'll lose his vision. Vidyadhar, I was very proud of that boy. Of course, he was very upset when he was told. But do you know what he said?'

'What did he say?'

'He said, "My sight may go, but my arms and legs are still intact. Blind people can do so much today."' I was telling an untruth.

'Doctor kaka, can I ask you something?'

'Sure, ask.'

'Doctor kaka, am I going to lose my sight?'

I started. It was Vidya who spoke on, 'Kaka, why did you jump? I only asked. Shall I tell you, why? There must be so many different incidents that you could have narrated, then why did you tell me about this specific case instead of the others? Ajoba has also become very quiet since yesterday. He just holds me close and weeps; caresses my head, kisses me.'

I got up and went to the balcony. He came behind me and held my hand with both of his. 'Tell me na, Kaka, this is true, na?'

I replied with my back still turned, 'It's true.' I did not have the guts, at least at that moment, to meet Vidyadhar's eyes and look into his face. He was weeping bitterly, hiccoughing between his sobs. I held him close. His shirt was soaked through in perspiration. His sobs lessened after about five minutes. In any case, each moment that passes away blunts the edge of the emotion of the previous moment.

'Kaka, blind persons can continue with their education, na? Aren't they able to perform all their tasks themselves? In our Marathi textbook, we have a lesson on Helen Keller. She was blind, deaf and dumb, but she became highly educated. She also got a very big award. I have read about her.'

'Vidyadhar, you can read, you can write. You can do everything. Helen Keller is a role model. Arrey, there is a play called "The Alchemist" based on her. It is a beautiful play.' I said this but changed the subject. There was little chance that he would see the play now! In all probability, Vidyadhar may not have heard me talk about the play, because he was asking me with the greatest composure! 'Kaka, I will study. You will help me, na? It's only eyes that I will not have. Then what is the need to be scared? Whatever is there to learn, I will enjoy learning it.'

I was overwhelmed by this boy's attitude. The news that the brave and strong may have not been able to digest, this little boy had accepted with composure; was it possible that he may not have comprehended how extremely shocking it was?

The page that I filled in my diary that night was of great import. 'It is no great achievement to do what one likes; it is greater to love what one has to do.' There may be many who hold on to such a philosophy, but what do we call someone like Vidyadhar who does not know what philosophy is, but decides to live it as a praxis?

Imperceptibly, unknown to myself, I was becoming deeply caught up with the case.

*

Vidyadhar was admitted to K.E.M. Hospital for his operation. General ward. Bed number 8. All the smaller tests were done. His general fitness was obtained. The surgery was scheduled for the next morning. Ajoba and his grandson passed the day somehow. The ambience in the hospital could never cheer anyone up. I took their leave at night in the same environment. Vidyadhar was gazing at me unblinkingly as if he wanted to capture in his heart all the seeing and looking of his entire life.

Who was I for him? An angel who would give him life or a monster who was going to snap his sight? I couldn't understand why I was thinking about it so much.

The next day dawned. Vidyadhar woke up early, finished his bath and other things and was set to pass into the world of darkness. Vidyadhar was about to be taken into the operation theatre when suddenly there was an emergency. When that operation was going on, there was an urgent call from Jahangir Nursing Home. That operation too had to be performed immediately. Therefore, Vidyadhar's surgery had to be cancelled. It was decided that it would be done early next morning (7 o'clock) and, after informing Ajoba about the new timing, I took the assistant along with me and turned my car, which was parked on the porch, towards Jahangir.

*

I wound up the surgery and went home at around 3 in the afternoon. I was exhausted. Had no energy to even eat. Because she was waiting, I had a quick wash and joined my wife at the table. It seldom happens that people like us have the comfort of eating a meal together. When it does take place as today, I silently blessed it and began to mix the rice on my plate. Even before I could eat the first mouthful, the mobile rang.

'Sssss r,' a trembling voice.

'Yes. Speaking.'

'Sir, sir please can you come immediately?'

'The operated case done in the morning?'

'No sir. She is all right.'

'What then?'

'Sir, sir your Vidyadhar is not in the ward.'

'Impossible! Where is Ajoba?'

'Both are not here.'

'Since what time?'

'We realised at 11 o'clock, but we were searching till now and waiting for them.'

For a moment, the world turned around me. But I had to collect myself. I put the food back on my plate and, washing my hands, set off immediately to K.E.M. Like the wheels, my thoughts were also turning round and round. So many kinds of possibilities were running helter-skelter, there was no count to them.

I reached the hospital. Everybody was waiting for me. I went straight to his bed. It was empty, but his meagre things were still there, where had the two of them gone? Why had they gone? Why had they left without telling me? The new shoot of love, the feeling of oneness that had taken root in the heart, was it all without substance?

I asked, 'Who has seen them since morning?'

'When I was scrubbing the floor, both of them were right here,' one help said.

'When I was sponging number 9, I saw them here,' the nurse said.

I went out to the waiting room. Enquired at the reception counter. The receptionist's account revealed that Vidyadhar and his grandfather had sat here for about an hour. Vidyadhar seemed sad. In some time, Ajoba had started reading the newspaper. No one knew where they had gone after that.

Where could they have gone? I am certain they would never have taken any decision without telling me. Where could one look for them? If a police complaint were to be filed, it would bring utter disgrace to the hospital. How can a patient run away? My head felt as if a beehive was set alive. A rage was building up. God knows how, but a journalist landed up exactly at the same time. A reporter and a phone are the same: never there when you need them and when you don't, they stand right before you. I told him to sit for 15 minutes. I saw the clock. It was past 7. I thought there might be perhaps a chit, a note below the pillow, I rushed inside. But there was nothing.

It crossed my mind that it was necessary to inform Dr Sharan about this matter. Should the occasion arise, he could go to Vidyadhar's house. His phone number was perhaps listed in the file containing the case paper. I was scanning the papers turning them this way and that to see if his number was there in the little note which he had sent me.

Just then, the nurse came running. 'Sir, sir, Vidyadhar and his grandfather have both come.'

'What?' I started again, but there was a world of difference between the two occasions.

'Yes, sir, they have just got off the rickshaw. Vidyadhar looks very happy. See, they are coming here.'

Vidyadhar looked like he had had a very good time. 'Doctor kaka, Doctor kaka,' he began and was going to tell me something; but gauging the mood, Ajoba stopped him. There was silence all around. A dramatic situation was at its climax. Other patients were standing stock still. Since I had come into this profession, this was the first such incident which they were seeing and handling.

'Where had you gone?' my voice was stern, harsh.

'...'

'Ajoba, I am asking you, where had you gone?'

Ajoba still hung his neck. I continued further, 'Ajoba, this is not an asylum. It is not a hotel where one can go and come at one's will. You, particularly Vidyadhar, are our responsibility since he was admitted. If you start behaving irresponsibly then what can we do?'

As my voice started getting sharper, Vidyadhar held Ajoba's hand with both of his and hid his face behind his grandfather.

Ajoba was mortified and stung to the quick. He kept quiet. So the question of where they had been was still unknown. The nurse said, 'Ajoba, please say something. Why are you so silent now?'

'I have conducted myself in a way I should not have.'

'I must ask for the police to keep guard for tonight. I will make arrangements before I leave.'

'No, Doctor, there is no need now for anything like that.'

'All right, then. But where have you been since morning?'

There was pin-drop silence for a moment. Everyone standing there had their ears pricked to what Ajoba might say. Ajoba started telling his story in a low tone.

'Please believe what I am going to tell you. Doctor, I cannot hide anything from a person such as you; you have been like a god to us. Before you left this morning, you told us that Vidya's operation would not take place today. You would do it in the morning tomorrow.

'That Vidya's sight was going to extend by 24 hours made that moment very joyful; but how to spend the day and those hours? There was a weight on me. And no cure. I sat with Vidya on the bench outside. But can the ambience in a hospital ever be joyful? Someone weeps, someone has had an accident, someone's being given blood transfusion or saline. Just then, Doctor sahib, the little boy you had spoken of who had lost his vision came towards us and Vidya began to cry. I consoled Vidya and took him for a short walk, but everywhere it was the same scene.

'Then I sat reading the papers on the bench for some time. Vidya saw an advertisement and almost jumped. "Ajoba, this is the play! Its name is "The Alchemist". Doctor kaka told me about it. It's a play about Helen Keller, the blind lady. I want to see it."

'I checked and saw that the play was at 11 o'clock in Balgandharv Rangmandir. But how was it possible? I was thinking.

'Vidya said again, "Ajoba please take me to see it. I will never get the chance to see it again. Let's go! I will never throw a tantrum ever again."

'He would never be able to throw tantrums again. The 24 hours we had were a bonus. With the thought that they were meant only for this, I rose. There was a sparkle in Vidya's dull eyes.'

'But how did you manage to get out?'

'I went inside and got some money. The lady in front got up for some work. There was not a single nurse nearby. At that point, I got into a rickshaw that someone had left in the front yard of the hospital first. In half a minute, Vidya got inside. I told the rickshawala, "Leave us at this theatre".'

'We reached there. We were scared in the pit of our stomach, but the play started and we forgot everything else. The kid forgot himself in the play; if I could show him a very important thing it was just because of you.'

'The Alchemist' which I had referred to so casually had wrought this transformation. It was unimaginable. Where could they have gone after the play was over? As I was thinking, Ajoba said, 'Doctor, the play got over. Our hearts were swollen and ennobled. Then I decided to show him only noble things. We came outside, sat in the rickshaw and went to the blind school. I narrated to the manager there the true account of our affairs. He escorted us through the blind school and showed us everything. Vidya saw the many things the blind make which the sighted cannot do. Vidya could see with his vision of 24 hours that there is so much to do in the blind people's world.

'A group of people was conversing animatedly. They were joking and laughing. But a part of the conversation shook me. The person taught me how to be contented. He was saying, "When the feet are bare, there's no point in weeping and crying that the thorns prick, one should be happy with the fact that one has legs to walk".'

'Why, what happened Ajoba?' Unknowingly I asked.

'One person was questioning another in the group, "Tell me, what a mother is like! I was born blind. Not mother, or father or sister, I have seen none," tears flowed from his eyes even as he spoke. The second person wiped the tears from his cheeks and said, "What a silly person you are, asking me what a mother and father are like? Arre, I am also like you, born blind, but man, you are more fortunate than me. You can weep because you have never seen your parents. You are at least able to weep water from your eyes. Run your hands over my face and check a little! Arre I have only two slits in place of eyes, slits that are closed. I can't even weep. Now you must laugh over this."

'And Doctor sahib, he laughed, just like someone with eyes and vision. Vidyadhar saw all this, heard it, he experienced it. We left the place. Vidyadhar said, "Ajoba, it's only six. Shall we see something else?" I fished around in my pocket. There was a little money. I waited a moment: tomorrow it may be required for medicines, but this moment of vision will never return. If there arose some need, the gold ring could be sold off. Of what use was it, safeguarding gold? He should see everything with his precious sight. We went to Shanivarwaada. Saw that. Outside, I showed him the statue of Thorle Bajirao sitting astride his horse. If you want to stand tall in the world, you must become like Bajirao, I told him, and then we went straight to Sarasbaag. It was as if something possessed me.

'It made Vidyadhar ecstatic with happiness to see all those trees, the flowers, the horses that carried children, their galloping and the colourful fountains. He was beside himself trying to see everything and contain the many different sights in his vision.

'You should also have seen his joy. Until today, the village in which we have lived for the past 19–20 years has never left the boy and he has seen little save hard work and difficulties. For a moment, his eyes livened up. He forgot even the reality that he was going to lose his vision tomorrow. Unbeknown, his will to live was strengthened. Doctor, as I live, so too I wanted him to have the strength and courage to live. I am not very educated. What do I know of books and what they say of courage? I tried to give it to him in this way. I think I have had a little success. At the very end, I made him prostrate himself at Ganapati's feet and surrender his future to that Vighneshwar, the one who overcomes obstacles.'

Ajoba stopped for a minute after his long speech and wiped his eyes. I was just going to say something to him, when he stopped me and said, 'You are going to ask me if it was necessary to go today, and without taking permission. I will answer that as well, and you can punish me as you wish.'

'If you had asked me this the day before yesterday, you would have had no answer. It has been immense trouble for all of you. I have done wrong to you. But it was crucial that he had to be shown all this today. You know well the ambience and scenes here. In his sight, the whole long day would be nurses dressed in white, green hospital clothes, the red blood and anxiety-ridden faces. From tomorrow morning, he will be in permanent darkness. I thought that even a man condemned to death is asked for his last wish. This darkness too is like death! Then why should his wish to watch the play not be fulfilled? A poor man may not find much respect, but he has a mind of his own. All that is lovely and beautiful, all things high and noble, all that can find a home in his eyes, all this, I decided, to show him and bring him back at night.

'To tell him stories as he eats. He will sleep. In the morning when he wakes up, there is the surgery; but instead of a melancholic atmosphere before he loses his sight, he must be in an environment that is high-minded, he will always remember Helen Keller, the blind school, Shanivarwada and Sarasbaag. I made the best of the bonus gifted to his sight, without taking your permission. Doctor, did I commit a mistake? Please tell me the truth. Was I wrong?'

*

Ajoba's passion had exhausted itself. The dam had breached. He held my feet tightly, and I? Truth to tell, his question had shifted the ground under my feet. By holding on tightly to them, Ajoba had given strength to my unsteady legs. Now I was neither a specialist nor a doctor; I was just an ordinary human being, defeated.

I held Ajoba's arms and raised him. I said, 'Please rise! Ajoba, stand up. Stand with your head held high. My anger has gone.' Ajoba glanced at me and smiled gently.

In that hour, Ajoba looked sublimely handsome. I had never seen such beauty before. What is beauty in the final analysis? A tall, well-built personality? Large eyes? A straight nose? A fair complexion? Never! Beauty is the capacity to envelop the other in oneself, the ability to understand that life is to be lived well; that is beauty. To live and enable others to live is a cohesive, inseparable act. This act, Ajoba practised without any bookish knowledge, as an innate part of his being. I was lost in thought. Ajoba was saying, 'Doctor, doctor, what are you seeing?'

'I see a grandfather taking the first step to conquer fate itself, Ajoba! I am seeing an alchemist.'

CIKITSA

(The Treatment)

By Raamaa Chandramouli

Introduction

By Editors

Published at the beginning of the millennium, Lynn Manning's *Weights* is an autobiographical play about the onset of his blindness (2000, written and performed by Lynn Manning; Premiere by Theatre of the Blind, 2004). For the most part, the play follows the more or less usual path that such (autobiographical) narratives of adventitious blindness take—a 'normal' life that is lived as commonly as possible till a singular event, in this case a gunshot wound, drastically changes the course of that life and flings it, body and soul, into a different state of being. What is rather peculiar about Manning's story, however, is his preparation for his blindness. Before he turns blind, Manning, believing in Murphy's Law (which states that anything that can go wrong will go wrong), keeps on practising being blind, preparing for such an eventuality, by either blindfolding himself or turning off all the lights around him. This preparation is governed by the received knowledge of the experience of blindness that sighted people like Manning are interpellated in. At one level, the playwright, before his impairment, seems to definitively know that blindness is, fundamentally, a lack; an absence that will not allow him to do the things he hopes to do. Thus, that state of existence requires practice so that he isn't rendered completely useless. At a second level, this act of practising itself reveals Manning's knowledge of the blind's existence. Manning seems to, once again, definitively know that a cold and immediate absence of sight is what blindness is about. However, both these levels of knowledge are undermined when Manning *does* lose his eyesight. In his own words, the onset of blindness brings with it a completely novel way of knowing the world: 'through [his] ears, through [his] nose, through [his] feet, through [his] pores … [and] light and shadow [take] on physical dimensions' (Manning 2000). Blindness, in essence, not only allows him access to a world that he had not, as an abled body, thought possible but also, simultaneously, ousts his erstwhile 'reality' of the blind as fundamentally fabricated.

The fabrication of the reality of blindness that the abled Manning partakes in, however, is not just a lie or a mistake. It has, as a rather powerful one, the force of reality behind it. Thus, as Titchkosky and others note, that reality becomes a simulation: that which is not only feigned but also conjured up as the 'real'. Unlike pretending, believing or faking, the reality of the simulated is never under question; it is, in very absolute terms, true. This simulated, hence, as Jean Baudrillard notes, creates the hyper-real: 'the generation by models of a real without origin or reality' (1995). This hyper-real, in other words, is an existential state of being, conjured up through simulations that do not (and can never) have a referential connection to the objective world and is, yet, unquestionably regarded as real. For the one who simulates, then, this distance from 'reality' is simply non-existent. The simulated *is* the real, no matter the lack of reference. Lynn Manning, thus, as he prepares for blindness by shutting off his visual sense, lives in the hyper-real. Insofar as his abled self is considered, Manning indisputably knows that blindness cannot mean anything else but an absence of eyesight. Later, being blind not only allows him access to the true reality of blindness but also propels him to a rather unique position where he can, now, understand the simulated nature of his earlier knowledge. His actual disability, and the consequent knowledge about blindness, therefore, completely shatters the hyper-real and drives in the simulated nature of the former knowing (that blindness is essentially like darkness).

Quite clearly, there is a political element to this hyper-real as well. Titchkosky and others, revealing this political dimension, write that '[o]ccluded sight [that] animates the simulation [makes] the normal authority of sight prevalent throughout these simulations.... [Thus], occluded vision as the simulation of blindness makes sight the authoritative figure, and blindness simulations teach us that it is bad news to mess with sight' (2019). What is of importance, then, is sight and its retention at whatever cost necessary. So, the abled world often makes itself feel reassured (that they have sight) by participating, rather willingly, in events that simulate blindness through the negation of vision. They put on blindfolds and try to navigate the world; failing to do so, more often than not, and re-establishing the need for vision. There is but a small jump between Manning's preparation for blindness and such 'sensitising' events organised the world over. Both seem to know, once again, in absolute terms, that blindness is nothing but darkness and all the failures that accompany that darkness. Titchkosky and others exemplify this through the #HowEyeSeeIt campaign run by the Foundation Fighting Blindness (FFB) where celebrities are asked to blindfold themselves as they try and be who they are. In their failure to do so lies the salvation of FFB. They can boldly declaim that the loss of sight disables not only physically but also by taking away 'the capacity to *do*' (Titchkosky, Healey and Michalko 2019). Blindness, thus, is the enemy and has to be, as the name of the organisation shamelessly declares, fought. Interestingly, the research that FFB wishes to carry on is 'not oriented to eyes already blind but rather to sighted eyes, since they are the only ones that can go blind' (ibid.). Blindness, in a sense, is not an option and the war against it, as Titchkosky, Healey and Michalko so eloquently put, has to be won. Movements like the #HowEyeSeeIt, in this way, establish the singularity of vision and disallow even the possibility of a knowing that lies outside the able-ist culture where blindness is not 'the "worst thing possible"' (ibid.). The hyper-reality of blindness as darkness and absence is, thus, entangled with the desire to always be able to see by creating situations that enforce the existential emptiness of blindness.

Having said that, it is important to note here that this hyper-real is a problem that neither begins nor ends with Manning or the FFB. Titchkosky, Healey and Michalko show how a simulation becomes the *only* way by which the knowledge of blindness is both established and unconditionally comprehended by the entire sighted world. In a sense then, the abled human that seeks to existentially and experientially capture the state of blindness (either out of curiosity, for political ends, or a genuine desire to know) inevitably ends up simulating it rather than 'understanding' it before 'knowing' it (2019). Such simulations, they point out, result from the able-ist world's institution of sight as not only the single-most-important sense to experience the world but also the normal state of being. An absence of sight, thus, can only be a deviancy and never an alteration. One state of the hyper-real, where sight becomes singularly important, can only give rise to another state of the hyper-real where blindness is a simple absence of sight. This problem, further, is a problem that exists in a global cultural arena. When Titchkosky, Healey and Michalko figure out the root of the hyper-reality of the blind in cultural moorings, they know and acknowledge a transnational singularity to this cultural causation. In a sense then, there is attendant naturality to this hyper-real that allows it to be the case everywhere. Thus, it is of little wonder that while both Manning and the FFB are combating blindness in their ways in America, exactly similar realities are being crafted in India as well. Raamaa Chandramouli's Telegu short story 'Cikitsa' is a case in point. In the story, a depressed and suicidal 17-year-old Ravi is made to 'see' the beauty of life (and thus not end it) by coming into contact with blind children and juxtaposing his own life (of blessed sight) against theirs (of accursed darkness). At the beginning of the story, Ravi's physics teacher Janaki shows Ravi how life has to be understood in relative terms. She makes Ravi draw a set of parallel lines and a set of 'stairs' connecting those lines so that they can see the drawing from multiple angles and impress upon the relativity of life in general. Suddenly, the metaphor, of the lines, become a reality of life. Both Janaki and Ravi accept that reality without ever contesting it or considering the metaphorical nature of the drawing itself. This, agreeably hyper-real, existence is carried over as Janaki drops Ravi at a special school for blind children. Like Ravi can 'know' the relative reality of life (in general) through the lines, he is able to 'know' the relative beauty of his life through the blind children. The deviancy that these 'unfortunate' children exude allows Ravi the comprehension of his completeness. Thus, the necessity of deviancy to ensure relativity impressed upon by the lines, originally meant to be a simple metaphor, ends up ensuring Ravi of the deviancy of the blind. For, insofar as Ravi is concerned, what else can their reality be? Suddenly, his life isn't so bad. If the blind children live, so can he. No wonder then that Ravi, in Chandramouli's story, is nothing but thankful that he can see. The blind children, for him, are a curse and can only be pitied because their lives are flooded by darkness. They are the punished and the condemned—fated to roam the world without ever knowing its beauty. The children themselves do not harbour such an idea. They are free and able to do everything that they wish to do. They play, study, eat, make merry and interact with other people as Ravi himself would have done at their age. But, that is a reality that Ravi refuses to accept. Spurred on by (the hyper-reality of) his teacher's diagram, Ravi knows that the children are miserable and suffering. Like the FFB and the #HowEyeSeeIt movement, Ravi is firm in existing in a reality where blindness is a blackening of being. He fails to notice not only the lack of any referentiality of his reality but also the irony where, in search for and the subsequent conquest of the real beauty of life, he ends up staying far away from it.

Works Cited

Baudrillard, Jean. 1995. *Simulacra and Simulation*. Translated by Sheila Faria Glaser. Michigan.

Titchkosky, Tanya, Devon Healey, and Rod Michalko. 2019. 'Blindness Simulation and the Culture of Sight'. *Journal of Literary and Cultural Disability Studies*, 13(2): 123–139.

Cikitsa: The Treatment[1]

Translated from Telugu by Indira Babbellapati

The doors were yet to open for the day. It was still dark outside; around 5 in the morning.

Seventeen-year-old Ravi had been sitting on a wooden bench with his head bent down in the room ... He was in a stilled silence.

Janaki, 35 years old, was sitting in a chair looking intently at Ravi. Janaki was a physics teacher.

Silence reigned between the two.

If only he hadn't knocked at my door! How he's faltering when I opened the door! If only I didn't open the door ... wouldn't he have turned into a dead body in puddles of blood on the rail tracks? Janaki shuddered at the thought. She's like a forest on fire in the middle of summer.

'I don't know what prompted me to meet Janaki teacher one last time! Had I not done that, I might have been dead by now....' Ravi thought. He's like a paper burning. Ravi simply burst as tears gushed forth; he went on weeping uncontrollably.

Janaki got up from the chair and walked towards Ravi.

'It's time you should know yourself, Ravi!' she said, patting his head. Ravi didn't understand her words. His face assumed a question mark.

'Draw a vertical line on the paper,' she instructed, pushing a sheaf of papers lying on the table towards him. Ravi drew.

'Now tell me how big or small it is...!' Ravi looked at her in confusion.

'You can't say, can you?'

'...'

'Draw another vertical line ... a little smaller this time!' Ravi followed her instruction.

'Now, tell me, which is big and which is small?'

'The line I drew earlier is bigger,' said Ravi confidently.

'Bigger than what...?'

'The other line, of course!'

'Sure it is! What do you understand from this?'

'To know ourselves, we should know clearly about what is around us...' replied Ravi.

Janaki looked into Ravi's eyes; they looked like just-lit lamps.

1 Translated with permission.

'Keep the paper in your pocket. Now, take another and draw two perpendicular lines.'

Ravi did.

'This line is the wall; this is the floor, okay?' she said, pointing at the lines on the paper. 'Draw a ladder with the lines as the base. The ladder-end on the floor is A and the end against the wall is B.' Ravi marked accordingly. 'Now, draw steps and number them,' she continued.

1 ... 2 ... 4 ... 6 ...12 ... Ravi had put down the numbers against each step.

'Ravi, what if you turn the ladder upside down?'

'A goes up; B comes down.'

'And the steps?'

'Twelve is at the bottom; 1 is at the top.'

'That means the numbers changed their order but the values and purpose haven't changed. Am I right?'

'Yes...'

'How about step number 6?'

'Neither the number nor its value changed!'

'Suppose we place the ladder horizontally'?

'There're no steps! Or is there any value or purpose; everything is equal?'

'What do you understand from this?'

'That values change depending upon the positions. Where the values remain constant, it's a fixed state!'

'Good.'

Once again, silence reigned between them.

'What does *with* mean?'

'Too ... accompanied by,' he replied.

'Within?'

'Too ... inside.'

'With people, within people ... Think!'

Silence again.

Ravi looked like a seed about to germinate while Janaki was like a fruit-laden tree.

'When you open your eyes, you're *with* people in a world and you in the world; close your eyes and, look, a world is *within* you! A world that is only in you. We learn of the world that belongs to all while, simultaneously, we learn about the world that's exclusively one's own—designed, constructed, destroyed and reconstructed only by one's self. That's life!'

Ravi listened in excitement like the earth absorbing rain.

Janaki went on...

'Get up! We'll now go into the world,' Janaki said after some time—Janaki, Janaki teacher.

*

The gates were just being opened.

'Space, Home for the Blind' read the board in large English letters.

Janaki stopped her scooter. Ravi got off the pillion and stood in front of Janaki.

'You go in... Go and see a new world, Ravi. We will meet again,' said Janaki, starting her scooter.

Ravi entered the gate.

Sun was just rising red beyond the compound wall; a thin golden glow had spread all over.

Old is the sun but how new the sky every morning

Old is the earth but how she welcomes with stretched-out hands like a mother

Old is the air but how like the caressing hands of a mother every moment

Ravi recalled Janaki teacher's words in one of the classes.

How new the world can look if only we developed new ways of looking at anything old, looking at old matters anew or looking at old life as a new experience, thought Ravi.

As Ravi stepped into the premises, he heard the morning hymn sung at its sweetest best for the lord—*Kausalya Suprajarama.*

A 20-year-old lady came walking to him. 'Come Ravi ... Janaki teacher had already informed me of your visit. Welcome! My name is Radha. I've been working here for five years. I just came to see the place and that's it. I settled here. I now feel I don't need anything else in life other than working for these blind children assisting Shobha madam, *tammi*,' she said endearingly.

Ravi looked into Radha's face in amusement; it glowed like a lighted bulb.

The compound was filled with morning activity. The visually challenged children were moving up and down in hurry. They were bathed, dressed and moving in groups with hands on one another's shoulders; they all looked normal and didn't seem bothered about their visual disability. *Sa, re, ga, ma* ... some musical notes were heard from one of the rooms.

It was a world of the visually challenged. They were all up even before the world outside was still slumbering. It was a world filled with vibrancy, excitement and a lot of movement...

Meanwhile, a Hero Honda bike stopped outside the gate. A 40-year-old man walked in carrying a heavy gunny sack. Radha rushed to share the weight.

'Radha, the bag contains 150 mangoes. Wash them clean and give them to all the children. I'll see you later,' he said; a group of seven to eight boys and girls came rushing and crowded around the man. 'Seenu sir, Seenu sir, stay for a while ... please, please!' said the children in chorus. They recognised him by his voice.

'Meet Thouta Srinivas garu,' Radha introduced the man to Ravi. 'He's our advisory committee member. Children love him,' she added.

'Do they recognise people by their voice?' asked Ravi.

'If they get to hear you once, even after six months, they will know you. If they touch you once, they know it's you even if you're in a crowd by merely touching you. They've unique retentive ability,' said Radha.

Thoutam Sreenu spoke to Ravi for a while and left. The children breathed in the sweet aroma of the fruit. 'Thank you, sir! Very sweet, our Srinivas sir ... Good sir!' they all shouted as Srinivas left.

Ravi turned into a tender leaf vibrating to a mild breeze.

Ravi looked clearly and closely into a few children's faces as he followed Radha into the home.

The children's eyes looked like sockets buried deeper into an empty eye ... Some of them had eyelashes but no eyeballs. Some had protruding white-coat filled eyeballs that looked similar to glass marbles; the rest of their bodies was normal like others'. Why like this? Who punished them like this? What sins have these kids committed that they should be condemned this way deprived of sight, with no eyes and unable to see the world! Ravi lost himself in deep contemplation.

These kids do not know anything; they've no idea of how they look. The shape, colour, structure of a human are beyond their estimates. All they have is darkness within and without. Mere black darkness. Flowers, things, trees, roads, hillocks, rivers, birds, mountains ... the entire living world is beyond their imagination. Everything, just every part of the world is nothing but black. All they know is to identify sound; sound is their pathway. Sound is their very breath. Sound is their walk. The world is only sound! What's the remainder? Touch. Touch is their knowledge. Touch is their memory. Touch is their education. Touch is their jnana. Ravi's thoughts brought tears into his eyes. What's this blindness that deprives them of even a blink of sight ... Blindness; renting sorrow? The overpowering darkness. Agonising sorrow; pity for those blind by birth. And, at the same time, choking joy for himself for the blessing of sight!

Those who can see will never know the value of eyes. It's only when one is deprived of vision, only upon seeing those without vision that one understands the value and blessing of being born with sight. When the realisation dawned on Ravi, he thought of the statement, sarveendriyaanam, nayanam pradhaanam ... of all faculties, eyes are of utmost importance. 'What am I doing having such valuable eyes,' now the question engaged Ravi's mind.

Ravi accompanied Radha to the tin-roof shed in the courtyard. There he heard children singing and a music sir training them in the adjacent room.

I'm a girl-child, amma, I'm a girl-child ... worry not that I'm a girl.... the popular song on the girl-child poured forth at its musical best from one of the girls. Her voice reflected the emotions of deprivation, sorrow, agony ... and heart. Ravi stopped to peep through the window. A 12-year-old blind girl standing with folded hands was singing in those dark worlds she alone knew!

Who's her father? Mother? What might be her place of birth? Where were her formative years spent? Since when had she come to sing the song? How could she sing the song with so much feeling that it melted the listeners' hearts?

'Ravi, that girl's name is Manjula. She reached the finals of a reality show in music. She'll present her song next week in Hyderabad at the Grand Finals. She's sure to bag the first prize. You know, even stones melt when she sings!' Radha's words broke Ravi's thoughts.

How inherent and unparallel are the qualities of an individual! How one shines when hidden talent is recognised, nurtured, refined, encouraged and supported! Is blindness an impediment to one's achievements...? Ravi was lost in his thoughts. He found a few children engaged in writing something on a Braille chart. Radha ran to them and whispered into their ears. When Ravi went nearer, they touched their scripts and in unison said, 'Welcome, Mr Ravi! Swagatam!'

Ravi bent down to touch the protruding letters; he looked into their faces intently in an inexplicable joy. The empty sockets were full of smiles. But his own eyes welled up with tears.

Ravi turned the pages written in Braille, their alphabet: 1, 2 made A; 1, 2, 3 made L; 1, 2, 3, 4 made P; 3, 4, 5 is aa in Telugu; 1, 3, 6 is U in Telugu; 1, 2, 3, 4 is pa in Telugu. All dots and symbols ... a system of coding and decoding. But then, isn't life itself a process of coding and decoding? Ravi felt himself like a piece of paper swirling in a whirlwind.

There was a photo hanging on one of the opposite faded walls, with 'AMMA' written below it.

'She's our founder, Shobha Madam. She's a mother to all of us,' said Radha pointing to the wall.

Just at that moment, Ravi heard a joyful commotion around. Children were found rushing towards the entrance.

'Shobha Madam must have come,' said Radha, rushing in the same direction.

Madam pushed the gates and entered the premises; she was around 40 years, fair and serene; she looked like a just-washed pearl.

Yes, she's Shobha!

All the blind children flocked around her. One of the boys was left behind panting and finding it difficult to go closer to Shobha. Shobha noticed him and freed herself from the others; she jumped to reach the boy.

'Jacob...!'

She quickly placed her cupped hands towards his mouth; struggling for breath Jacob puked in her hands. She drew the child closer to her and rested his head on her shoulders.

Ravi stood stunned. Shobha looked at the boy and Radha, taking the cue, rushed to fetch a bucket of water.

Ravi pulled the paper that he hid in his pocket in the morning…

He likened himself to A and on the next page drew two vertical lines. Below one line he wrote 'Janaki' and, below another, he wrote 'Shobha'.

He then struck out A that represented him and made it flat. At that moment, a new dimension seemed to have revealed itself to him; he began to observe the children in a new perspective!

Some have eyes but no vision; some have no eyes but are gifted with vision.

'Me?' wondered Ravi, 'do I have eyes or vision?'

Ravi began to understand...

MOONNU ANDHANMAR ANAYE VIVARIKKUNNU

(Three Blind Men Describe an Elephant)

By E. Santosh Kumar

Introduction

By Editors

Painted by Pieter Bruegel the Elder in 1568, *The Blind Leading the Blind* depicts a line of five blind men, each, following the leader, in a progressive process of losing their balance and falling. At the bottom right of the painting, the leader of the five, himself blind, is already lying in a ditch with his arms and legs flailing wildly in the air seeking help against, what one can assume, a sudden and unexpected fall. Beside him lies a hurdy-gurdy, a musical instrument often used by beggars. Following from the fallen ones, the left end of the painting shows the last blind man of the line, still upright and seemingly unaware of his inevitable fall. The six are, or, have had been till before the fall, connected by multiple wooden staves linked together like a chain. The linkage allowed them connection as they guided themselves by holding the shoulder of the man in front. Behind the six men, in the background of the painting, is a more or less desolate pastoral landscape with a small church at a distance. This landscape has been painted primarily in a yellow desert-like tone with hints of proper greenery only on a distant hill. While the six, then, still have some colour to them, they are put in a world that is primarily barren and, enforced by the fall, immediately hostile.

On the face of it, then, Bruegel's painting functions as a tragicomic rendering of the fates of the six as they follow each other, both literally and metaphorically, blindly. Looked at more critically, however, this tragicomic presentation rips open a discourse that is far more serious than what the painting betrays at first glance: a seriousness that is accorded by a fundamental juxtaposition between the subjects of the painting and their compositional presence (both in terms of their painted nature and definitive literary/biblical allusion). On the one hand, there is a grounding of the six men in clinic reality. It is, as Philip McCouat shows, possible to distinguish the medical nature of each person's blindness against that of the others:

> So, for example, starting from the follower on the far left, we have a case of pemphigoid (scarring of the conjunctiva); a non-identifiable ailment obscured by the second man's hat; phthisis bulbi (shrunken non-functional eyes); corneal leukoma (wall-eye); and enucleation (removal of eyes) in the case of the man turning sightlessly toward the viewer' (2018).

Each character, therefore, is 'real-ised' in his disability. This realisation, on the other hand, does not extract either the painting or the blind men in it from the complex matrices of structures that render disabled subjects as disembodied metaphors. There is, in other words, a simultaneous unreality to the blind men despite (or perhaps because of) their medical propriety. Consider, for example, the colour pattern of the painting. There is a perceptible darkening of the palette as one moves from left to right. While the last blind man, upright and yet unaffected, is still standing against a light and bright yellowish background, the leader, having already fallen, is both placed inside and surrounded by a blackened and shadowy ditch. There is an explicit 'message' that the painting intends to tell; a message that not only visualises the biblical problem of the blind leading the blind, where blindness is not a real physical phenomenon but rather a moral–intellectual one, it also draws upon a history of similar treatments of disability. Bruegel's painting, failing to situate blindness in and as real human-bodied condition, hence, much like the subjects in it, falls. The reality, in it, is restricted to the vagaries of moralising metaphors that consciously chose to delimit the blind human as a mere idiom. That the blind, even as an idiom, is shaded in blackened tones of immorality (for the blind is the one who is not able to 'see' the good and proper path) is a strong point in itself.

Notwithstanding the attendant negativity of this denotation, what is of importance here is the de-realisation of the blind; a phenomenon where the human being is stripped of their human existence to be turned into an abstraction. It is of little wonder, then, that E. Santosh Kumar conceptualises his story, translated here as 'Three Blind Men Describe an Elephant', as a definite response to Bruegel's painting. Unlike *The Blind Leading the Blind*, Santosh Kumar's story figures the blind not simply in their clinical reality but their experiential and existential one. The story, in a sense, manages to circumvent the problem of, as Georgina Kleege puts it, the 'Hypothetical Blind Man' (2005) where the blind human is a medium of exemplification—either moral or philosophical. As Kleege puts it, this 'hypothetical' is a smorgasbord of experimental subjects always tending towards productions of comparative knowledge—of comprehending the world through the presentation of the absence of one cognitive sense and, as a sigh of relief, knowing that this absence is conjectural. Kleege, thus, writes that the hypothetical is

> ...a prop for theories of consciousness. He is the patient subject of endless thought experiments where the experience of the world through four senses can be compared to the experience of the world through five. He is asked to describe his understanding of specific visual phenomena—perspective, reflection, refraction, color, form

> recognition—as well as visual aids and enhancements—mirrors, lenses, telescopes, microscopes. He is understood to lead a hermit-like existence, so far at the margins of his society, that he has never heard this visual terminology before the philosophers bring it up. Part of the emotional baggage he hauls around with him comes from other cultural representations of blindness, such as Oedipus and the many Biblical figures whose sight is withdrawn by the wrathful God of the Old Testament or restored by the redeemer of the New. His primary function is to highlight the importance of sight and to elicit a frisson of awe and pity which promotes gratitude among the sighted theorists for the vision they possess. (ibid.)

Bruegel's painting, fitting rather snugly inside Kleege's theoretical framework of the hypothetical, gives its viewers the hypothetical metaphorised blind men (five, in fact) who have chosen to follow yet another blind man. The resulting fall is, hence, inevitable. But, Santosh Kumar's story, as already mentioned above, not only not falters and ends up giving another hypothetical but also manages to go the complete opposite of Kleege's blind man and allow something very real and very human to germinate. It is important here to note that Kumar writes a reply to the historical hypothetical and not just the one from the painting. While, on the one hand, there is a shadow of Bruegel's moralistic fallen blind in Kumar's narrative, there is, on the other, another hypothetical residing closer home that's been systematically deconstructed. The story recreates the rather widespread and famous Indian parable of the three blind men (the number varies as per different versions) trying to describe an elephant by touching and ending up knowing only the individual parts: one finds the trunk and likens it to a snake, another thinks the leg is a tree and so on. For each, in the parable, the elephant primarily becomes the part they are touching. Like Bruegel's blind men, the ones here are also similar hypotheticals that create forms of meaning. In thus choosing to allude to such characters from across space, time and narrative/artistic form, Kumar effectively writes against all such tendencies of hypothesisation and ensures a grounding of not just blind characters but all those whom they represent in the real. This realisation happens in two fundamental ways. In the first, Santosh Kumar does not allow the absence of sight to govern the realities of the three characters in the story. In other words, while they are blind, they are not just blind. Unlike the painting, all of them have a name, an avid interest in cricket and, more importantly, a vocation which is not restricted by their disability: Shekhar is a telephone operator, Raghuram, a music teacher, and Chandran (to the utter disbelief of the narrator), a tourist guide. They are allowed, in a sense, an existence that is not defined by their impairment. This accreditation of the involvement of the three 'blind' men with the world at large, either through their hobby or their vocation, allows Kumar to present, at the very least, a universe within which these men are real human beings and not just moral and hypothetical mannequins and, at its hopeful most, an inclusive world where such involvements are commonplace. The second way by which Kumar responds to Bruegel (and, by extension, those that require the blind to be hypothetical) is by, in quite literal terms, dismantling the hypothetical. The narrator, ever so comfortable in his abled life, can think of the three as nothing but an experiment. Having heard the aforementioned parable about the blind men trying to describe an elephant, he wishes to recreate it. For him, Shekhar, Raghuram and Chandran are nothing but mediums towards the confirmation of the hypothetical blind as it exists in his head. But, when the three describe the elephant, the narrator realises that they not only do not live in the world of a parable but have, like him, immediate emotive associations with the world. The three show him that the elephant (which itself has to be understood as a stand-in for all objects) is not just an inert thing floating in the world but something that affects. One of them invokes fear, the second indifference and the third reverence. That, towards the end of the story, the narrator himself falters at describing an elephant and later on feels a similar imposing presence of the animal as the three do, betrays his reckoning not only with the reality of the blind but his own as well. Till he interacts with Shekhar, Raghuram and Chandran, the real world finds a cosy divide between the disabled other and the abled self. By the end of the story, however, he comprehends and perhaps apprehends the fragility of the divide. Through the narrator, finally, Santosh Kumar can speak to the world and, especially, his non-disabled readers, to present a disabled world that is as realised and affected as can be.

Works Cited

Kleege, Georgina. 2005. 'Blindness and Visual Culture: An Eye-Witness Account'. *The Journal of Visual Culture*, 4(2): 179–190.

McCouat, Philip. 2018. 'Perception and Blindness in the 16th Century: Bruegel's "The Blind Leading the Blind"'. Available at: http://www.artinsociety.com/perception-and-blindness-in-the-16th-century.html (accessed on 7 April 2021).

Three Blind Men Describe an Elephant[1]

Translated from Malayalam by Shalini Rachel Varghese

Now and then our journalism classes were engaged by Kuruvilla, the man who had served a brief spell in a foreign newspaper. A sense of contempt prevailed in his treatment of India and Indian journalism. At whimsical intervals, he prescribed novel assignments for us as if to provoke us—a report on a thoroughly unexplored topic, a scoop with no hint of obscenity, an imaginary interview, two different points of view of a single problem … and so went his array of projects. Our responses, however different, always met with the same air of disdain from Kuruvilla Sir and so some of us looked for that rare and opportune project to floor Kuruvilla.

My stay was taken care of in a relatively inexpensive boarding house. I was the only student there. The rest were either government servants expecting a transfer or small-scale merchants. The boarding house comprised a pair of double-storied buildings which faced each other. The distance between these buildings was meagre and there was even a broad cemented bridge between the upper storeys of the buildings. The way up was through a flight of wooden stairs. One had to be extra cautious while going up or down as the bannisters kept rattling noisily.

I knew that somewhere opposite my room in the lodge there were three blind men. But I never made the effort to get acquainted with them. Sometimes I even spotted one of them in some corner of the city, and that was that. I noticed nothing that distinguished them from the rest of the human world except that they were blind.

But then I did notice them on that Saturday when I huddled around lazily in my room with nothing to do. They were going out. One of them closed the door and slid the latch to lock it when all three had got out of the room. He had taken the key out and inserted it into the keyhole very carefully. The three of them filed out along the corridor, crossed the connecting bridge between the buildings and reached the stairs at the other end. They tapped the wooden stairs gently with their walking sticks, which I had never seen them put to use before, as though to crosscheck something. And then the rattle of the bannisters was heard for quite some time.

I was surprised. These three blind guys stayed together without help or support on the second floor of a lodge. Who are they? How

---

1 Translated with permission.

did they end up together? Seeing them considerably well dressed and living in rented premises, the impression of beggars and vagrants that we normally associate with blind people vanished from my mind. My curiosity aroused, I must have felt prompted to think of other blind men known to me. Racking my brains, I found none worth remembering except one or two beggars. The only familiar image left then was the blind character played by actor Kala Bhavan Mani in that famous film.

I got up and walked down till the end of the corridor looking for the threesome. They had crossed the not-so-crowded road and reached the other end. Two of them boarded a bus that came along in a little while. The third one tapped his stick to examine a few places around him and walked along the side of the road in the opposite direction. I stood right there till the man disappeared from my sight. Not many people were there at the bus stop. Even the ones who were there paid no attention to them.

Back in the room, I sat remembering Kuruvilla Sir's boastful classes. Why, I could make a theme of these blind men! The life of three blind men. Their jobs, stay, food, conversations. On second thought, I wondered if I'd present myself as easy prey to Kuruvilla's high-handed ridicule. That's when the adage about the three blind men seeing the elephant rang in my mind. I realised that it was a criticism more than an adage—that indeed blind men cannot view an elephant in totality. This was just the topic I was looking for, it seemed. What did my blind neighbours imagine the elephant to be after all? They must be aware of the age-old saying. So, if I suggested the idea to them, they might misunderstand it as an attempt to ridicule. I must be careful in approaching them with the subject.

I sat around lazily till about 4 in the evening, even skipping lunch for the day. I then had a bath and got out of the room to wander about the city aimlessly. It looked like there was some cricket match and a consequent crowd in front of every TV shop. While the crowd had begun to disperse in front of a particular shop, I noticed the three blind men and remembered my prospective interview with them all over again. How on earth did they end up amidst these cricket fans? I started studying them from a distance. They began discussing among themselves as they slowly walked towards the next bus stop and I stood watching them. It was past 6 o'clock then.

I was back in the hostel by 7:30. Instead of heading for my room, I turned at the verandah and reached the entrance of the room occupied by my three neighbours. The door was closed. I could vaguely hear the conversation inside. I knocked at the door gently.

'The door isn't closed. Do come in,' the voice from inside could be heard.

I opened the door. The three were seated on a reed mat. They sat a little closer to each other than regular people do. The room was brightly lit. A high voltage bulb was fixed to beat the low voltage menace of the cities. I was mildly struck by the sheer unnaturalness of these three blind men beneath such bright lights.

Not just that. Anybody would be attracted to the ordered and tidy manner in which things were arranged in the room. Even the walking sticks the three used were neatly propped up in a corner of the room. Only a table and chair served for furniture in the room. There was not even a bed. Except for the hum of the ceiling fan, the atmosphere was perfectly quiet. The table had a few carry bags and a harmonium that was not so new.

'Hello,' one of the blind men addressed me.

'Do be seated,' another pointed in the direction of the chair.

'I live in the room close by…' I attempted to introduce myself while sitting on the chair.

'We know.' The threesome said in a chorus. 'We noticed that you were coming.'

'How is that? You have not seen me before, have you?' I wondered how they would interpret the term 'see' despite my question.

'The sound of the footfalls on the stairs helps us recognise,' one of them said.

'You study here, don't you?'

So they knew me.

'We were discussing the match today,' he continued. 'This chap here is a die-hard cricket fan. He laid a bet that India would win today's match. He didn't have to part with his money because it was us.'

'If it weren't for that unexpected run-out, the story would have been different,' the other two blind men contended with a smile.

'I don't have my earlier enthusiasm anymore.' The cricket fan turned to me. His eyelids were permanently closed. I could see them twitch now and then. He continued, 'When Gavaskar retired, my interest retired too.'

'Why is that?' I asked a natural question.

'All the rest seem mediocre. Who else could stay longer in the game?' There was a considerable silence. I coughed to make my presence felt again.

'I still remember the day Gavaskar made 10,000 runs,' he continued, 'it was a late cut. Two runs.'

'He remembers this kind of stuff distinctly,' one of them mocked. 'Earlier there was good commentary. With the arrival of television, no one seems to care for it anymore.' The cricket fan voiced his disappointment.

'We must buy a television.' The one who had been quiet commented.

'Whatever for? We'll have the mad game in here too then,' the other man quipped with a gentle smile. 'You must excuse us. This chap is crazy about the game. He won't stop if you set him off on cricket.'

'Oh, that's alright. I came only to meet you and get acquainted.'

'That's wonderful. Something we forgot to do.' The cricket fan extended his hand towards me.

'My name is Shekhar. I am a telephone operator.' He mentioned his company while shaking my hand. I realised that I had shaken hands with a blind man for the first time.

'I am a music teacher,' the man sitting next to him informed, 'I tutor students in about four or five homes.'

'What is your name?'

'Raghuraman. That harmonium is mine.' He got up, found the harmonium and returned to sit on the reed mat, beginning to finger on the keyboard. The white portion of his eyes moved in tune.

I introduced myself too, 'My name is Chandran.'

The third one spoke this time. 'I don't have much of a job. My education is not much to speak of either.' There was a tinge of disappointment in his voice.

'I am a tourist guide now.'

'A guide?' I couldn't help asking. But the disbelief in my question did not affect him a bit.

'I am not the roaming kind of guide by the way,' he explained. There was an ancient temple a few roads away and his job was to show the tourists in and around its premises.

The temple was famous for its formidable sculpture. He showed it to tourists though he could not see himself.

When I felt that I had bonded long enough with these men, I presented my topic as though it were a very important mission, with as much humility as I could assume. I was scared all along that they might take offence. But the three of them regarded the idea quite seriously. The limitations of the blind man as presented in the oft-repeated adage of the blind men seeing the elephant did not bother them at all. I seriously felt that they were thinking only of the real inquiry in my research, beyond the negativity of the old proverb.

Shekhar deserted the happy disposition he wore while discussing cricket and reminisced, 'It was a long time ago when I was a boy. Mine was a big family. A lot of people it had. And when the temple festival went on for seven days in our village, more people would come.

People moved up and down the festival grounds irrespective of whether it was night or day.

'One of my distinct memories of the festival is the smell of sweet dates. I was never taken to the festival ground. If at all I was taken, I would be made to stand at a distance to listen to the varying drumbeats of the percussionists and brought back soon afterwards. Once, one of the bigger boys took me to the festival ground for a change. He was one of my relatives who stayed and studied in a distant town.

'Our walk to the ground was constantly impeded by the ruckus of people returning from the festival. Some of them passed with loud laughter. Some kids perhaps cried aloud and played with their toy flutes in irritating tones. Horns were blown loud from the bicycles selling ice cream. The crowd swelled by degrees as we neared the festival ground. I held my chaperone's hand tightly as I walked.

'Thus I heard the sound of musical drums from such close quarters for the first time. I felt the music of the drums reach a crescendo like the mad hum of cockroaches around me. In the crowd, the people stood brushing against each other. You could smell the odour of your neighbour's sweat as you breathed.

'And all of a sudden…', as Shekharan said these words, his face grew taut. He was seized by unexplained fear. His irises, white in colour, flitted about rapidly. Probably he imagined there was no one else in the room and his illusion of solitariness seemed to have inspired him.

'My dear friends, it was all of a sudden that I felt the still environment around me move. And how quick it was! The people who stood and walked around began to scatter all over. Someone said an elephant had run amok. I fell in the middle of the stampede. Several people jumped and knocked over me and surged ahead. My hand had lost its hold of my relative. I kept attempting to get up from the ground. Each time I would be knocked over by the mad rush of fleeing people. My bruises were smarting now. After a while, I felt a quietness and emptiness as though I were the only one left on the premises. I sat up. I could not do any more than that. I cried as I did not know which way to go.'

I felt transfixed in the momentary world of his helplessness; we must have forgotten that it was only he who lay there alone.

'I then heard the earth quaking around me. It came closer, albeit not very fast. And yet with every step, there was a frightening noise. Very slowly, it came near. Would you believe it, friends, that noise went right past me—or shall I say across my body?' He then tried to mimic the sound of the movement that he had heard. His closed eyelids kept twitching in powerful fervour.

He kept quiet for some time then. It was as if everyone around him was smitten into a web of fear.

'After that, I have never been to temple festivals. When this friend asked me about the elephant, I heard that noise all over again. As far as I am concerned, the elephant is that mind-blowing movement, my friend. It is not an isolated entity. But a spate of events. Drumbeats that came to a sudden halt, the fall, the people running amok, the voices floating above the shocked silence … when I lay there without a soul to turn to, the reverberations of that world which crossed me....'

Shekharan did not speak after that. Was he recalling the sequence all over again?

'My experience is not a singular one as Shekharan's,' Raghuraman, the music teacher, broke through the silence, 'it happens to me again and again.'

'What are you saying?' I asked.

'I dream of the elephant now and then.'

'You dream of the elephant?'

'Yes, I do. A couple of times I even saw a herd of them.'

'How do you dream?' My curiosity had been roused. Leave alone the elephant, how could a blind man dream at all! But I was also scared that my question might upset him.

'There are some things I cannot explain,' he turned to me and continued, 'What I said is true. I have surely dreamt of an elephant herd. But it has never frightened me as in Shekharan's case.'

'How do you see?' I asked. He looked at me as though he had not followed what I meant.

'I mean…' I began to elaborate, 'How do you see without light that aids vision?'

'Why must you have light in a dream?' Raghuraman asked pausing in between. 'What after all is this light as you call it?'

'Light … What I mean is…' In groping for a word, I tried to point at the bulb in the room and then gave up realising the futility of the attempt. I then said softly, 'This room has light.'

'Yes, indeed,' one of the remaining two agreed.

'And that is why we see,' I elaborated.

'But what is seeing?' The earnest curiosity in Raghuraman's voice quite bewildered me.

'You still see dreams,' I added.

'I am convinced of that. But you don't seem to understand that.'

'I have not dreamt of elephants.' I felt I had landed back to square one, a bottleneck where I had begun.

'But you have seen elephants, haven't you? Don't take me amiss when I ask this.' He hung his head in humility and continued, 'How does your elephant look, my friend?'

I felt my interview had hit a crisis. I began to wonder how I would describe an elephant to this poor man. I felt a pall of gloom over the dimming world of my language, increasingly aware that I was as helpless as the carpenter with an array of tools he did not know how to use.

The blind men continued to listen to me carefully.

'You probably know that the colour of the elephant is black?' I looked at them. 'Only the tusks are white.' And then I spoke as I searched for something they would be familiar with. 'It is just the size of a bus. A bus you know.'

'You mean it looks like a bus?' Raghuraman asked.

'Not that it looks like a bus. But the size is much the same.'

'The elephant is a quake, a tremor,' Shekharan recalled, 'Have you not heard the rumble of a bus, Raghu?'

'Well my friend,' it seemed to me that Raghuraman was inviting me in his loving manner. 'If only you come along with me to my place where I dream, I could show you the elephant herd I spoke to you about.' He continued with a loud chuckle, 'That's all I can do as I have always been a bad storyteller.'

I could only laugh along like a fool.

'Ganapathy is my favourite god,' Raghuraman happily declared. He then went on to tune the harmonium while he sang a stanza from Dikshitar's invocation to Ganesha. He sang with an outlandish expression on his face.

'Elephants are my particular favourites too,' Chandran the guide spoke up. He adjusted his spectacles. 'I know all the 49 sculpted elephants of the temple by their lineage. Some of them in the front row do not have tusks and some have broken ones.'

'That must be Ganapathy,' Raghuraman speculated.

'No. The tusks were broken during some invasion in the past. Now the government is taking care of them.' He corrected us and continued his rumination. 'I have been crazy about elephants since my childhood. No, I did not pick it up at the pageants or festivals. Just watching the elephants being brought to the river for a bath. Mahouts coming home asking for palm leaves for feeding them. The double-spiralled finger ring made of hair from the elephant's tail that I had back then. The commands of the trainers taming the elephants. The occasional trumpet calls. I even touched an elephant once.'

'Wow,' Shekharan, the man who was introduced to the elephant with an earthquake was full of wonder and awe.

'But I felt no apprehension. I knew that that was not my elephant. For me, it would have to be an elephant that I could fathom completely, hold in my hands, feel and touch.'

'Like the sculpted elephants,' I said.

'Not even that. Something I could call my own.' He paused for a moment.

'Most people in my village got themselves tattooed in those days. It was done by running the needle over the skin. Burnt images were formed using a chemical. They looked green and stayed indelible. They stuck forever, idol-bearing figures on the skin. Hanuman, Vishnu and Devi the goddess, mostly godheads.'

He removed his dark glasses. There was a certain nakedness in his eyes. Something pale in colour.

'I have seen conch shells tattooed,' I remarked.

'Oh yes, they do that. But I wanted an elephant. The tattoo man refused at first. He asked me if I could not be satisfied with the gods. But I was stubborn in my demand for the elephant. The image that disturbed my sleep and waking hours. I would not budge.' Chandran proclaimed proudly, 'Finally he came around.'

'Show us!' The three of us cried in a chorus. Chandran was hesitant for a moment. Gradually, with a hint of coy submission, he lifted the lungi that he wore above his knee, exposing his hairless thigh.

I was shocked to find an utterly disfigured image on the fair skin. The image that one could suit oneself to regard as the elephant stood oblivious of its stature, breaking all boundaries of common conception. A patch that could be regarded as the trunk rose in the air, like an erect phallus. A terrifying trumpet sound pierced through my ears.

Chandran slowly ran his fingers over the tattoo mark. The other two stood hesitant as though unnerved by my presence. Soon they began to feel the tattoo with their fingers in minute detail and got acquainted with the elephant. When their fingers touched his skin, Chandran felt visibly ticklish I thought. The disfigured, measureless elephant seemed to challenge me in turn.

He let his lungi fall back and displayed a smile of satisfaction though mysterious. He then wore his dark glasses and looked at me dispassionately.

Everyone fell silent for quite some time. The old clock in the room chimed 9:30.

I stood up and thanked the men. The three blind followed me to the door. When I said goodbye and reached beyond the door, I heard Shekharan say, 'Wasn't that 9:30 on the clock? It rang at least five minutes in advance. Make it fast my friend, at 9:30 we have our power cut.'

I walked slowly and reached my room. The moment I reached the room, the lights went off. I was drowned in unfathomable darkness. In the room I felt the menacing presence of an elephant full-bred in darkness, waiting.

DRUSHTI

By Bolwar Mahamad Kunhi

Introduction

By Editors

Charles Taylor, in his book *The Sources of the Self,* notes how constructions of the self are always contingent on the moral frameworks the said bodies are put in. It is, in fact, impossible, according to Taylor, to have a notion of the self without finding topological placements within moral structures. This impossibility owes to the fact that these structures function on two fundamentally 'human' planes: finding, firstly, reactive legitimacies through and as human instincts, and, secondly, the positional loci of a natural being of humans. To this end, Taylor writes that 'moral reactions … have two facets … on one side, they are almost like instincts, comparable to our love of sweet things…; on the other they seem to involve claims … about the nature and status of human beings' (1989). Human ontologies, therefore, are always revealed from within a system of immediate and natural judgements which, in turn, allow discriminations of the good and the bad through 'strong evaluations' (ibid.). This moral judgement, as Taylor writes later, '[orients] us' by 'providing the frame within which things have meaning for us, by virtue of the qualitative distinctions it incorporates' (ibid.). Human identity, thus, finding itself tied rather intimately to moral frameworks, allows a definition of 'what is important to us and what is not' (ibid.). This conception of the location of the Self inside morality becomes rather important when one considers the distinction drawn between the abled human against the disabled one. Given that, as Taylor notes, there is an instinctual and natural impulsion towards the judgement of the good and the bad, the 'natural' body of the abled automatically becomes the strongly evaluated good, rendering the disabled body as something that needs to be discarded as bad and abhorred. This naturalness, and the instinctual drive, subsequently, is derived from the ostensible quantitative advantage that the abled bodies have. In other words, because abled bodies are seemingly or, as Lennard Davis would suggest, at least, temporarily, larger in number than the disabled ones, the former allot themselves a naturalness of being thus forming their selves as morally superior.

This morally inferior location that is evaluated onto the disabled subject, then, goes on to decide and define the multivalent ways in which they are 'handled' by society. That they are considered as a curse and in an immediate need for correction (either religious or medical) is a discourse, for example, that draws its legitimacy from the phenomenon that Taylor conceptualises as the inexorable moral construction of human selves. Even the re-presentations of disability suffer from this moral impetus. Stories and narratives, as Ato Quayson notes as well, never fail to impress upon the immorality of the disabled subjects. They are, more often than not, depicted as evil and generally unwanted. This position becomes all the more tenable in a country like India where, unlike the West, logics of moral frameworks are never tempered with other forms of rationality. Bolwar Mahamad Kunhi's short story 'Drushti' is a rather palpable example of the situation of the disabled being as moral corruption that generates nothing but societal guilt or shame and is always in an immediate need of concealment. The story, set in a village in Karnataka, revolves around a man who has just returned from Muscat. The story told from the perspective of the different characters whom this man meets from the moment he enters the borders of the village, relates how all these characters find themselves ashamed and unable to tell him that his son, born in his absence, was born blind. He wasn't given the news earlier because the elders of the village decided that the news would discombobulate him, make him angry and shame the village to which he married into. On his return, the situation gets worse as the villagers feel guilty about not only harbouring a disabled child (as one would while concealing a criminal) but also keeping the father in the dark. This feeling of shame and guilt that the entire village, including the child's mother and grandparents, feel, displays the inherently immoral position that has been lobbed onto the child. He is never really allowed to be fully human and is always thought of as something that should not have been. In not telling the father, the villagers find respite, believing that they have contained the secret of their disgrace.

The immediate effect of this moralisation, when concerned with the disabled subject, shows itself in the processes of stigmatisation that these people are made to go through. The creation of stigmatised traits goes hand in hand with allocations of immorality. Stigma happens when 'prevailing social practices treat particular "undesirable" traits as universally discrediting' (Bagenstos 2000). These social practices, however, are constructed in consideration of the aforementioned moral framework. For, this framework not only creates human identities but also, to ensure its upkeep and allow further human identities to find a basis for creation, delineates social rules for these identities. Therefore, those who find favour within the framework find specific social performances in accordance with these rules that they need to play out for the maintenance of both society and morality. One such rule is to always ensure that those, as Bagenstos says, with 'undesired' traits, are kept out of the process of the upkeep of society. This is an ontological exclusion because any such inclusion, in light of the undesirability of their being, would threaten the stability of the framework within which both the individual and the society finds subsistence. It is of little wonder that these 'undesired' people are also the ones who find themselves at the negative end of the moral spectrum. These two aspects are, obviously, not mutually exclusive. Their immoral situation is within and by a moral framework that does not want them for its survival. As a result, Bagenstos, quoting Erving Goffman, writes, 'people with stigmatized traits are not considered to be among the "normals" for whom society, and its institutions, are designed' (2000). Finally, in not being the norm, the stigmatised are also not accounted for by those who 'design social and physical environments' (ibid.), thus, ensuring a complete effacement of all beings undesired. Bagenstos is quick to note, however, that stigma is far more insidious than simple prejudice. Even when people are not prejudiced against the 'undesired', stigma, in spreading alongside the moral framework, ensures that 'unnatural' existences are never considered or remembered in the construction of the world. This completes their universal disqualification as they are not able to participate in society even if they want to.

Impairment, often being physical, becomes a very apparent trait that is 'undesired'. Owing to the fact that the impaired human is (visibly) incomplete, they are immediately disqualified as existences that need to be accounted for. This incompleteness is further accentuated by the impaired human's perceived inability to perform social roles. In other words, society refuses to allot them positions because it believes that the impaired will not be able to do it in the first place. This is but a mere perception. Even when it is not, this inability, as shown above, stems from society's refusal to construct its institutions in a way that would allow the impaired to perform any duties. This fundamental stigmatisation is, as disability scholars have tried to show, what creates 'disability'. Bagenstos too writes that '"the entire physical and social organization of life" is frequently structured as though everyone were physically strong, as though all bodies were shaped the same, as though everyone could walk, hear and see well, as though everyone could work and play at a pace that is not compatible with any kind of illness or pain, as though no one were ever dizzy or incontinent or simply needed to sit or lie down' (2000). It is important, here, to note the circular nature of the stigmatisation of disability. It begins by delineating the undesired state of impairment as immoral, especially because it cannot be included within systems that uphold the moral framework. Due to this, the impaired are then rendered unnatural (for the moral condition betrays systems of naturalness) and are not taken into account as society is structured. This furthers the disability of the impaired by once again disallowing them to perform social roles, thus, demarcating them, once again, as immoral. Thus, as Arthur Kleinman and Rachel Hall-Clifford show, the stigmatisation of disability 'decays the ability to hold on to what matters most to ordinary people in a local world, such as wealth, relationships and life chances' (2009). In Kunhi's story, this stigmatised universal disqualification is shown, once again, through the villagers' refusal to tell the father. Yes, it is done so because they feel ashamed and guilty. But, alongside the moral angle of this shame and guilt, also lies an apprehension that the child will never be able to live a life that human beings are meant to live. This apprehension, the villagers believe, will haunt the father and make him angry. In fact, in the middle of the story, as the family of the child is pondering how to tell the father about the child's blindness, the maternal grandmother laments the fact that the boy will not be able to see the world, the love, his mother or his father. At the core of her lamentation lies a profound belief that disability has robbed her grandson of a life that everyone else is living; a life that is normal and, thus, coveted. She does not understand that it is people like her and the villagers who are responsible for not allowing the disabled human, like her grandchild, to live a 'normal' life.

Interestingly, the coda of the story shows that there is, at least, one person who accepts the child's blindness. Turns out, the father already knew about his child's condition even before he came to the village. It is true that, upon hearing of his son's blindness, he roamed around Muscat looking for a cure. But, unlike the villagers who keep on lamenting and feeling guilty about the child's disability after they fail to find a cure, the father accepts him. He brings, for his son, a pushcart the likes of which he would have brought anyway. The father's acceptance of his son's condition, if nothing else, generates hope.

Works Cited

Bagenstos, Samuel R. 2000. 'Subordination, Stigma and "Disability"'. *Virginia Law Review,* 86(3): 397–534.

Kleinman, Arthur and Rachel Hall-Clifford. 2009. 'Stigma: A Social, Cultural and Moral Process'. *Journal of Epidemiology and Community Health,* 63(6): 418–419.

Quayson, Ato. 2007. *Aesthetic Nervousness: Disability and the Crisis of Representation*. New York: Columbia University Press.

Taylor, Charles. 1989. *Sources of the Self: The Making of Modern Identity.* Cambridge, Massachusetts: Harvard University Press.

Drushti[1]

Translated from Kannada by Keerti Ramachandra

Sayyed, chatting desultorily with Podiyajja in Andu Kaka's tea shop, looked out of the window and exclaimed, 'Who's this, coming to our village at this time of the day?'

From where he was sitting, washing glasses, Andu Kaka turned to look towards the hill slope below. In the deepening dusk, the green grass had acquired a bluish hue. Crinkling his eyes, he tried to make out who the pant-clad man trudging towards his hotel was. The man was carrying a large suitcase in one hand, while a richly embroidered leather bag hung from his other shoulder. After peering into the darkness for a few seconds, Andu Kaka shrugged and returned to his washing, 'Why speculate? Everyone who comes to our village must pass this way. When he gets here we will know.'

Podiyajja was seated cross-legged on the bench, leaning against the wall. Slowly, he disentangled his legs, supported himself with a stout stick, straightened his back and shuffled to the door. He took in the whole darkening hillside through the thick lenses of his spectacles and stared at the hazy figure approaching them. He jogged his memory to match the blurred image he was seeing with the features of someone he knew. Then he turned to Sayyed beside him. 'Isn't it one of the forest rangers?' he said, his eyes twinkling.

Sayyed's heart went *dhasak* as if a tiger had pounced on him. But he quickly wiped the fear off his face and, with a calm he did not feel, stared out of the doorway. He examined the figure carefully, then, more to reassure himself, scoffed, 'Heh! Forest rangers, I believe! You pickled ambatekai, it takes you half an hour to recognise what is in front of you and now you can see what is one furlong away, is it? Nonsense!'

Only the previous week, Sayyed had succumbed to his sister's bullying and illegally cut down six tall bamboos from the neighbouring forest. He knew Podiyajja was aware of his misdeed and knowing fully well how scared Sayyed was of the forest rangers, had deliberately taunted him. That's why he had mocked him earlier. But Podiyajja was equal to Sayyed's mockery. '*Hun hun*, don't let your tongue grow so long ... When you reach my age, you won't be able to tell your wife from your mother!'

1 Translated with permission.

'You two started your great badr* battle again?' interjected Andu Kaka. 'When you have nothing better to do, this is what happens.' Looking up at Sayyed he scolded, 'Really, Sayyed, he is as old as your father. Is this any way to talk to him?' That was how Andu Kaka was. He disliked rudeness and insolence. He stayed a yard away from quarrels. And he was very helpful. It was these qualities that had made him everybody's much loved Andu Kaka. A stranger to these parts, he had come from who knows where, and opened the little tea shop in Muthuppady, and was now an integral part of Muthuppady life.

Situated on the brow of the hillock beside the national highway like a bottu, the red dot on a forehead, Andu Kaka's tea shop was not visible from the main road. However, if you walked a few yards along the path perpendicular to the tar road and turned to the right, you would see it on the hillside, sitting like a crown above a row of eight houses. Even if the panchayat record showed that this hillock was part of Muthuppady, the fact is that the village boundary starts at the lake adjoining the Jumma Masjid. The masjid was a good half-mile walk from the highway.

As mentioned earlier, no one who came to Muthuppady could bypass Andu Kaka's tea shop. The foresters had planted a subabul forest along the highway, but the trees were only waist-high still, so anyone waiting for a bus was forced to take shelter at Andu Kaka's hotel. The village postman came here to sort out his letters. It was here, too, that petty quarrels and disputes among the locals, too trivial for the time and effort of the Jamat president, were resolved by Andu Kaka under the guidance of Podiyajja. Such was Andu Kaka's standing in the community. It would not be wrong, therefore, to say that Andu Kaka's small eight-bench hotel was the second headquarter of the village Panchayat.

On his way to touching 40, had Andu Kaka so wished, he could easily have been the most sought-after prospective son-in-law in all of Muthuppady. Finding him a wife would have been as simple as boiling water for tea. There was even a murmur that Podiyajja was planning to get his second daughter married to him. But before the rumour could blossom, the resourceful Andu Kaka fixed up an alliance for her with Ismail, the contractor who supplied farm labour! After that, Podiyajja had taken to spending all his time in Andu Kaka's tea shop. Between chasing away the crows and sitting behind the munda, collecting cash from the customers, Podiyajja kept himself fully busy. Now that his elder daughter's husband had begun to send a draft every month from Muscat, Podiyajja did not have to worry about relishing fish curry and rice every day.

In a short while, as they had expected, a thin, six-foot-tall youth entered the tea shop. He set his luggage down, looked around the room, and then, seated himself on a bench. Drawing out a checkered kerchief from his pocket, he wiped the sweat on the back of his neck. As he did so, the gold watch on his left wrist glinted in the fading light. Sayyed's eyes were dazzled. He glanced at Podiyajja who was muttering something under his breath, ignoring the stranger. Sayyed's brows shot up in surprise.

Andu Kaka, sitting on his haunches in front of the fire, gave the stranger a long hard look and felt his stomach churn. As if it were a cauldron of boiling milk. His fingers became limp and the wood chips, he was feeding the fire with, fell to the ground. He took a couple of deep long breaths, composed himself and stood up. Going up to the young man he smiled and said, 'When did you arrive?' He tried to laugh to show his pleasure but it sounded false even to his ears. To hide his embarrassment, he turned to Podiyajja. 'You remember him, Podiyajja, Fakir Saab's son-in-law Sulaiman? You recognise him?'

'Why wouldn't I remember him? I see Fakir Saab's face every day, how can I forget him?' Andu Kaka was perturbed even more by Podiyajja's cryptic retort. He thought he saw an expression of mild curiosity sweep across the young man's face. Quickly he tried to distract him, 'Only one minute, Sulaiman, I will make you a first-class cup of kadak cha. When you go back to Muscat you will remember my tea.' In his anxiety, Andu Kaka's words came out in a rush.

As Andu Kaka picked up the pot of boiling water, he could see Fakir Saab's round button-eyes in the rising steam. His insides felt as if they were filled with the dregs from the pot. What devilish drama was going to be played out in Fakir Saab's house tonight? He didn't even want to imagine it. Keep the young man here somehow till the night, then escort him to the village and Fakir Saab's house, Andu Kaka told himself. He went out into the backyard, pretending to empty the tea vessel, and called out to Sayyed.

Sayyed came out with a puzzled frown on his face. Andu Kaka placed a hand on his shoulder and, in a conspiratorial whisper, said to him, 'Do something for me. Go straight to Fakir Saab's house…' he stopped, corrected himself, and continued, 'No, first go to the masjid and tell Moulvi Saab to come to Fakir Saab's house for dinner tonight. It is better to have four-five elders around when this fellow lands up there. From the masjid go straight to Fakir Saab's house and inform him. Tell him there's no need to panic, that elephants will not turn to horses ... and—one more thing—tell them, dress the child up in a nice shirt and chaddi and put him in the cradle inside. I will bring this bridegroom fellow there around dinner time. As for everything else, as Allahu desires.'

Sayyed nodded as if he understood everything clearly and, waving his newfound courage like a currency note in Andu Kaka's face, ran down the hillside.

*

The panchayat committee had been fed … Aisabi's burkha-clad photograph with the minister was published in the papers also … Shettar's orchard was raided by thieves … With this and that piece of gossip, Andu Kaka had managed to detain Sulaiman at the tea shop until it was fully dark. It had been easier than Andu Kaka had expected.

What had surprised him, though, was that Sulaiman had gone out to the top of the hill with Podiyajja, saying he wanted to watch the sunset. He had been gone for more than an hour and, when he returned, he was alone. Seeing the questioning look in Andu Kaka's eyes, Sulaiman had replied tersely, 'He went back to the masjid.' This made Andu Kaka even more uneasy.

Even as he served tea to his customers Andu Kaka kept a watchful eye on Sulaiman, monitoring the conversation between him and the customers who did not know who he was. When Sulaiman finally said, 'Shall I go now? Andu Kaka hastily replied, 'It is my responsibility to take you to your destination, is it not? You cannot walk all that distance alone, in the dark, carrying those two heavy bags, can you, tell me? If the car could take you right up to there, would you have come to my hotel in the first place, han? As soon as we hear the aazaan calling for the night prayers, we will set out. All right? Who knows if you will have time to talk to me once you are there? And I have so much to ask you. I can't even dream of your Dubayee, Muscat, can I Sulaiman? I believe Mecca–Madina are very near to there. Is that so?' In this way, Andu Kaka stretched the conversation. Regardless of whether Sulaiman replied or not, he kept sprinkling questions at him. If Sulaiman made any mention of Fakir Saab's household, Andu Kaka would shrug it off with a laugh. 'That is for another time,' he'd turn his tongue in another direction.

By the time the azaan sounded, the moon had climbed to about three arm-lengths above the horizon. Before Sulaiman could remind him it was time to go, Andu Kaka gathered the cinders from the wood fire, took them to the yard and doused the still glowing embers. He arranged the vessels neatly, washed his hands and feet and put on the shirt hanging from the peg in the wall. He opened the drawer, picked up all the cash and stuffed it into his pocket. Then he handed a torch to Sulaiman, placed the two bags outside the door and told Sulaiman to start walking. Finally, Andu Kaka released the pin of the gaslight. A thick blanket of darkness fell upon them. He pulled the door shut, locked it, then ignoring Sulaiman's protests, hefted the two bags onto his head and directed Sulaiman to walk ahead of him. Sulaiman followed the beam of the torch and Andu Kaka walked behind him with measured steps, staring thoughtfully at Sulaiman's back.

It would take about half an hour to get from the tea shop to Fakir Saab's house. They would have to go past the well by the primary school, along a mud track through the government-owned cashew plantation for about two furlongs down the masjid hill where they would cross Tyampanna Shetty's areca nut plantation. If they kept to the right of this field and walked to the end of it, the first house they would come to was Fakir Saab's.

Fakir Saab had lived in Muthuppady for the last 30 years and owned about three and a half acres of agricultural land. From trading in buffaloes at the cattle fairs in several towns like Seethaanadi, Kulkunda and others, Fakir Saab had made himself a small fortune and acquired a certain standing in the village. He had only one daughter, Zulekha. She had studied up to class V in the Kannada school and Fakir Saab was not about to marry her off to any good-for-nothing, illiterate fellow. He, who was looking for an SSLC-pass groom for his daughter, landed himself a PUC-pass son-in-law!

The boy lived with his mother in a six-rupees-a-month rented house. He had no recollection of his father. His mother had brought him up and educated him by supplying local hotels with homemade rice-flour akki rotis. The boy was her only asset. He dreamt of going to Dubai and sending money to his hard-working mother. His friends assured him that for 8,000 rupees they would get him a visa.

Fakir Saab sold off one and a quarter acres of land to Tyampanna Shetty and solved the boy's visa problem. After spending four months with Zulekha, Sulaiman deposited his mother in his father-in-law's house and flew off to Muscat. For him, a four-year contract, no leave during that period. For Zulekha, only memories.

When Zulekha delivered a baby boy, Fakir Saab distributed sweetened avalakki—beaten rice and pieces of fresh coconut—to the entire village. Within a month, a parcel arrived from Muscat, packed with brightly coloured clothes for the child. Letters, drafts, parcels followed regularly. Truly, he was a gem of a son-in-law…

*

Until they crossed the school, Andu Kaka did not separate his closed lips. With two bagsful of worries on his head, he dragged his feet mechanically behind Sulaiman. The moon had climbed high above the horizon. In the clear rain-swept sky, stars glinted sharply. The squelching sound of their feet as they walked through the slushy field mocked the silence of the two men. This path, which he had crossed hundreds of times held no terrors for Andu Kaka even on the darkest night.

But that one blazing hot afternoon when Fakir Saab had appeared at the tea shop and burst into uncontrollable tears, Andu Kaka was alarmed. 'Chhe! How could this happen?' he had exclaimed. And then, more calmly, he comforted Fakir Saab. 'Don't be afraid, Sayebre, I am there, am I not? Finding a remedy is my responsibility. Don't worry.' For two weeks, there was a lock on the tea-shop door. Andu Kaka accompanied Fakir Saab to more than 10 or 15 places. But they met with no success. They lit agarbattis at every dargah, sought the advice of innumerable astrologers, but no solution was found. Now and then Fakir Saab would get dejected and say to Andu Kaka, 'Shall we write to Sulaiman and let him know?' But Andu Kaka would find some excuse to dissuade him. 'No point rushing into anything, is there, Sayebre?' he would say. 'Let us wait for a few more days. If Allahu chooses, everything is possible. Why write to the boy and destroy his peace of mind? He won't come and perform magic, some maya mantra, will he? Horses won't become elephants, will they?' So Fakir Saab waited. He waited for three whole years. Not only did he regret not informing Sulaiman at the outset, but he was also now agonising about how he would explain the delay in revealing the truth. No matter how hard they had tried to keep it a secret, the news had spread through the whole village. Embarrassed and afraid, Fakir Saab stopped crossing his threshold. Andu Kaka however would visit Fakir Saab, offer him a few words of comfort and give the child a sweetmeat or a toy, and leave.

On that muddy slope that night, Andu Kaka's feet began to falter. Like his confidence in himself.

'When are you going back?' he asked Sulaiman, although it didn't concern him at all.

'Why?' Sulaiman countered.

'Nothing, I just asked.'

'Must I tell the truth?'

'What does that mean?' Andu Kaka was annoyed with himself. Till a couple of minutes ago, he thought the silence was oppressive. Now he wanted no conversation at all. But Sulaiman wanted to talk.

'You must be visiting my father-in-law's house often, isn't it?' Sulaiman turned around, but he couldn't see Andu Kaka's face. 'Though there is a moon it's so dark, isn't it?' Sulaiman remarked.

'Yes, very dark,' Andu Kaka replied. He was worried about how he should answer the first half of Sulaiman's question. If he told the truth, that he went there twice a week, he would have to explain why. A stream of questions would flow. Better to say, 'no', he thought. And then he remembered that he hadn't visited Fakir Saab's house for two weeks. He felt better. 'Where do I have the time, Sulaiman!' he said, calmly. 'I had gone there a month or so ago. They'd asked for 100 banana leaves, you know. When I went to deliver them, I also saw your son,' The minute the words were out of his mouth Andu Kaka bit his tongue.

'The child must have grown big now, isn't it?' Sulaiman sounded as if he was going to say something more. Andu Kaka's heart started beating faster. 'Do you know Andu Kaka,' Sulaiman was saying, 'I had written to them asking for a photograph of the child. But they never sent it to me. They made some excuse that if you take a photo, the child's life span would be reduced! Does anyone believe such things in this day and age? What do you say?'

'Really? I didn't know!' Andu Kaka replied putting more surprise into his voice than necessary. 'Had I known I would myself have taken the photographer to the house and got a picture of the child for you. Such a lovely child, you know, Sulaiman. So very fair, so lovable, you just want to pick him up and hug him. Honestly, I haven't seen such a beautiful boy anywhere else!'

When Sulaiman asked most casually, 'Are you telling me the truth?', Andu Kaka was indignant. 'What do you think? If I were telling a lie, my eyes would be deceiving me, wouldn't they?' His words, though true sounded like an exaggeration. They had almost reached the beginning of the cashew plantation. Somewhere in the distance, a jackal was howling. It was joined by many voices from different directions. The eerie sounds in the pitch blackness might scare Sulaiman, thought Andu Kaka, so he began to grope for words to engage him in conversation.

But before he could speak, Sulaiman asked, 'Why didn't you ever get married?'

The question was so unexpected, it startled Andu Kaka. He had to say something, so he laughed and said, 'Who will give me their daughter, Sulaiman? What do I have? A house, land, property?'

'What do I have Kaka? I'm also just like you.'

'Chhe .. chhe … what are you saying, Sulaiman? You are a Muscat-dweller. You spend as much money on one cup of tea as I earn after washing glasses for a whole year. People go looking for boys like you, you know.'

'They must be regretting it now, isn't it?'

'Why? What great tragedy has befallen that they should do that?' Andu Kaka panicked.

Sulaiman didn't seem keen to answer Andu Kaka's question.

Now that they had entered the cashew-nut grove, they could walk side by side. Two pairs of feet marched to the *kirr kirr* rhythm of the chirping crickets, crunching dry leaves as they went along. Staggering under the burden of his worries, Andu Kaka's legs felt leaden. His anxious eyes strained to catch a glimpse of Tyampanna Shetty's areca plantation. Somehow he dragged himself to the end of the cashew-nut grove. In the distance, he could see the lights from Shetty's house twinkling like stars. Suddenly, Andu Kaka felt exhausted. His head throbbed.

'What have you got in your bags, Sulaiman?' he grumbled, as he slid the bags off his head and squatted on the overground roots of the jackfruit tree. 'Have you filled them with iron bars or what? I need to catch my breath before going on.' Even if Sulaiman, who was a few steps ahead, was annoyed by Andu Kaka's sudden protest, he did not show it. He came back, spread his towel on the thick black grass and sat down opposite Andu Kaka. The dense foliage of the tall-as-ten-men jackfruit tree had hidden the moon so they couldn't see each other's faces. The darkness was fearsome. Andu Kaka was breathing heavily. Sulaiman started absently throwing the pebbles he had gathered in his right fist, one by one, into the jungle slope. An owl flew out flapping its wings and sailed off towards Fakir Saab's house.

Andu Kaka shut his eyes and opened the door to a carefully kept secret. 'Look Sulaiman, I want to tell you something,' he said. Making up a story as he went along, Andu Kaka clutched at words as a drowning man would at a straw. But he didn't want to see Sulaiman's reaction to his words so he kept his eyes closed.

*

When Sayyed neared Fakir Saab's house, he found several people gathered there. It looked as if all the eggs of grief had broken upon the chavadi. He could hear Fakir Saab's wife wailing even as he turned the corner of the garden wall. Sayyed was not unfamiliar with this house. As a toddler, he had been fed by Fakir Saab's wife Ummatumma. As he grew older, he ran small errands for her since she had no son to do it. Now that Saab went out less and less, Sayyed's responsibilities had also multiplied.

'No need for you all to weep and wail,' he burst out as he stepped into the courtyard, gasping for breath. 'Andu Kaka says he will sort everything out and only then bring him here.' Sayyed made this announcement loudly, several times, but the people gathered at the chavadi were too engrossed in squabbling and wailing to pay attention to him. Fakir Saab was sitting on the cot hugging his knees, trying desperately to silence his wife. But all the pent-up words which Ummatumma had stored within herself found an outlet and gushed out in an endless stream of accusation and acrimony to drown Fakir Saab.

'As for you, a woman's opinion is worth the mud under your feet. Look what's happened now. With what face can we ask him to come inside? What great joy must he come home to? Hadn't I told you a hundred times? Hadn't I begged you, pleaded with you…? But for you, that Andu Kaka's advice was more precious than my tears? What does he know of a woman's pain, he has no wife, no family? Yet, you heeded his words. Write him a letter, we said to you, but did you listen? Instead, you went from village to town to city … and what purpose did it serve? Not even one-quarter worth of success. You came back empty-handed.'

'Enough, Ummatumma, I beg of you, I will hold your feet … be quiet for a while,' said an exasperated Fakir Saab, slapping his hands over his ears. 'Assuming that I had written him a letter. Had he gone to the tea shop for a cup of cha that he would come running back as soon as he received it? Do you know how much a return ticket costs? Ten thousand rupees! All right, even if he did come, say. What great miracle would he have worked? And then, was I just sitting here blowing into the fire? He must be thinking we are all decking ourselves in gold ornaments with the money he sends every month. Have I got myself even one glass of single cha in the last two and a half years? Most of the cash went in bus fare, didn't it?'

Ummatumma got even more fierce in her accusations. 'Whatever I say you bring it down to money, you cannot think of anything else. It's been so long. Did anyone even bother to cuddle the child? It is not destined to see its mother's face. Even the father is not near it. He of course has gone to collect gold bricks. Is my daughter a piece of stone? Should she put all the money he sends in a box and offer duas to Allah? Nothing we say matters one bit to all you men.'

'Ummatumma, let it be … why are you putting him under the grinding stone like this?' Sulaiman's mother, Zainamma said, trying to comfort Ummatumma. 'It's all over and done, isn't it?' she said thickly. 'All in all, it is a defeat for me. I was thrown into this house, no! Even if I wanted to go to some corner and die, there's this child, no!'

Too emotional to continue, Zainamma stuffed her sari pallu into her mouth and rushed into the inner room.

Poor Fakir Saab! Only when Podiyajja and Moulvisaab stepped into the chavadi, did he get his breath back. As soon as she saw the two men, Ummatumma drew her sari over her head and disappeared behind the curtain. From the steps leading to the courtyard, Sayyed stared at the street corner, waiting for Andu Kaka to appear.

The Moulvisaab was apprised of everything, so there was no need for Fakir Saab to say anything. As for Podiyajja, he sat there staring at the ceiling, completely detached from his surroundings. For almost 10 minutes, the only sound in the courtyard was the *phuk phuk phuk* of the petromax lamp, the gaslight.

As soon as Sayyed saw the beam of the torch at the bend in the road, he dashed out. He took the load off Andu Kaka's head and carried the bags to the main entrance of the house. Fakir Saab almost stopped breathing. His head hung low on his chest and all he could see in the yellow light of the lamp were two pairs of feet step into the courtyard and approach him. His eyes refused to rise.

Andu Kaka brought out a wooden chair which was lying by the inner door, placed it near the suitcase and told Sulaiman to sit down. Sulaiman paid his respects to Moulvisaab, pulled the bags closer to him and his seat. Pushing Fakir Saab's legs aside Andu Kaka made some space for his backside on the cot. Podiyajja gave everyone a long, measured look, took off his spectacles, put them in his pocket, leaned back against the wall and closed his eyes. In no time at all, he was dozing. Sulaiman watched the curtains on the inner door billowing. After a few minutes, he drew the big bag towards himself and started drumming his fingers on it.

'Everything about this place is the same as it was when I left for Muscat,' he thought as he looked around. Only, the green colour slapped on the walls at the time of the wedding had acquired a film of soot, making it look bluish. The glass bead ornament on the door frame with 'Welcome' woven into it, had turned black with grime. The only thing that looked new in the chavadi was the crisp white clothes Moulvisaab was wearing.

Andu Kaka began to squirm and fidget as if he was sitting on a hot pan. He hadn't been so agitated even when he had shut his eyes tight, afraid to confront the truth when he and Sulaiman had walked through the cashew plantation, the darkness made thicker by the jackfruit tree. He was expecting Sulaiman, who had maintained a grim silence so far, to explode any minute now. Just watching him calmly playing with the key of the strapped suitcase made his blood run cold.

The silence of the graveyard was broken with a sudden snap of the suitcase latch. Addressing them all Sulaiman said, 'Will somebody bring the child out?' All the blood left Fakir Saab's face. He placed his hand on Andu Kaka's thigh and silent tears began to flow down his cheeks. Andu Kaka shook his head helplessly.

Just then Ummatumma appeared in the doorway of the inner room, a baby nestling against her neck. The sight of that chubby little back sent waves of alarm through the chavadi. Not knowing what to do next, Ummatumma came out and stood leaning against the wall next to the pillar.

Sulaiman slowly opened the suitcase. All eyes rested on his dancing fingers. One by one, he took out different shaped pieces of shiny steel and as he put them down they made a musical *khun khun* sound. Carefully he began to put the pieces together. First, he made a square frame. To it, he attached four wheels. Andu Kaka's heart was flapping about as he watched Sulaiman engrossed in the task.

In a short while, before their very eyes, a beautiful little pushcart took shape. It stood in the centre of the chavadi in all its gleaming glory! Fixed on the black canvas seat was a soft red cushion. Behind it were attached two vertical handles. Sulaiman stood up and moved the pushcart back and forth to test it. As it moved, the little golden bells on the wheels tinkled merrily. Shifting his gaze away from the cart to his right, Sulaiman walked straight towards his mother-in-law. He plucked the child from her arms as he would a flower, and lowered it gently onto the seat of the pushcart. Alarmed by the unfamiliar touch, the child let out a piercing shriek. Poor Sulaiman was startled. He didn't know what to do. Just then, Zulekha shot out of the inner room, shoved past Sulaiman, grabbed the screaming child and rushed inside. Sulaiman collapsed into the chair as if struck by lightning, his face pale.

Andu Kaka leapt to his feet, grabbed Sulaiman by the shoulders and shaking him asked, 'So … So … Er, so you knew all along?'

Gently disengaging Andu Kaka's hands and taking them into his own, Sulaiman said softly, 'Yes, Andu Kaka, I got the news two months ago from Podiyajja's son-in-law in Muscat. Because of some nerve disorder, the child will never be able to see. Even the doctors in Muscat said nothing can be done about it. There is no cure.'

Sulaiman stood up, placed his hand on Andu Kaka's shoulder, pressed it lightly and whispered, 'Thanks.' He shook his legs out as if to get the strength back in them, walked to the billowing curtains and disappeared behind them. Andu Kaka turned around to stare at Podiyajja. His eyes were full of admiration and respect for the old man.

With an embarrassed laugh, he said, 'Whoever says you cannot see must have chappals made out of their tongues!'

'Tell that to your Sayyed,' retorted Podiyajja. He then took his spectacles out of his pocket, wiped them on his shirt and carefully placed them on his nose.

GLOSSARY

Aein-aein	sounds of a baby crying
Agarbatti	incense stick
Agyan	ignorance; used as an antonym for gyan
Alvida	last Friday of Ramzan
Akki-rotti	a type of bread
Ambatekai	hog plum
Amma	mother
Apanjrapol	animal shelter
Appa	father
Avalkshanam	unpleasing
Ayah	nurse
Azaan	call for namaz
Ba	word in Gujrati to address elder women
Baba	a godman
Badr	the first holy war between believers and non-believers in Islamic history
Baisakh	a month of the Hindu calendar coinciding roughly with April of the English calendar
Baithak	an outer room in a traditional north-Indian house, to host guest
Beta	son, also used as an endearing word by elders
Bhuvas	quack healers/witch doctors
Biswakarma	An Odiya god
Bon	sister (in some Gujrati dialects)
Chaddar	shawls
Chaddi	underwear or shorts depending on the context
Chadra	a long waist-wrap cloth for men
Chappal	sandals
Chaturmas	the holy period of the four months from July to October; chatur means four and mas means month
Chavadi	booth, a place for people to meet
Chhod Do Yaar	let it be friend
Chironji	edible seeds of a deciduous tree, used as a spice in India
Chillum	a pipe to smoke tobacco/hashish/marijuana in
Chowkdi	a squat

Chunari/Chunni	a piece of stole-like cloth that women wear above their blouses or around their head
Dada	an elder brother; also a sound that babies make
Dal	a dish made with lentils and water
Domni	a woman from the Dom caste, they are known for their dances
Dudhu	milk, primarily used by and/or for babies and children
Eidi	money given by elders on Eid
Ekantha	peace
Faakas	a fast without prayers and therefore pointless; usually used in a derogatory sense to dismiss someone's fast as mere starvation
Fakir	Muslim ascetics who live on alms
Farz Namaz	the mandatory prayers to be offered five times a day
Fitra	the charity that must be given to the poor by every Muslim at the end of the holy month of Ramzan
Ganapati	God Ganesha
Ghee	clarified butter
Gond	acacia gum; used as an edible item
Gungiya	mute
Gyan	knowledge
Halwaayi	one who runs a confectionary or a sweets shop
Happa	sounds of a baby; usually made while playing
Haramzadi	a swear word in Hindi
Harira	caudle
Ilanje	cardamom
Jalebi	a type of Indian sweet made by dipping coiled batter in sugar syrup
Jamat	an Islamic congregation
Jnana	life force
Jutti	traditional Punjabi shoe made from leather and embroidered with intricate patterns
Kaaka	a little child; commonly used for the young heir of a Punjabi family
Kadak Cha	strong tea
Kaka	paternal uncle; used as a respectful call sign for elders as well
Kaki	paternal aunt; used as a respectful call sign for elders as well
Kardhan	ornamental girdle
Kavya	poesy
Kheer	a sweet dish usually made out of rice, milk and jaggery

Kheer-Puri	fried bread served with kheer
Kund	a holy pond
Kunje	a kid
Lakshmi-Narayana	a Hindu goddess and god
Lohini sagai	ties of blood
Ma	mother
Maasi/Mausi	maternal aunt
Magshar	months in the Hindu calendar that coincide with November and December of the English calendar
Maiya	mother; also used endearingly for elder women
Mandap	a tent erected in celebration or an event
Mari atha	pox
Maya Mantra	magical chant
Monal	a type of pheasant
Moulvi Saab	an Islamic priest
Multani Mitti	Fuller's Earth; known for its cosmetic uses
Nagadawala	nagada is a type of drum usually played on both ends; nagadawala is the drummer
Namaz	the ritual Islamic prayers that must be mandatorily performed five times a day by all Muslims
Neem	*Azadirachta Indica*; trees found in India and Myanmar known for their medicinal properties
Nyaya	law/justice
Paan	betel leaf, usually chewed with lime and tobacco
Panchayat	a village council
Pillai	used to denote a child or a Malayali caste
Poda	a Malayalam informal retort to ask someone to either stop doing what they are doing or call someone in exclamation
Prasad	eatable offering to a god; usually made with sweets and distributed among devotees after being offered to a deity
Qalma	the Muslim confession of faith
Ramzan	The 9th month of the Islamic calendar lasting 30 days. During the month, strict fasting is observed from sunrise to sunset.
Randi	a derogatory term for a prostitute
Rickshawala	the driver of a rickshaw
Risis	saints
Saale	an abusive Hindi slang

Sanyasi	an ascetic
Sardar Bahadur	an order of merit in British India
Sehri	the pre-dawn meal consumed by Muslims before the fast
Seth	a term by which the ostensible rich are called
Sherwani	a long coat-like garment worn in the Indian subcontinent, especially amongst Muslims
Shilajit	a sticky substance found in the Himalayas, it is known for its medicinal properties.
Shishya	disciple
Shuklapaksha	dates when the moon waxes
Subabul	river tamarind
Taraabi	special prayers offered at night during the month of Ramzan to recite the Qur'an
Tammi	an endearing call sign for an adult woman
Tehsil	an administrative area, an office.
Tejasvi	majestic
Tilla	a shiny thread used for embroidery
Tithi	date, usually auspicious
Tulasi	basil, considered sacred in Hindu religious tradition
Valonaa	a butter churn.
Vyakaran	grammar.
Vedanta	the study of Vedas
Vuzu	ablution ritual before the prayers
Wan	a small tree or shrub with a crooked trunk
Zaildaar	a feudal title; in charge of a zail, a rural administrative unit extending between 20 and 40 villages in British Punjab
Zenana	a part of the house to seclude women from the world

INDEX

ABOUT THE EDITORS

Someshwar Sati

Someshwar Sati is an Associate Professor of English at Kirori Mal College, Delhi University. He has been singularly responsible for the creation of multiple Disability Studies courses in the university and the conduction of multiple disability-centric programmes. He is currently the chairperson of the Indian Disability Studies Collective. His publications include *Disability in Translation: The Indian Experience* with G.J.V. Prasad (2019), and two volumes of *Warble of Postcolonial Voices* (2016). He is also the recipient of the 2016 C.D. Narasimhaiah Prize.

G.J.V. Prasad

G.J.V. Prasad, formerly Professor of English at Jawaharlal Nehru University, is a poet, novelist and translator. His teachings and research have focused on Indian English literature, modern drama and translation. His recent publications include four edited volumes—*Violets in a Crucible: Translating the Orient* co-edited with Madhu Benoit and Susan Blattes (2019), *India in Translation Translation in India* (2019), *Disability in Translation: The Indian Experience* co-edited with Someshwar Sati (2019) and *Reading Dalit: Essays on Literary Representations* (2020—and a short monograph on Khushwant Singh. His latest publication is a translation of Ambai's stories, *A Red-Necked Green Bird* (2021).

Ritwick Bhattacharjee

Ritwick Bhattacharjee is an Assistant Professor of English at the Sri Guru Tegh Bahadur Khalsa College, Delhi University. His research has been located around fantasy, philosophy, phenomenology, horror fiction, science fiction, Indian English novels and Disability Studies. He has done his MPhil from Delhi University and written a thesis on the fantastic phenomenology of Stephen King's *The Dark Tower* series. He is the author of *Humanity's Strings: Being, Pessimism, and Fantasy* (2020) and co-editor for *What Makes It Pop? An Introduction to Studies in Popular Fictions* with Srinjoyee Dutta (2020) and *Horror Fiction in the Global South: Cultures, Narratives, and Representation* with Saikat Ghosh (2021). He has been awarded the 2020 Prof. Meenakshi Mukherjee Memorial award for his essay titled 'Politics of Translation:

Disability, Language, and the In-between', published in the book *Disability in Translation: The Indian Experience*. He is also the treasurer of the Indian Disability Studies Collective.

ABOUT THE AUTHORS

Bolwar Mahamad Kunhi

The credit for introducing Kannada readers to the ethos of the Muslim community goes to Bolwar Mahamad Kunhi. Primarily through his short stories set in the small imaginary town of Muthuppady in the Karavali region of Dakshina Kannada, he has highlighted the syncretic culture, the mutual respect, affection and inter-dependence of the Hindu (80 per cent) and Muslim (20 per cent) communities. His story 'The Fish Seller' is one of the finest examples of this. It is interesting to note that the Byari or Beary community, that is portrayed in his works, has its own officially recognised dialect, which is mostly Malayalam mixed with Urdu, Kannada, Tulu and Tamil. This is evident in the speech of his characters, though Bolwar writes in standard Kannada.

This extremely sensitive, deeply insightful and gentle writer says he never thought, even in his dreams, that he would become a writer! His first short story came out of a challenge when a writer-friend declared that writing stories was not child's play. Later, at a function to felicitate Bolwar, the same friend took credit for making Bolwar a writer!

Bolwar has edited *Tattu Chappale Putta Magu*, one of the finest collections of 100 poems for children, *Santammanna*, an anthology of 40-odd illustrated poems and 12 outstanding children's plays. For his book, *Paapu Gandhi Bapu Gandhi Aada Kathe,* '...one of the best books on Mahatma Gandhi for children and adults,' (U.R. Ananthamurthy), he received the Sahitya Akademi award in 2010.

In 2016, the Sahitya Akademi was awarded to him a second time, for *Swatantrada Ota* (The Run for Freedom), a novel that grew out of a humorous short story he had written 20 years earlier—*Ondu Tunda Gode* (A Piece of Wall). His later work, *Odir*, was perhaps the first historic account of the Prophet Muhammad's life. The book has been very well received. Bolwar compliments the readers of Kannada literature and attributes the success of this work to their maturity. Bolwar says he was always concerned about the women of the past—How did they express their feelings? How were their opinions formed and what value did they have? How did they assert their rights? Exercise their preferences? To delve into these issues, he embarked on a novel *Umma* inspired by the life of Aisha, the young wife of the Prophet. Bolwar hopes that *Umma* is read with the same spirit as the stories of Sita, Savitri, Ahalya, Tara and Mandodari.

For his contribution to Kannada literature, Bolwar has received almost all the major awards, from the Sahitya Akademi, Central Sahitya Akademi, the Bala Sahitya Puraskar and other prestigious institutions. Bolwar, a gold medallist in Kannada literature from Mysore University, retired as the Chief Manager Syndicate Bank, Bengaluru. He lives in Bengaluru with his family.

E. Santosh Kumar

Among the leading writers in Malayalam today, E. Santhosh Kumar stands out as a contributor to the genres of novels, novella, short story and children's literature. He has won numerous awards, including the prestigious Kerala Sahitya Akademi award for best novel for his work *Andhakaranazhy* in 2012. Born in 1969 in Pattikkadu, Kerala, he studied in the Government High School Pattikkadu, Sree Kerala Varma College, Trichur and St Thomas College, Trichur. His first published short story is 'Galapagos'. He won his first Sahitya Akademi award in 2006 for *Chavukali*, a collection of short stories. In 2011, he also won an award for the best children's novel, instituted by the Kerala State Children's Literature Institute, for his *Kakkara Desathe Urumbukal*.

Attracted to literature from a very early age, E. Santhosh Kumar has established his unique status among the new generation of littérateurs with his craft and powerful imagery and his inimitable ability to engage the readers' mind with startling and panoramic visuals. Santhosh Kumar contemplates new characters in each of his stories for it is admittedly the urge to imagine a new world that keeps him going as an inspired writer. The conversations one listens to, a peculiar scene one encounters or a unique person that one comes into contact with, often act as catalysts leading to a moment of realisation and an idea that assumes the shape of a story for the writer. In Santhosh Kumar's own words, 'If you can imagine the writer's mind as a fully loaded gun, these circumstances act as a trigger; but no more than that. You've to load the gun beforehand.' Santhosh Kumar admits to being inspired to write the story 'Moonnu Andhanmar Anaye Vivarikkunnu' after contemplating Pieter Bruegel's painting 'The Blind Leading the Blind'. All popular proverbs about the blind manifest the hegemony of the world of the sighted. As against this, 'Moonnu Andhanmar...' steps out of the closet to expose the visual capability of the sighted as merely a minuscule segment of the spectrum of perception beyond which there is an entire universe. The stunning insight of the blind protagonist(s) poses a kaleidoscopic challenge to the limited imagination and understanding of the sighted world. Hence, what matters is not sight, but insight.

Gurdial Singh

Gurdial Singh began his writing career in 1957 with a short story titled 'Bhaganwale'. It is only with the publication of his novel *Marhi Da Deeva* that he became a well-known Punjabi author. His first novel was also adapted into a film of the same name in 1989 by Surinder Singh. His most acclaimed novel *Anhe Ghore Da Daan* was also adapted into a film by Gurvinder Singh. Before his demise in 2016, Gurdial Singh was awarded the Padma Shri in 1998 and the Jnanpith Award in 1999.

Ishwar Petlikar

Ishwar Motibhai Patel (1916–1983), better known by his *nom de plume* Ishwar Petlikar was a journalist, school teacher, storyteller, essayist, novelist, social chronicler and reformist who wrote in Gujarati. Rural concerns, the web of urban entanglement, social and cultural issues and the spirit of social reform permeate his works. He was a prolific writer and wrote more than 40 books. In his novels and novellas, he offers a slice of the life of those at the margins of society, the depraved, the deprived and the oppressed. His keen eye records the minutest of details of village life, the manners and mores and his sensitive depiction of their deprivations, their trials and tribulations accord him a prime position in the terrain of Gujarati literature. *Bhavsagar* (1951), considered his best novel, poignantly etches out the inner workings of the mind of a long-suffering woman in a harshly orthodox rural mileu. The simple aphorisms and sayings, the idioms and phrases that echo in the villages make for the colloquial simplicity of his language and account for his popularity as a writer. 'Lohini Sagai', his most popular short story, was in 1980 made into a Gujarati film of the same name. Besides his novels and four novella collections, he also has four biographical works and several essays.

He was a fearless and prolific journalist and wrote hundreds of columns and articles in various dailies and journals including *Loknaad*, *Nirikshak*, *Stree*, *Gujarat Samachar* and *Sandesh*. He edited several magazines and the periodical, *Patidar*, which urged for social reform in the Gujarat of his time.

Kalindi Charan Panigrahi

Kalindi Charan Panigrahi (1901–1991) is one of the foremost writers of 20th-century Odia literature who has not left any department untouched. Panigrahi is renowned for his epoch-making novel *Matira Manisha* (1931) which has run into several editions and has been translated into several languages. It was made into a movie by Mrinal Sen in 1966, which won the national award as the best film of the year.

Panigrahi came to the limelight when he was still a student of Ravenshaw College for a literary group called 'Sabuja Sahitya Samiti' he created along with his friends, Annada Shankar Ray, Baikuntha Nath Patnaik, Sharat Chandra Mukherjee and Harihar Mohapatra. 'Mansara Bilapa', one of his very well-known short stories, has been dramatised several times and has been made into a movie in 1972. *Matira Manisha* has been translated into English by Lila Ray (*A House Undivided*, 1973) and by Bikram Das (*Born of the Soil*, 2016). In 1971, he was bestowed with the Fellowship of Sahitya Akademi and honoured by the Government of India with Padma Bhushan. In 1976, Sambalpur University conferred on him DLitt *honoris causa*. Some of his poems like 'Gandharira Ashirvada' ('The Blessing of Gandhari') have become classics of sorts.

Panigrahi's works include *Amara Chita* (1932), *Muktagadara Kshudha* (1932), *Luhara Manisha* (1947) and *Ajira Manisha* (1957) [novels]; 'Mo Kathati Sari Nahin', 'Dwadashi, Shesharashmi', 'Rashiphala', 'Sagarika' [short stories]; 'Chhuritie Loda', 'Mane Nahin', 'Mahadeepa', 'Kshanika Satya', 'Mo Kabita' [anthologies of poems]; *Priyadasshi, Soumya, Padmini* [plays]; 'Sahityika', 'Netrutwa o Netrutwa', 'Prabandha Sahitya', 'Sahitya Sanchayana', 'Samayika Sahitya Sameekshya' [essays/criticism]; *Ange Jaha Nibhaichhi* [autobiography], *Dinalipi* [diary], *Gali Aili Russ Germany* [travel writing]. His autobiography was rendered in Hindi by Pt Shankar Dayal Sharma who later became the President of India. Besides these, he also wrote in English: *Glimpses on Art and Literature: Orissa* (1976) and edited periodicals like *The Mayurbhanj Chronicle*.

Panigrahi was the elder brother of Bhagabati Charan Panigrahi, the founder of the Communist Party in Odisha and the harbinger of the Progressive Writers Movement in Odia literature. His daughter ,Nandini Satapathy (1931–2006), an eminent writer and journalist, was a minister under Prime Minister Indira Gandhi and later the Chief Minister of Odisha (1972–1976).

The included story, originally titled 'Pangu', was probably written in the late 1940s and later included in his short story collection *Rashiphala*.

Khalid Jawed

Khalid Jawed is a leading contemporary novelist and short-story writer in Urdu. He teaches in the Department of Urdu at Jamia Milia Islamia, New Delhi. As a literary critic, his academic interventions are mainly focused on exploring the relationship between literature and philosophy. As a writer, his novels *Maut Ki Kitaab* and *Namatkhaana* as well as his short story collection titled *Aakhri Daawat* have been well-received in the Indian subcontinent where his experiments with magic realism have been applauded for their coherence and lucidity.

Madhavi Gharpure

Madhavi Gharpure is a lecturer in Marathi literature. She is the author of two anthologies of short stories. *Shwaasani Itar Katha* was first published in 2005. Her second volume of stories *Davabindu* was published in 2015.

Mahadevi Varma

Mahadevi Varma (1907–1987) was a renowned poet, essayist and critic. Considered one of the premiere writers of the Romantic period in Hindi Literature, she was the recipient of the prestigious Jnanpith Award for her poetry in 1982, the Padma Bhushan in 1956 and the Padma Vibhushan, posthumously, in 1988. Her works are marked by a tender, emotional tone. Her prose writings carry a spirited critique of societal norms and stigma against the oppressed, voiceless women and men. One of her most significant contributions to society is in the area of women's education. She helped establish, and later headed, Prayag Women's College in Allahabad.

Manik Bandyopadhyay

Manik Bandyopadhyay was born on 19 May 1908 in Santhal Pargana, West Bengal. His real name was Prabodh Kumar Bandyopadhyay, Manik was his nickname. His family was from Dhaka, Bangladesh. He was the fifth son of his parents, Harikar Bandyopadhyay and Niroda Devi. Harikar was a government employee and he had to travel all around undivided Bengal. Manik Bandyopadhyay's childhood was spent seeing and learning about every aspect of life in rural Bengal. His acquaintance with the hardships of life and intricacies of relationships made him represent these than romanticise village life like many of his contemporaries did.

After finishing his Matriculation in 1926 from Midnapore, Manik Bandyopadhyay moved on to complete his ISC Examination from Wellesylan Mission College in Bankura. He went to Presidency College, Calcutta, for his BSc course, which he did not complete. He joined the Mymensingh Teacher's Training School as its headmaster. He became the assistant editor of *Bangoshree* in the year 1937. He married in Vikrampur, Dhaka.

He is considered one of the leading figures of modern Bangla fiction. His works deal with the harsh realities of human life. In a short lifespan of 48 years, plagued simultaneously by illness and financial crisis, he produced 36 novels and 177 short stories. His important works include *Padma Nadir Majhi* (1936), *Putul Nacher Itikatha* (1936), *Shahartali* (1941) and *Chatushkone* (1948). His works also deal with complicated human psychology.

Medha Trivedi

Medha Trivedi is a Mumbai-based writer who is a commerce and law graduate from South Gujarat University. She writes short stories and articles mainly in her mother tongue, Gujarati. She has published two collections of short stories, *Prathamakshar* (2010) and *Aksharbeej* (2014). She has also written a biographical novel, *Bharat Ratna Sthapati: Sardar Vallabhai Patel* (2016). All her books have been published by Navbharat Prakashan, Mumbai. Her short stories and articles have also been regularly published in Gujarati magazines and the biographical novel on Sardar Patel was serialised in the Gujarati newspapers, *Janmabhoomi* (Mumbai), *Phoolchhab* (Rajkot) and *Kutchmitra* (Bhuj) simultaneously in 2016.

P. Padmarajan

P Padmarajan (1945–1991) is one of the most celebrated writers of Malayalam literature and cinema. Even though he bagged his first Sahitya Akademi award for his very first novel, *Nakshatrangale Kaaval* in 1971 (when he was just 26), and went on to write several critically acclaimed novels and short stories, it needs to be underscored that his brilliance as a scriptwriter and moviemaker overshadowed his achievement as a writer. Some of his notable novels are *Itha Ivide Vare, Udakappola, Kallan Pavithran, Peruvazhiyambalam* and *Prathimayum Rajakumariyum*. Many of his scripts are based on his short stories and novels, *Thakara, Kariyilakkaattu Pole, Itha Ivide Vare* and *Aparan* being just a few. Padmarajan teamed up with Bharathan to create some of the most popular movies in Malayalam which are generally termed the Middle cinema. These movies dealt with sexuality, relationships and disability which touched a chord with the masses but used innovative techniques and aesthetic styles to present the story.

Padmarajan's works are known for their psychological detailing and his adept depiction of complex relationships. His characters are from around him, but his sensitive observation is inclusive of the marginalised. They are at some level most relatable but, very often, they are caught up in the most unusual of circumstances. These circumstances bring out the best and the worst, and the unexpected. The vicissitudes, ironies, inequalities and existential complexity of life are pitted against a human character that sometimes tides over challenges but also many times gets crushed under the weight of the adversities. This quality of his stories raises them to the level of tragedy where misery leads to wisdom. Thakara's story is a brilliant example of Padmarajan's intricate characterisation, his perceptive sensitivity, his narrative excellence and his tragic vision.

Raamaa Chandramouli

Prof. Raamaa Chandramouli born on 8 August 1950 is a post-graduate in mechanical engineering. A recipient of the Rashtrapati Award as the Best Teacher, he has authored six textbooks for mechanical engineering students. Chandramouli, who published his first story as a 13-year-old, is an eminent poet in Telugu known for his surreal verse. He is also a short-story writer, a literary critic and a novelist. His works are highly valued by critics and book lovers for the poetic prose and unique experimentation with language, social concerns and reflections of the contemporary society that he authentically represents both in his fiction as well as poetry. He has 50 published books which include more than 305 short stories, 30 novels, 10 anthologies of Telugu poetry and 4 anthologies of Telugu literary essays and also a regular reviewer of Telugu works for *India Today's* Telugu version. He has penned stories and dialogues for five Telugu movies. Several of his works are translated into English, Hindi, Tamil, Malayalam and Bengali. He has participated as an Indian delegate at the '22nd' World Congress of Poets' in Greece in 2011 and Taiwan in 2016. He is a recipient of the Swarna Nandi Puraskaram from the Government of Andhra Pradesh (2011), the Andhra Pradesh Sahitya Akademi Award 1984, the Telugu University Kavitha Purskaram (2007), the Cinare Kavitha Puraskaram (2008), Kolakaloori Bhaageeradhi Kavitha Puraskaram (2012), Dr Avansta Somasunder Kavitha Puraskaram (2012), Citizen Extraordinaire Leadership Award (2007–2008) to name a few.

Rabindranath Tagore

Rabindranath Tagore (1861–1941) is unarguably one of the most influential figures of India. He was born into an affluent Brahmo family. Although he did not receive any formal education, he was well-versed in Sanskrit, Bengali and English literature, and was also acquainted with French and German languages. He wrote during the late 19th and early 20th centuries. A multifaceted personality, Tagore was a creative writer and a critical thinker. In a remarkably prolific literary life, he wrote poems, plays, essays, short stories, novels and songs. His literary works deal with love and nature, and subsequently with mysticism and the divine, and are characterised by a strong humanist ethos. His philosophical musings and social thought also permeate the other genres he wrote in. Tagore was also a painter and an actor, as well as a political thinker and educationist. He founded the Visva Bharati University at Santiniketan and a rural centre at Sriniketan. Tagore was awarded the Noble Prize for literature in 1913 for *Gitanjali.*

Rashid Jahan

Rashid Jahan (1905–1952) was a writer of short stories and radio plays. Rashid Jahan was known, first infamously and later lovingly, as 'Angareywali' because of her critical role in the ground-breaking Urdu writing anthology *Angarey* that was published in 1932. The anthology, widely considered as the precursor to the Progressive Writers Movement, consists of the writings of three other writers, all men, Sajjad Zaheer, Ahmad Ali and Mahmud Zaffar, which probably explains why only Jahan gained the epithet. Though the story translated here is not from the anthology, it registers Rashid Jahan's expression of controlled anger, a recurring emotion in her work, that responds to social injustices she observed and recorded in her writing. Born in Aligarh in 1905, Rashid was the oldest of five children in a family that was deeply invested in women's education in India given that her father was responsible for establishing the Women's College at Aligarh Muslim University. A doctor by profession, Jahan was a vigilant documenter of the lives of women who surrounded her, thus, making perspicuous structural inequities by vividly portraying anecdotal, incidental and rebellious aspects of their lives. Rashid Jahan's commitment to communist politics is embedded in her short stories and plays which underscore the peculiar nature of social disadvantages and advantages that are inextricably related to people's class locations. At a time when colonialism and the resistance to it preoccupied writers and thinkers of pre-Partition India, the attention to class differences emerged as a refreshing literary feature. Rashid Jahan's work came to be included within the oeuvre of feminist writing only belatedly when her writing received recognition for its literary explorations of Muslim women's lives at a time when colonialism and communalism had successfully silenced any discourse of hardships of women who belonged to a minority community. Remembered as the first 'angry young woman' of Urdu literary circles, Rashid Jahan is widely celebrated today for being the inspiration behind Ismat Chugtai. She died in 1952 in Moscow where she had gone for treatment after having been diagnosed with cancer in 1950 in Bombay. Rashid Jahan was 47 years old. She was keen that the knowledge of her disease be used for further medical research and insisted that the doctors at the Kremlin Hospital in Moscow treat her as a colleague as well as a patient. Fittingly, the tombstone on Rashid Jahan's grave in Moscow reads 'Communist Doctor and Writer'.

Sachidanand Hiranandan Vatsyayan

Sachidanand Hiranandan Vatsyayan or as he is popularly known, Ajnyeya, is a revolutionary writer of modern Hindi drama, poetry, novels and stories primarily because of his instrumental role in the introduction of the *Nayi Kavita* (New Poetry) and *Prayog* (Experimental) movements of Hindi literature. He has also been the editor of *Saptaks*, a literary series and several newspapers like *Sainik* (1936), *Vishal Bharat* (1936) and *Prateek* (1947) before becoming the founding editor of *Dinaman* of the Times of India Group in 1965.

Ajnyeya was born on 7 March 1911. His father Hirananda Shastri was an archaeologist. In the beginning, Ajnyeya was taught Hindi, English, Persian, Bengali and History at home. Subsequently, he learnt Tamil and Sanskrit from a monastery in Udupi. He passed his intermediate from the Madras Christian College in 1927 with Maths, Physics and Sanskrit as his major. Thereafter, he completed his BSc in Industrial Science from Forman Christian College, Lahore, in 1929. He shifted his career for his post-graduation and joined MA in English. Before he could finish his MA, however, he became involved in the dissident actions of the Indian freedom movement with Bhagat Singh, Lala Lajpat Rai, Chandrashekhar Azad, Sukhdev and Yashpal. He was arrested by the British in November 1930 at Amritsar and charged with an apparent connection to the Delhi Conspiracy Case. Subsequently, Ajnyeya spent three and a half years in different prisons across the country. His trilogy *Shekhar: Ek Jiwani* is a product of his prison days. In the wake of the Second World War, Ajneya joined the Allied forces as a Captain where he spent almost three years mobilising people's resistance against the fascist incursions.

After the end of the war, Ajnyeya travelled to Japan in 1957–1958 to learn about Zen Buddhism. The philosophies of Zen influenced him and his writing style to a great extent. 'Khitin Babu', written around that time, becomes exemplary of such an influence where Ajnyeya stresses the importance of the soul in the construction or the becoming of the human self. Like Kalidas can see into the emotions of the trees behind their facelessness, Ajneyaya too can move beyond Khitin Babu's impairment and connect to his soul. In 1961, he moved to America where he held the position of visiting faculty at the University of California, Berkley, till 1964. He returned to Berkley in 1969 as a Regents Professor for a year. In 1976, he served for eight months at Heidelberg University as a Visiting Professor before joining the University of Jodhpur back in India as Head of the Department of Comparative Literatures.

His writing career has been equally impressive. To his great credit, he has 28 poetry anthologies (both Hindi and English), 8 novels, 15 short-story collections, 1 play, 3 travelogues, 27 critical essays, 7 diaries and memoirs and 9 translations (among many more). His verse play *Uttar Priyadarshi* was first staged in 1966 at the Triveni theatre in Delhi before being adapted into Manipuri by Ratan Thiyam. For his contributions to the literary world, Ajnyeya has been awarded the Sahitya Akademi Award in 1964 (for his poetry collection *Aangan Ke Paar Dwar*), the Jnanpith Award in 1978 (for his poetry collection *Kitni Naavon Mein Kitni Baar*), the Baratbharati Award and the Golden Wreath Award in 1983. Ajnyeya passed away on 4 April 1987 in New Delhi.

Saurabh Kumar Chaliha

Saurabh Kumar Chaliha was the pen name of Surendra Nath Medhi (1930–2011), a renowned short-story writer in the Assamese language. With more than a dozen short-story collections to his credit, Chaliha was honoured with the Sahitya Akademi Award in 1974 for his anthology *Ghulam* (Slave).

T. Jayakanthan

Jayakanthan writes about people from the margins such as rickshaw-pullers, masons, sex workers and coolies. For a significant part of his life, Jayakanthan was an official member of the CPI. He was also deeply influenced by the Tamil poet Subramanya Bharathi and modern Russian literature in general. The story *Kurai Piravi* appears in a short-story collection *Jayakanthanin Siru Kadhaigal Thoguppu1* (2008).

ABOUT THE TRANSLATORS

Aneesa Mushtaq

Dr Aneesa Mushtaq is lecturer of English at Islamic University of Science and Technology, Awantipora in Kashmir. She has a PhD in English Literature from the Department of English, Maulana Azad National Urdu University, Hyderabad. In her doctoral work, she explored critical responses in Northeastern women's writing to conditions of conflict. Her research interests include women's writings, conflict literature, writings from the Northeast of India, eco-criticism and postcolonial literature.

Banibrata Mahanta

Banibrata Mahanta is Professor of English at Banaras Hindu University. His areas of interest are Indian writing in English, the development of Indian nationalist thought and cultural theories, especially Disability Studies. He is a theatre enthusiast who has organised a few amateur theatrical productions and is an occasional translator. His most recent work is the edited volume titled *English Studies in India: Contemporary and Evolving Paradigms* (Springer 2019).

Brati Biswas

Dr Brati Biswas teaches English at Dayal Singh College Evening of Delhi University. She is an author, a poet and a translator with multiple publications under her belt. She is the editor of *Women and Empowerment in Contemporary India* (with Ranjana Kaul) and *Essays on Text and Performance* (with Geeta Budhraja) among others. She has published several poems across multiple publications: 'Pariah' and 'Furies' for *The Commonwealth Review*, 'Gaze' for *The Indo-American Review* and 10 poems for Anne George Sandhya's book *Roots and Wings* being a few of them. She has also translated several poems and short stories from Bengali to English. Currently, she is in the process of translating Bengali Dalit Women writings into English.

Hemchandran Karah

Dr Hemachandran Karah teaches English Literature at the Humanities and Social sciences faculty of IIT Madras. He is interested in researching themes such as disability, health, the language question, literary criticism and musicology. The hallmark of humanities scholarship lies in its rare capacity to enrich responsible worldviews, empathy, justice and care. Karah's activism as a teacher and a scholar caters to such a goal. In addition to academic writing, Karah regularly contributes to newspapers and magazines.

Indira Babbellapati

A retired professor of English from Andhra University College of Engineering, Andhra University, Visakhapatnam, Indira Babbellapati is a widely published poet and translator.

Jasdeep Singh

Jasdeep Singh is a technology worker, translator and film-writer based in Chandigarh. He curates 'Parchanve', a blog on translated Punjabi poetry, Kirrt, a visual archive of Punjabi labour and *Trolley Times*, a newsletter of farmers protests, 2020–2021.

Keerti Ramachandra

Keerti Ramachandra has been a teacher of English language and literature, a translator of long and short fiction and non-fiction from Marathi, Kannada and Hindi and has edited over 75 books for leading publishers. She has won the Katha A.K. Ramanujan Award for translating from two languages and her translation of a Marathi novel *A Dirge for the Damned* was shortlisted for the Crossword Award in 2016. Among her Marathi translations are *A Dirge for the Dammed* and *Mahanayak* (Vishwas Patil), 'A Faceless Evening and Other Stories' (Gangadhar Gadgil's short stories), 'The Song of Life and Other Stories' (Vijaya Rajadhyaksha) and 'Of Closures and New Beginnings' (Saniya) Marathi. From Kannada, Hindutva or Hind Swaraj (U.R. Ananthamurty) with Vivek Shanbhag, and several short stories by Bolwar Mahamad Kunhi, Sara Aboobacker, Jayant Kaikini, which have appeared in anthologies and magazines in India and abroad. From Urdu/ Hindi, *A Dying Sun and Other Stories* (Joginder Paul) with Usha Nagpal and three stories by Joginder Paul appear in *Land Lust*. She has translated and edited several stories by Premchand for Jamia Milia's projects on Premchand. Presently, she is a visiting faculty at Mount Carmel College, Bangalore, where she teaches postgraduate courses in translation and PG and UG courses in Communication Skills.

Nilufer E. Bharucha

Professor Nilufer E. Bharucha is Director and Scientist in Charge of the CoHaB Indian Diaspora Centre, University of Mumbai. She is former Head and Senior Professor, Department of English,

University of Mumbai. She is Visiting Professor of Humanities, Centre for Excellence in Basic Sciences, University of Mumbai. She is also a Visiting Professor at the WW University of Muenster, Germany. She is on the Global Faculty of the Fairleigh Dickinson University, USA, and is Faculty Associate Emeritus, South Asian Studies Institute, University of the Fraser Valley, Abbotsford, Canada. Her current research interests are focused on literature and cinema of the Indian Diaspora, Law and Literature and Writing of the Parsees. She has been a Visiting Professor at Universities in Europe, the USA and Canada. She has initiated academic collaborations between Mumbai University and universities in Europe and Canada and has been in charge of resultant faculty and student exchange programmes from 1997 to 2014. She has also been a member of several international research projects at British, German and French universities. From 2012 to 2015, she was the Coordinator and Scientist-in-Charge of the European Union's Marie Curie international project on the Diasporic Constructions of Home and Belonging, of which CoHaB IDC is the second phase. She has received several professional awards such as the British Council Scholarship for study at the University of Manchester, the Commonwealth Academic Staff Fellowship for post-doctoral research at the Queen Mary and Westfield College, University of London, the DAAD (German Academic Exchange Service) Visiting Professorships at German Universities, the Indo-Canadian Shastri Institute's Visiting Lectureship and the ICCR (Indian Council for Cultural Relations) Rotating Chair at the University of Muenster, Germany. She has been on the juries of the Commonwealth Literature award, the Sahitya Akademi, Delhi's award in English Literature and on the Selection Committee for the Rhodes scholarship. She has supervised 15 students for their PhD theses and eight students completed their MPhil Dissertations under her guidance. She is a creative writer and has published several short stories. She also translates poetry and fiction from Gujarati into English.

Rajashree Bargohain

Rajashree Bargohain currently teaches at the Department of English, Cotton University, Guwahati, Assam. She previously worked as lecturer in the MA English Programme at Yonphula Centenary College of the Royal University of Bhutan, located at Yonphula, Trashigang, Eastern Bhutan. She has presented research papers at several conferences within India and abroad, and her work has been published nationally and internationally. She is currently engaged in compiling an edited volume of scholarly essays, tentatively titled *Eastern Himalayas and Border*

Thinking in a Post-COVID-19 World, to be published by Routledge, India, as a part of the proposed Routledge book series—'Academia, Politics and Society in a Post-Covid World'.

Ritwick Bhattacharjee

Ritwick Bhattacharjee is an Assistant Professor of English at the Sri Guru Tegh Bahadur Khalsa College, University of Delhi. His research has been located around fantasy, philosophy, phenomenology, horror fiction, science fiction, Indian English novels and Disability Studies. He has done his MPhil from Delhi University and written a thesis on the fantastic phenomenology of Stephen King's *The Dark Tower Series*. He is the author of *Humanity's Strings: Being, Pessimism, and Fantasy* and a co-editor for *What Makes It Pop? An Introduction to Studies in Popular Fictions* (with Srinjoyee Dutta) and *Horror Fiction in the Global South: Cultures, Narratives, and Representation* (with Saikat Ghosh). He has been awarded the Prof. Meenakshi Mukherjee Memorial Award for his essay titled 'Politics of Translation: Disability, Language, and the Inbetween' published in the book *Disability in Translation: The Indian Experience*. He is also the treasurer of the Indian Disability Studies Collective.

Rohini Mokashi-Punekar

Dr Rohini Mokashi-Punekar is a Professor of English at the Indian Institute of Technology, Guwahati. Her notable works include *Vikram Seth: An Introduction, Untouchable Saints: an Indian Phenomenon* and *On the Threshold: Songs of Chokhamela.*

Sania Hashmi

Sania Hashmi is pursuing her PhD in the English Language and Literature programme at the University of Michigan, Ann Arbor.

Sanju Thomas

Dr Sanju Thomas is an Assistant Professor in the School of Letters at Ambedkar University, Delhi. Her areas of interest are Indian literature, Translation Studies, Malayalam fiction and cinema and women's writing. Her publications include the English translation of the memoirs of Ajitha (*Kerala's Naxalbari*, 2008) and an edited anthology of Malayalam short stories by women writers (*Myriad Mirrors*, 2003).

Shalini Rachel Varghese

Shalini Varghese is Assistant Professor and Head of Department of English, Christian College, Chengannur, Kerala. She has been reading, teaching and publishing in areas such as postcolonial literature and cultural studies for the past 16 years.

Shilpaa Anand

Shilpaa Anand is Associate Professor at the Department of Humanities and Social Sciences at BITS-Pilani, Hyderabad Campus. She researches in the field of Disability Studies and is interested in cultural conceptualisations of disablement as well as disability historiography. She holds the honorary position of Distinguished Research Fellow at the Centre for Disability Studies at NALSAR University of Law, Hyderabad, and moderates a lively email list called Disability Studies India.

Shilpa Das

Dr Shilpa Das is Principal Faculty, Interdisciplinary Design Studies, Chairperson, International Programmes and Head, PhD Programme at NID. Since 2004, she has been heading Inter-Disciplinary Design Studies and Science and Liberal Arts Studies at NID. An alumnus of JNU New Delhi (MA) and TISS Mumbai (PhD), she has cumulative work experience of almost 30 years in the education, publishing and voluntary sectors. Shilpa has been the founding co-editor of two prominent publications brought out by the Research and Publications department of NID—The Trellis, a research-based publication and a magazine called *D/signed*. She is the editor, author and creative visualiser of the book *50 Years of the National Institute of Design: 1961–2011* (2013) and co-editor of the book *Indian Crafts in a Globalizing World* (2017). She has authored several published research articles in journals, chapters in books and school textbooks. She has been editorial consultant to Collins Cobuild Dictionaries, UK, and the Gujarat State Textbook Board, Gandhinagar. She teaches courses such as Comparative Aesthetics, History of Design, History of Art, History of Objects, Narrative Theory, Indian Story Telling Traditions, Design for Disability, Approaches to Indian Society, Cultural Studies, Form, Emotion and Culture, Disability Studies, Feminist Disability Studies, Craft Documentation and Research Methodology. She has been visiting faculty at several universities in India and overseas. Among her notable outreach and consultancy projects are those for the Department of Health and Family Welfare for the Government of Gujarat; Ministry of Women and Child Development; Department of Telecommunications, Government of India; the Department of Posts and Telegraph, Government of India and the Indian Navy. She is on the advisory board of many disability collectives. She was on the Board of Advisors in 2018 to the Bill and Melinda Gates

Foundation to create public good on human-centred design (HCD) in global health. She was also on the Core Advisory Board of the Core Project (2018–2020) at the Bill and Melinda Gates Foundation which aimed to gain new insights into women's sexual and reproductive health (SRH) needs in India, Kenya, Nigeria and Tanzania.

Shubhra Dubey

Shubhra Dubey teaches at the Delhi University. Her research interests include literacy, pedagogy, everyday writing practices, gender and Disability Studies.

Subhendu Mund

Dr Subhendu Mund, a well-known Odiya poet, critic, lyricist, translator and lexicographer, was also a universally acclaimed scholar in Indian English literature, Odiya literature and Culture Studies. He is the author of 80 research papers and 40 books in Odiya, English and Kannada (in translation). In addition to his anthologies of poems, short stories and critical essays, Dr Mund has published scholarly books like *Atibadi Jagannath Das: A Quin-Centennial Tribute* (edited with a critical Introduction, 1993), *The Indian Novel in English: Its Birth and Development* (1997), the scholarly reissue of Toru Dutt's 1878 novel *Bianca: The Young Spanish Maiden* (2001), *The Young Zemindar* (omnibus of the fictional works Shoshee Chunder Dutt; Sahitya Akademi, 2017), *Odia Identity: History, Language, Culture, Literature* (Odisha Sahitya Akademi, 2017) and *The Making of Indian English Literature* (Manohar, New Delhi, 2021 & Routledge/Taylor and Francis, UK, 2021). Dr Mund has translated extensively from Odia to English, as well as from Hindi, English and Bangla to Odia. He has translated for Sahitya Akademi, Odisha Sahitya Akademi, NBT (India) and other organisations. His poems and short stories have been translated into most of the Indian languages and included in representative anthologies.